Representing and Reasoning with
Probabilistic Knowledge

Representing and Reasoning with Probabilistic Knowledge
A Logical Approach to Probabilities

Fahiem Bacchus

The MIT Press
Cambridge, Massachusetts
London, England

This book was printed and bound in the United States of America.

Library of Congress Cataloging-in-Publication Data

Bacchus, Fahiem.
    Representing and reasoning with probabalistic knowledge : a   logical approach to probabilities / Fahiem Bacchus.
        p.   cm. — (Artificial intelligence)
    Includes bibliographical references (p.   ).
    Includes index.
    ISBN 0-262-02317-2
    1. Probabilities. 2. Logic, Symbolic and mathematical.
    3. Artificial intelligence. I. Title. II. Series: Artificial
    intelligence (Cambridge, Mass.)
    QA273.B24   1990
    519.2—dc20
                                                          90-13555
                                                            CIP

for Liz

Contents

Contents

Series Foreword

Artificial intelligence is the study of intelligence using the ideas and methods of computation. Unfortunately, a definition of intelligence seems impossible at the moment because intelligence appears to be an amalgam of so many information-processing and information-representation abilities. Of course psychology, philosophy, linguistics, and related disciplines offer various perspectives and methodologies for studying intelligence. For the most part, however, the theories proposed in these fields are too incomplete and too vaguely stated to be realized in computational terms. Something more is needed, even though valuable ideas, relationships, and constraints can be gleaned from traditional studies of what are, after all, impressive existence proofs that intelligence is in fact possible. Artificial intelligence offers a new perspective and a new methodology. Its central goal is to make computers intelligent, both to make them more useful and to understand the principles that make intelligence possible. That intelligent computers will be extremely useful is obvious. The more profound point is that artificial intelligence aims to understand intelligence using the ideas and methods of computation, thus offering a radically new and different basis for theory formation. Most of the people doing work in artificial intelligence believe that these theories will apply to any intelligent information processor, whether biological or solid state.

There are side effects that deserve attention, too. Any program that will successfully model even a small part of intelligence will be inherently massive and complex. Consequently, artificial intelligence continually confronts the limits of computer-science technology. The problems encountered have been hard enough and interesting enough to seduce artificial intelligence people into working on them with enthusiasm. It is natural, then, that there has been a steady flow of ideas from artificial intelligence to computer science, and the flow shows no sign of abating.

The purpose of the Artificial Intelligence series is to provide people in many areas, both professionals and students, with timely, detailed information about what is happening on the frontiers in research centers all over the world.

Patrick Henry Winston
J. Michael Brady
Daniel Bobrow

Preface

Contents This book is a study of how probabilities can be applied in AI. In particular, we will examine the application of probabilities in the formal design and specification of intelligent systems. It has already been demonstrated, in various works, that probabilities are a useful tool for managing uncertainty in applications like expert systems. However, our aim here is much more general: we aim to show that probabilities have an important role to play in the design of intelligent systems in general.

This goal brings to the fore a number of issues:

1. The problem of epistemological adequacy (McCarthy and Hayes [88])—formalisms that require exact numeric information are not reasonable for the analysis of intelligent systems that do not have access to this type of information, e.g., systems that have access to the same kinds of information we do.

2. The problem of generality—intelligent systems whose range approaches our own require very general forms of knowledge. To analyze such knowledge we need the expressive power of at least first-order logic; therefore, probabilities will not be of use in analyzing general intelligent systems if we cannot integrate them with at least first-order quantifiers.

3. The problem of the interpretation of probabilities—although the formal behavior of probabilities is for the most part uncontroversial, their interpretation is not. Probabilities have two distinct interpretations (at least): they can be interpreted as statistical statements, e.g., "More than 10% of the world's population lives in China," and they can be interpreted as statements of graded belief, i.e., degrees of belief, e.g., "I think that it is highly unlikely that the Toronto Maple Leafs will win the Stanley Cup."

4. The problem of the source of an agent's degrees of belief—the truth of statistical assertions is determined by the objective state of the world, but the truth of assertions about an agent's degrees of belief are determined by that agent's subjective state; what, then, determines the agent's subjective state and how is that state related to the objective state of the world? This is, of course, a

very general question, but what interests us in particular is the relation between the agent's degrees of belief and the information he has about the statistical state of the world.

These are the main issues addressed in this book.

We want formalisms for describing and analyzing how probabilities can be used in intelligent systems. The key component of such systems is the knowledge they contain and the inferences they can make from that knowledge. To treat the knowledge component formally, then, is the most important goal of any formal analysis of intelligent systems. For this task logics are the most natural and powerful tool, and all of the work here is based on the use of this tool. Since we are concerned with systems that have probabilistic knowledge, we will develop *logics for probabilities*.

Logics for probabilities have the essential advantage, for our purposes, of allowing us to overcome the first three problems described above. First, we solve the problem of epistemological adequacy by developing logics capable of expressing a wide range of *qualitative* probabilistic assertions. Second, we develop *first-order* logics for probabilities, thus providing a smooth integration with first-order logic. Third, since logics have a precisely defined semantics we can be unambiguous about the exact interpretation given to the probabilistic knowledge. It turns out to be most productive to develop two distinct types of probability logics, each suitable for representing and reasoning with a distinct interpretation of probability.

Having developed logical formalisms which are clear and precise in their interpretation of probabilities, we then examine the last problem— the connection between the two types of probabilities. We propose a system of direct inference in which degrees of belief can be inferred from statistical knowledge, and demonstrate how this mechanism can be applied to the study of default reasoning.

Chapter 1 is a general introduction and justification of our methodology. In Chapter 2 we develop a logic for probabilities where the probabilities are interpreted as degrees of belief. In Chapter 3 we do the same for probabilities interpreted as statistical assertions. In Chapter 4 we demonstrate how these two probability logics can be combined into a unified formalism for both types of probabilities. In Chapter 5 we develop a formal system of direct inference that connects the two types of probabilities.

Contributions Various parts of our work may be useful in other disciplines, particularly in philosophy, but the main contributions are to AI.

The logics we develop for probabilities are a contribution to the study of knowledge representation. These logics are a significant advance in the formal tools available for representing and reasoning with probabilities. They have the ability to represent an extensive variety of qualitative probabilistic assertions and can also represent first-order logical information. The logics also have proof theories which give a formal specification for a class of reasoning that subsumes and integrates most of the probabilistic reasoning schemes that have been developed in AI. These formal tools should be of use in the development of more advanced practical applications of probabilities.

The second major contribution is to the study of default reasoning. The mechanism of direct inference developed in Chapter 5 operates as a powerful system of default reasoning. Its most important contribution is to demonstrate that statistical notions play an essential role in default reasoning, and to offer a statistical perspective on the problems that exist in this kind of reasoning.

The logics for probability may be of interest to mathematicians as an application of logic and probabilities. However, these logics would probably be of more interest to philosophers, since they frequently use probabilistic and logical models. In addition, they may be interested in our approach to direct inference, as this work has its roots in philosophy.

Audience The book is intended for researchers and graduate students in AI, but the material should be comprehensible to anyone with some degree of logical literacy. If one's background in logic is weak, or if one is not particularly interested in such matters, the material on proof theories, Section 2.6, 3.4 and 4.4, can be skimmed without much damage to one's understanding of the rest of the material. And the proofs can be avoided, *if* one is willing to accept the claims on faith; however, I strongly encourage the reader to look at the easier proofs (at least) as they can significantly increase one's understanding of the formalisms. The material in Chapter 5 presupposes some familiarity with work on non-monotonic reasoning. The unprepared reader should still be able to understand our approach to this type of reasoning, but might not understand some of the references to other work.

Although the book is about probabilities one does not need to know much probability theory. The probability theory we use here is usually what is covered in the first couple of weeks of an introductory course. An appendix is included in Chapter 1 which explains most of the probability theory that one needs to know.

History This book started out as a copy of my Ph.D. thesis, but by some mysterious process (and a great deal of effort) became totally different. All that remains intact from the original thesis is the material in Chapter 3 and the title.

The thesis contained two major contributions: (1) it addressed the issue of representing statistical information, a neglected area in the study of probability logics, and (2) it contained the idea of making the probabilities into terms of the language, thus allowing the representation of qualitative probabilistic assertions. Subsequent to the thesis Joe Halpern refined the idea of letting the probabilities be terms of the language and applied it to the development of a logic for representing degrees of belief. He also demonstrated how the two types of probability logics could be combined into a logic capable of dealing with both types of probabilities simultaneously. This work was such a natural extension of what I had done in my thesis that I felt that a description of it had to be included in the book. This inspired Chapters 2 and 4.

My thesis also addressed the issue of direct inference, but what was developed there was more heuristic than formal. The new logic that combined the two types of probabilities provided the tool I needed to address this problem more rigorously. The result is Chapter 5. The material in this chapter appears for the first time in this book.

Acknowledgements A number of people have given me valuable comments on this work, and I am pleased to acknowledge their contributions. Among them are Hector Levesque, Scott Goodwin, Craig Boutilier, Peter van Beek, and Ray Reiter. Len Schubert, my thesis supervisor, and Henry Kyburg, who funded a postdoc visit to Rochester, deserve special notice. Diane Wudel did an excellent job of proof reading. I owe a special debt to Joe Halpern who provided very useful comments on the drafts I sent him, and whose contributions stretch back to my thesis work for which he was external examiner. Finally, this work would not have been possible without the generous support of the National Science and Engineering Research Council of Canada.

1 Introduction

1.1 Logic for the Analysis of Knowledge

Knowledge plays a key role in intelligence. Knowledge of its environment is an essential resource for an intelligent agent, a resource that is used for various purposes in the processes that comprise intelligence. For example, such knowledge may allow the agent to infer additional information pertinent to the task at hand, or the recognition of a common situation may allow the agent to bring to bear stored knowledge about that class of situations, or about analogous situations, that might be useful.

Since an intelligent agent must typically deal with many different aspects of its environment, it must have broad knowledge of its environment. This knowledge will include knowledge about various objects in its environment, e.g., knowledge about an object's intended use. It will also include knowledge about other agents that are part of the agent's environment, e.g., knowledge about the typical behavior of other agents, and even knowledge about the knowledge possessed by those other agents. The agent is itself part of its environment, and as such will have knowledge about itself: knowledge about its own knowledge, about its capabilities, its desires, etc.

On a less general scale, even AI programs that perform some sort of intelligent processing in a very specific domain can be analyzed in terms of the knowledge that they possess and the manner in which they use that knowledge. Such an analysis examines these programs at the knowledge level (Newell [97]).

These observations motivate a desire for formalisms which can be used to analyze knowledge and its uses. Such a formalism should provide a mechanism for representing knowledge in an implementation independent manner; it should provide a mechanism by which the "meaning" (or propositional content) of that knowledge is clearly and rigorously specified; and it should provide some insight as to how that knowledge could be used. Logics continue to be superior formalisms for such work.

From this perspective a number of controversies about the use of logic in AI become irrelevant. It does not matter whether AI programs represent their knowledge explicitly, as a declarative knowledge base, or implicitly, embedded in the working of their procedures; whether they use symbolic structures similar to the syntax of logic, or conventional data structures with no surface resemblance to logical syntax; whether deduction lies at the core of the way in which this knowledge is used, or the knowledge is mainly used in other ways.[1] Logics are still good tools for analyzing this knowledge, its content, and its use. Clearer understanding of the role of knowledge in an intelligent agent gained through such analysis cannot but help us in our eventual aim of constructing an AI.

The reader may wonder about the use of logics for analyzing various non-deductive uses of knowledge. Logic in itself is not sufficient to explain the processes involved in, for example, analogy. However, the formal specification of meaning given by logics can still provide an essential tool in understanding the "reasonableness" (or underlying justification) of such uses of knowledge.

There are many areas in AI which require formal tools other than logics, e.g., the tools of algebraic topology used for reasoning about solid objects (Hopcroft [51]). Even if we restrict ourselves to the specific problem of understanding the role of knowledge in AI, logics seem to be insufficient. There are the aforementioned non-deductive uses of knowledge, like analogy, which require reasoning mechanisms beyond the traditional deductive reasoning offered by logics. Furthermore, problems which arise from the complexity of reasoning and reasoning with inconsistent knowledge point out other inadequacies of the analysis that logics alone can provide. However, these inadequacies do not refute the superiority, and perhaps necessity, of using logics to analyze certain key aspects of the role of knowledge in AI.

1.2   The Need for Transparent Semantics

There are some obvious reasons why logics are an important tool for analyzing the role of knowledge in AI. One reason is their expressiveness. For example, Hayes [47] argues convincingly that when it comes to representing knowledge, first-order logic (FOL) is strictly more expressive than many alternative representations, like frames, scripts, or semantic

---

[1] I am not agnostic on these issues, as will probably become apparent at various places in the text. Clearly, however, a definitive resolution of these controversies will require significant empirical evidence, evidence which we are still a number of years from accumulating.

nets. These representations can be *formally* reduced to FOL.[2] The most important advantage of logics, however, lies in their formal semantics.

It has been claimed that the importance of model theoretic semantics is vastly overrated (e.g., Pollock [106]), such semantics being simply a mapping from one mathematical structure, a recursive language, to another mathematical structure, a set theoretic model. This criticism rests on the point that it is possible to construct model theoretic semantics for even the most outlandish logical theories. Hence, formal semantics does not provide a guarantee that logics will represent our knowledge accurately or clearly. Although it is certainly true that we can construct model theoretic semantics which are very far removed from any intuitive understanding, this does not mean that all formal semantics are unintuitive. Nothing stops us from using logics for tasks other than representing knowledge. For such tasks there may be legitimate reasons for wanting to study "outlandish" theories, and model theoretic semantics, unintuitive or not, provide an indispensable tool for pursuing such studies.

The criticism does, however, point out that it is important to keep one's aims in mind when using logical formalisms. If we want to use logic to analyze the knowledge used by an intelligent agent, it is clear that there are some strong constraints on the types of logics that will be useful. An intelligent agent has knowledge *about* its environment. This means that if our logic is to provide insights into the "content" of this knowledge and its justifiable uses, then there must be a clear link between expressions in the logic and properties of the agent's environment.[3] This is where formal semantics play a vital role.

Formal semantics reduce an impossible problem, that of understanding the meaning of arbitrarily complex sentences of a recursive language, to a more tractable problem, that of understanding the meaning of an atomic set of primitive semantic features and functions. The compositional semantics of logics allows one to break down the interpretation of a complex expression into the interpretation of primitive functions applied to primitive features. An analogy can be drawn with the role of a proof in mathematics. A proof allows one to accept the validity of a

---

[2] Here we should be careful to differentiate between *practical* and *formal* reduction. Hayes was not claiming (on my reading) that, for example, the practical benefit of indexing provided by semantic nets is reducible to FOL.

[3] As we noted before, the agent's environment includes other agents and the agent itself.

complex assertion by breaking it down into a sequence of intuitively clear steps. It is important to note, however, that formal semantics do not by themselves provide "meaning." That is, they do not provide a *direct* explication of what the expressions in the logic are asserting about the agent's environment. We still have to rely on our intuition to provide the final mapping from the primitive semantic features to properties of the environment.

It is for this reason that logics suitable for the analysis of knowledge must possess *transparent* semantics. That is, the relationship between the primitive semantic features and properties of the environment must be intuitively clear, and this depends on the way in which we perceive and understand our environment.[4] Of course, intuitive clarity is a highly subjective notion: what would be called intuitive by some may be rejected as hopelessly complicated by others. Despite these problems we can often agree on at least relative notions of clarity; some logics possess simpler, clearer semantics than others.

It is from the point of view of transparent semantics that first-order logic stands out. Its primitive semantic features are very closely related to the manner in which we perceive our environment. We identify individual objects and classify them according to their properties. FOL is similarly built up from a collection of individual objects, and from the grouping together of individuals that share some common property into sets. The primitive semantic functions which serve to build up complex assertions are equally transparent: the ability to refer to the union or intersection of two sets, the ability to refer to the non-members of a set, the ability to assert that a set to which we can refer contains every object, and the ability to assert that a set to which we can refer is non-empty.[5]

Some readers may balk at the suggestion that FOL is transparent. We must examine some of the roots of this reluctance.

---

[4]It is the way *we* perceive and understand our environment that matters. It is we, not (necessarily) the AI itself, who must understand the role of knowledge in an AI in order to construct one. It would be very difficult for us to construct an AI which would function in an environment that was fundamentally different from our own (e.g., obeying different physical laws). In fact, it would be difficult to even understand what would constitute intelligent behavior in such an environment.

[5]A good demonstration of how closely related these notions are to the manner in which we perceive the workings of our environment can be obtained by duplicating these set theoretic manipulations with a collection of multi-colored geometric shapes.

FOL is not simple. Although the semantic primitives of first-order logic are simple, first-order logic itself is not. It takes a great deal of effort to understand how it can be used and its mathematical properties. This results from the fact that the primitives can be composed together in arbitrarily complex ways. For example, it can require a great deal of effort to understand sentences with extensive quantifier nestings. However, the point is that such complexities can be reduced to a sequence of intuitively transparent primitives, like the proof of a complex mathematical theorem. In fact, this is the best that we can hope for. If some aspect of our environment is complex we cannot expect that an accurate representation will be any less complex.

Describing a domain is difficult. It may well be very difficult to describe certain aspects of our environment in FOL. For example, it may be difficult to decide whether we should classify a particular object as a chair, as a piece of modern art, or as a modern device of torture. Again this is a complexity that we cannot expect to solve with any formalism. If we are trying to represent some aspect of our environment, we will usually have to do a lot of work to gather the information which will be used in our representation. The existence of a formalism will not reduce the effort required for this task. A *good* formalism, however, will be expressive enough to represent the information that we have gathered, and will be sufficiently transparent to allow us to check that the fidelity of the information has been preserved by the formal representation.

FOL can only model. FOL like any other formalism can only *model* aspects of our environment. Any model will necessarily involve certain simplifications and abstractions when compared to "reality." For example, it may well be a simplification to divide the world up into discrete individuals, and to assert categorically that they have certain properties. However, such simplifications and abstractions do not affect the utility of formal models. In fact, the simplifications are the reason that formal models are useful: they free us from unimportant complexities. However, one must keep in mind the simplifications that are being made. In this way one can decide whether or not accuracy is being excessively compromised.

Because the primitives of FOL are so simple there are restrictions on the types of knowledge it can represent with reasonable accuracy. For example, iterated concepts of knowledge, like knowledge about another agent's knowledge, cannot be captured in FOL without giving up a significant degree of clarity. These kinds of knowledge concern aspects of our environment which cannot be easily modeled by standard first-order semantics. Nevertheless, it is quite surprising how much knowledge can be effectively modeled by first-order semantics.

FOL can be used technically. FOL is formally capable of representing almost any kind of knowledge, including the above mentioned iterated concepts of knowledge. But such formal uses of FOL may compromise the transparency of some of its primitive semantic features. The compositional notions of forming sets of individuals and the functions which can be applied to those sets remain transparent. However, the primitive individual objects in the semantic domain may become obscure. For example, if we use FOL to represent an agent's knowledge about another agent's knowledge, we may have an primitive object in the semantic domain which denotes a bit of knowledge possessed by the other agent. There is no longer any way in which the semantics can capture the content of that piece of knowledge. That is, the other agent's knowledge concerns aspects of that agent's environment. When we bundle up that bit of knowledge into an individual object, we no longer have access, in the formal semantics, to the propositional content of that knowledge; there is no longer a clear link between the primitive individual objects and actual objects in the environment. Similar remarks hold when we encode modal logic in FOL by admitting "possible worlds" as individuals, or when we admit predicates and concepts as individuals. In other words, FOL like most other logics can be used in a very "technical" manner. However, this does not mean that it cannot also be used in a transparent manner.

1.3   Statistical Knowledge

Transparency, then, is important in formal semantics, and first-order semantics have this property. However, there are a number of important features of our environment which cannot be accurately modeled by first-order semantics. The main limitation of first-order semantics lies in its range of quantifiers. FOL can only model the extremes: one can assert that all individuals in the domain satisfy a particular formula or that at least one individual satisfies a formula. One cannot assert simple concepts of quantity like most, almost all, a certain percentage, a few, etc.

In fact, it seems that much of our knowledge about our environment is couched in a manner which involves some notion of non-extreme quantity. This includes: knowledge about objects in the world around us, e.g., knowing that dentist's offices are *usually* in pastel colors; knowledge about other agents, e.g., knowing that professional mathematicians *usually* have a broad knowledge of basic mathematics but are also *usually* very specialized in their knowledge of advanced mathematics; and knowledge about our own knowledge, e.g., knowing that you don't know the answers to *most* of the questions on the game show Jeopardy. The ability to understand basic notions of quantity seems to be part of our fundamental cognitive skills. Even our perceptual abilities are geared to recognize statistical information. For example, when shown a board with a mixture of red and white pins, subjects are surprisingly accurate in their estimates of the proportion of each type of pin on the board.

Universals and existentials are important, especially for terminological or otherwise analytic assertions, e.g., assertions like birds are animals, or animals are living creatures. But as the above examples demonstrate, information in the form of empirical generalizations which admit exceptions or in other quantitative forms, e.g., knowing that more politicians are lawyers than engineers (we often have only qualitative information about the underlying quantities) is also an important part of our knowledge. FOL's inability to represent and reason with such knowledge has been one of the motivations in the development of various formalisms for non-monotonic reasoning. Unfortunately, these formalisms have not seriously addressed the issue of transparent semantics.

There is, however, a simple and intuitive extension to first-order semantics which allows the modeling of these quantitative features of our environment. To the transparent notions of identifying individuals and grouping them into sets we could add the equally transparent notion of counting the number of individuals in each set, i.e., the cardinality of the sets. The notion of cardinality, although transparent, does not have much utility for us, however, since it is an absolute not a relative concept. When we examine the kinds of knowledge that we have about our environment, it is clear that absolute quantities are not as prevalent as relative quantities. For example, we are more likely to possess useful information about the proportion of birds that fly than useful information about the absolute number of flying birds. Fortunately, a natural extension of the notion of cardinality is the notion of relative cardinality, i.e., proportion or relative frequency. Extending first-order semantics to include a notion of proportions among the sets of individuals gives a semantics which has considerable additional modeling power with no loss of transparency.

We can use such semantics to model a wide class of exception-allowing generalizations and other qualitative assertions. For example, using proportions from among the set of all domain individuals we can assert that a certain proportion of the individuals in the domain satisfy a certain formula, or using proportions from among the set of individuals which satisfy a certain formula we can assert that a certain proportion of these individuals satisfy another formula. For example, we can assert that some large proportion of the individuals that satisfy the formula Bird(x) also satisfy the formula Fly(x), i.e., "Most birds fly."

It is important to note that we can add the notion of proportions to first-order semantics while preserving the standard features of first-order semantics.[6] Hence, one can still make a universal assertion that all individuals satisfy a certain formula, or an existential assertion that a formula is satisfied by at least one individual. Furthermore, one still has access to the same set theoretic manipulations on the primitive predicate sets; i.e., one can still form intersections and complements. We will also have proportions defined over the new sets of individuals formed in this manner.

Bringing a notion of proportions into the semantics of FOL puts one directly into the area of probabilities; proportions obey the calculus of probabilities. One of the main contributions of this work is to develop a logic whose semantics include a notion of proportions. This logic can be used to represent, in a transparent manner, empirical knowledge like that described above. Instead of using proportions directly it is far more convenient to use the more general concept of probabilities. This allows us to generalize the notion of proportions, if we wish, to something

---

[6]There are certain technical limits, however, on the cardinality of the domain of individuals. In particular, in infinite domains the notion of proportion becomes problematic. However, we can generalize from proportions to probabilities, and this allows us to deal with infinite domains.

which makes sense in infinite domains. It also allows us to generalize from strictly cardinality-based proportions that correspond to uniform probability distributions, to non-uniform probability distributions. This turns out to be useful in certain contexts (Section 3.6).

1.4   Probabilities as Degrees of Belief

We will use the terms *statistical* and *propositional* probabilities to denote two common but quite distinct notions of probability.[7] Statistical probabilities are those we have just discussed. They are probabilities defined over sets of individuals; they relate properties not particular individuals. For example, we can discuss the probability of a 40 year old smoker contracting lung cancer. This probability is not about any particular smoker, it is about the *proportion* of 40 year old smokers who contract lung cancer. Propositional probabilities, on the other hand, are probabilities attached to propositions about particular individuals. For example, we can refer to the probability that John, a *particular* 40 year old smoker, will contract lung cancer. There is no proportion involved here; John either will or will not contract lung cancer.

It is important to note the crucial difference between these two types of probability.[8] Assertions of statistical probability represent assertions about the objective statistical state of the world, while statements of propositional probability represent assertions about the subjective state of an agent's beliefs.

For example, the statement `More than 75% of all birds fly` is a statistical assertion about the proportion of fliers among the set of birds; its truth is determined by the objective state of the world. We may have various reasons for believing or not believing this statement and we certainly do not have any certifiably correct access to its truth value, but its truth or falsity is independent of whether or not any particular agent believes it. On the other hand the statement `The probability that Tweety flies is greater than 0.75` is an assertion about a degree

---

[7] These two types of probabilities have also been termed indefinite and definite probabilities (Pollock [105]). However, it is also possible for a particular *type* of probability to have a definite or indefinite *value*. I have chosen a different terminology to avoid this possible confusion.

[8] The failure to distinguish between these two notions of probability is quite common in AI. For example, the blurring of this difference elicited a number of complaints from the respondents to Cheeseman's position paper on probabilities [13].

of belief; its truth is determined by the subjective state of the agent who made the statement. The truth or falsity of this statement is independent of whether it is actually true or false in the world. That is, there is no *necessary* connection between the agent's subjective state and the objective state of the world, although we would clearly like there to be some connection.

Propositional probabilities, although different, are very important. One of the main uses of probabilities is as a guide to action in the face of uncertainty. The major formalism for using probabilities in this manner is decision theory, and decision theory requires propositional probabilities. One is always faced with making a decision in a *particular* situation (although the situation will usually be a member of a class of similar situations). Similarly, other more cognitive decisions, which may not involve the execution of any physical actions, require propositional probabilities. For example, if we wish to analyze default or defeasible reasoning in terms of probabilities, we need propositional probabilities; we are interested in the probability of propositions about particular individuals, e.g., "Tweety flies," not in assertions about proportions, e.g., "Most birds fly."

Since propositional probabilities are so important, it is useful to construct a logic suitable for representing and reasoning about an agent who has probabilistic degrees of belief. We will explore such a logic in Chapter 2. We will also demonstrate that logics suitable for representing propositional probabilities (probabilistic degrees of belief) are not naturally suitable for representing statistical probabilities (notions of proportion) and vice versa. The formal differences between these two types of probability logics reflect the fact that these really are two distinct notions of probability.

1.5   Direct Inference

Although propositional and statistical probabilities are distinct types, it is clear that there is, and should be, a connection between the two. The connection is most apparent in actuarial reasoning, which often equates the two. When you apply for life insurance, for example, the insurance company gathers information about your health, job risk, sex, etc., and then consult statistical information to determined the average life expectancy from among a set of individuals similar to you in the relevant aspects. They quote you a rate by assuming that you, a particular individual, will have the same life expectancy. That is, they have equated a function of a statistical probability, average life expectancy among some set of individuals, with a function of a propositional probability, their belief about your particular life expectancy: they believe that the probability of you dying after any particular number of years is equal to the proportion of individuals in their reference set who die after that many years.

In non-actuarial situations the connection between these two types of probabilities is not as obvious. Nevertheless, it would be of great utility if a general connection could be made, applicable to a wide class of situations. The reason is that it is the statistical probabilities that are directly related to features of the environment. Propositional probabilities, on the other hand, are not. They are relative to an agent's internal state. If we cannot find a general connection between empirically founded statistical probabilities and propositional probabilities it becomes extremely difficult to say where those propositional probabilities come from, or what values they should have.

After we present a combined logic suitable for representing and reasoning with both propositional and statistical probabilities, we will present a formalism for connecting the two. This formalism is based on the principle of direct inference. Direct inference is a technique for inferring propositional probabilities from statistical information. This technique has been explored by various philosophers. As will be demonstrated, the formalism we develop for direct inference yields a powerful and flexible approach to default or defeasible reasoning. The probabilistic approach of direct inference provides important information about the process of default reasoning.

The propositional probabilities that are the result of this system of direct inference are quite different from the probabilistic degrees of belief that have been touted by some proponents of probabilities in AI. Many of these probabilists have tried to advance the theory of subjective probability.

1.6   Subjective Probabilities

Some proponents of probability in AI have attempted to sidestep the
issue of the empirical foundation of propositional probabilities (or perhaps have been naive about the complexities of the problem) by recourse
to subjective probabilities (e.g., Cheeseman [13]). Subjective probabilities are degrees of belief whose only constraints are that they obey the
axioms of probability. In essence, subjective probabilities ignore the issue of where the probabilities come from and the problem of how these
probabilistic degrees of belief are related to our empirical experience.
Instead, as Kyburg phrases it, subjective probabilities are "undogmatic
and antiauthoritarian: one man's opinion is as good as another's" [72]
Subjective probabilities have a number of philosophical shortcomings,[9]
but their use in AI is even more problematic. If we suppose that ev-
erybody has subjective degrees of belief which they use as guides to
action in their day to day interaction with their environment, then at
least we have some assurance that those degrees of belief cannot be too
outlandish. Selection through evolution would have eliminated those
people with high degrees of belief in things like "I can fly," or "Lions are
harmless." However, unless we are willing to wait a few million years
for our intelligent machines to evolve, or somehow encode in them "reasonable" degrees of belief in *every* proposition, it is difficult to see how
we can have any assurances about the rationality of an AI with purely
subjective degrees of belief.

Subjectivists attempt to surmount this problem by appealing to the
mechanism of conditionalization. It does not matter what degrees of
belief different agents start out with, as long as they are probabilities.
If they always revise their degrees of belief by conditionalizing on new
empirical evidence they will eventually converge to the same degrees of
belief. It is through the process of conditionalization that the subjectivists try to achieve an empirical foundation for subjective probabilities
and try to explain agreement between different agents. As a practical
solution, however, conditionalization does not offer much more than evo-
lutionary selection. All the results about agreement are results which

---

[9] Kyburg gives a good critique in [72]. His conclusions on the matter are un-
wavering: "I conclude that the theory of subjective probability is psychologically
false, decision-theoretically vacuous, and philosophically bankrupt: its account is
overdrawn."

hold only in the limit. That is, we have no guarantees as to how long it will take before some reasonable level of agreement is reached. Even as a theoretical solution the mechanism of conditionalization is problematic, as discussed in detail by Bacchus et al. [6].

Another problem with the prescribed use of subjective probabilities in AI lies in its requirement for numbers. Every proposition must be assigned an exact probability. This is an old problem; it led to McCarthy and Hayes's rejection of probabilities as being epistemologically inadequate [88]. It is very difficult to see how exact degrees of belief in every proposition could be available to an agent. Representations which require unavailable information are, on McCarthy and Hayes's definition, "epistemologically inadequate." Subjective probabilists have tried to solve this problem by calling for the use of "maximally-uninformed" probability distributions. The idea is that the correct probability distribution is the one that satisfies the known constraints but is otherwise "non-committal." For example, it might be a maximum-entropy distribution. In this way the agent need not know "all the numbers;" instead the approach is suitable given whatever constraints on the numbers the agent does know: the slack in the constraints is taken up in an "uncommitted" manner. However, the end result of these uninformed distributions is still an assignment of an exact, point-valued probability to every proposition.

There remain a number of problems with this recourse. First, there is the problem of how these maximally uninformed distributions can be computed when the constraints on an agent's degrees of belief are complex, e.g., when the constraints are inequalities or functional relationships. This problem has only been solved for simple equality constraints using methods from the calculus of variations (e.g., Cheeseman [12]). It is also known that maximum-entropy distributions (one of the most plausible candidates for maximally ignorant distributions) are dependent on the representation used (Seidenfeld [121]). So if the agent chooses to represent his beliefs in a different language, say one with an additional primitive predicate chosen to represent a non-atomic formula in the agent's old language, then the maximum-entropy distribution over the new language may assign a different probability to a logically equivalent sentence.

Even if we can overcome the problems inherent in finding a maximally ignorant distribution, we are still faced with a number of problems which

result from a commitment to a point-valued probability for each proposition. Some of these problems have been identified by Kyburg [68]. We
briefly mention two of the most severe difficulties. The first is a lack of
a notion of *strength of evidence*. Say there is an urn which we are told
contains black and white balls and we are asked what is our degree of
belief that a ball drawn at random will be black. We do not know the
proportion of each type of ball, but we might have a degree of belief equal
to 1/2, based on, say, indifference. Now we start to draw balls from the
urn, replacing them at each turn and drawing at random in such a way
that each trial is "identical."[10] After we draw a few thousand balls from
the urn we find that half the trials resulted in a black ball being drawn.
At the end of all of this accumulation of empirical evidence we are again
asked about the probability that a ball drawn at random will be black,
and again we answer 1/2. Now, however, we are much more confident
about our answer. Unfortunately this increase in strength of conviction
cannot be represented in our point-valued degrees of belief. In order to
represent this we require something much more complex, for example,
probabilities on our probabilities, with all of the attendant difficulties of
answering the question of where these second-order probabilities come
from. Are they also subjective? If not, how are they related to our
empirical experience?

As will be shown later, in the formalisms for representing probabilities
that are developed in this work we do not claim that there is one true
probability value for every proposition. Instead we construct logics in
which various qualitative constraints on the agent's degrees of belief
can be expressed. Such constraints admit a whole family of probability
distributions—all those which satisfy the constraints. It is by examining
the size or variety of this family that we can hope to find reasonable
measures of strength of evidence, although that task is not undertaken
here.[11]

---

[10] Technically, the requirement is for exchangeable trials, a notion due to de Finetti
(see [68]).

[11] It has already been noted in AI that there is a need for a measure of belief and
a separate measure of strength of evidence. For example, Ginsberg develops multi-
valued logics in which there are orthogonal dimensions for values of belief and values
of strength of evidence [38]. Unfortunately, he offers no clues as to how either of
these quantities are to be related to the agent's empirical experience. The advantage
of looking at the family of distributions as suggested here, is that there is already
a range of possibly applicable methods from statistics which relate the number of
empirical observations with strength of evidence. For example, the larger the sample

The other major problem which results from a commitment to point-valued probabilities lies in an overcommitment to highly empirical propositions. To use another one of Kyburg's examples, say that we are presented with an urn that has different colored balls in it. We are told that it contains balls of many different colors, but we think that purple is a pretty rare color so we accord a probability (degree of belief) of 1/100 to the proposition that a purple ball could be drawn from it. At the same time we feel that if we do draw a purple ball our belief that another one could be drawn will increase slightly. Thus we might have an initial conditional probability of 2/100 that if a purple ball is drawn from the urn then we could draw a second one. With these prior probabilities it can be shown that the agent will have a prior probability of at least .99 that in the arbitrarily long run not more than 11% of the balls drawn (with replacement and drawn in identical random trials) will be purple, *without ever having drawn a single ball from the urn* [68]. This is an absurd level of commitment to an extremely empirical assertion. Again this type of absurdity does not occur when a family of probability distributions are admitted.[12]

1.7   Outline of what is to come

As suggested in the previous sections the rest of this work consists to a large part in presenting different logics suitable for representing and reasoning with probabilities, both propositional and statistical, in exploring their properties, and in discussing their uses for AI.

In Chapter 2 a first-order logic suitable for expressing propositional probabilities will be presented. This logic is due to Halpern [43], but we try to present it in a manner suitable for a more general audience. Various properties of this logic will be explored, including its relationship with standard (Hintikka-style) logics of belief.

In Chapter 3 a first-order logic for expressing statistical probabilities is presented. This work originates from my Ph.D. dissertation [5]. The properties of this logic are explored and various examples of its repre-

---

size the more constrained will be one's estimate of the proportions (the intervals will be narrower) at every fixed level of strength of evidence (confidence level).

[12]Although the numbers used in the example are quite arbitrary, the theorems from which the conclusions are demonstrated [68] can be used to show similar types of results for any numbers that one may wish to use.

sentational power are presented.

Chapter 4 demonstrates how these two logics can be combined to yield a logic capable of dealing with both types of probabilities in a unified formalism. This logic is based on ideas first developed by Halpern [43], but it contains features which extend his work. A number of its properties are demonstrated.

With this combined logical tool in hand we then attack the problem of direct inference in Chapter 5. We develop a mechanism for performing direct inference in the combined probability logic. We can reason about the consequences of direct inference by reasoning *inside* of the combined probability logic. We then demonstrate how this mechanism can be used as a powerful and flexible system of default reasoning. The resulting default reasoning system is compared with standard approaches and its advantages are pointed out. The material in this chapter is a completely reworked approach to direct inference from what originally appeared in my dissertation, and this is the first time that this material has appeared.

The key features of the work presented here are:

1. The first-order logics of probability developed generalize the propositional probability tools that have been used in AI. These logics may also be useful in other disciplines.

2. Our formalisms combine logic and probability in a comfortable manner. The probability logics developed are quite capable of representing ordinary categorical information, and are capable of reasoning about the mutual constraints probabilistic and categorical knowledge place on each other.

3. The probability logics developed do not require an unrealistic commitment to point-valued probabilities. A wide variety of qualitative assertions about probabilities can be represented and reasoned with in these logics.

4. A powerful system of default, or defeasible, reasoning is developed which, unlike other systems of default reasoning in AI, gives a palatable treatment of the empirical foundations for such reasoning.

1.8   Limitations and Non-Limitations

As the above list indicates, this work is very much in the spirit of the "logical" approach to AI. Two common criticisms of logic in AI are that reasoning is too complex and that logic is paralyzed by inconsistent knowledge. We close this chapter with a brief discussion of these issues.

Complexity—Deductive Reasoning

As will be seen, in the most general case where we allow unbounded domains, deductive reasoning in our probability logics is more complex than deduction in first-order logic. And first-order logic is itself only semi-decidable; i.e., one can eventually find a proof for every sentence that is provable, but one will never know if a sentence is not provable.[13] These complexity results raise questions about the suitability of such logics (or even first-order logic) for analyzing constructible agents. After all, no constructible agent will be capable of performing such complex reasoning.

The point is, however, that these complexity results are worst case results. They imply that no constructible agent can compute *all possible* deductions. But it is obvious that no agent will ever need to make all possible deductions; many deductions are highly irrelevant, e.g., deducing bird(T) ∨ dog(T) from the knowledge bird(T). There is no convincing reason to believe that we cannot construct an agent that possesses the computational ability to make the deductive inferences that it *needs* to make in its normal day to day functioning. Of course, there may well be deductions that the agent may wish it could make that it does not have the ability to, but this is not so different from human agents; e.g., many mathematicians want to find a deduction (proof) of Fermat's last theorem. Fortunately, such deductions are typically not vital to our functioning. When was the last time that tenure was denied because of a failure to prove Fermat's last theorem? To be sure, there will be those extreme situations when the agent's most vital needs may be compromised by its limited deductive ability. But again, this is not so different from human agents. This will always be the case for any agent with bounded computational resources and limited control over

---

[13]The issue of the complexity of logical reasoning has always been a topic of interest in theoretical computer science, and recently it has received a lot of attention in AI, e.g., Kautz and Selman [123,58], Levesque [79].

its environment, regardless of whether the agent is using its computational resources to perform deduction (and not necessarily in the sense of symbolic theorem proving) or to run some ill-specified program.

Although there is no conclusive argument that such "deductive sufficiency" can be attained, there are various pieces of empirical evidence that add support to this belief. For example, there is the work on special purpose methods by Schubert et al. [119,89]. For a number of fundamental natural problems they have developed fast procedures (linear or even constant time) for making deductive inferences. It seems that there are many naturally occurring types of problems which have additional structure that can be used to speed up inference. Sometimes, as in Schubert et al.'s work, this additional structure can yield an algorithm which can serve as a "theory resolver" (Stickel [126]); at other times very powerful heuristics can be developed that can be used to rapidly find answers to problems which are in the worst case intractable. For example, heuristics have been developed from studies of the structure of the traveling salesman problem which are so powerful that tours of hundreds of cities can be solved on laptop computers. It seems that all naturally occurring instances of the salesman problem have this additional structure. It is important to note that we are not referring to fast procedures which are restricted to specific domains; these are procedures for specific problems which occur often and in many different domains, e.g., procedures for temporal reasoning, or procedures for problems with the structure of the traveling salesman problem, which occur in many different domains.

Although the fact that people can perform certain inferences almost instantaneously indicates that special purpose procedures will be essential, there is also evidence that even when such a procedure is not available, general deductive reasoning may not be totally impractical. This evidence comes from work in automated theorem proving. For example, general theorem provers have been developed which can solve Schubert's steam-roller problem in a few seconds. The deductive reasoning required to solve this problem is far more complex than that required for most ordinary tasks of understanding natural language. It seems that most naturally occurring problems simply do not have worst case complexity. In fact, there has been an interesting series of studies (see Goldberg et al. [41] and references within) which indicate that such worst case problem instances may be very sparse. Goldberg et al. studied the average case complexity of the Putnam-Davis procedure, a decision procedure for propositional satisfiability.[14] It is well known that propositional satisfiability is NP-complete and that propositional unsatisfiability is co-NP-complete, implying that it is highly unlikely that an decision procedure can be developed with tractable worst case behavior. Goldberg et al. have demonstrated that under a variety of probability distributions (over the instances of the satisfiability problem) the average time complexity of deciding satisfiability is in fact polynomial. This means that the instances which take exponential time are very sparse: there cannot be more than an exponentially small fraction (under those distributions) of such worst case instances; otherwise, the average time complexity would be exponential.

There are, in addition, other approaches being investigated which promise to control (but not tame) the complexity monster. These include vivid reasoning (Etherington et al. [27]) and various techniques for reasoning using analogues (Selman [122]).

In summary, the evidence supports the conclusion that worst case complexity results are *in and of themselves* insufficient reason to conclude that deduction is too complex to be of use to a resource bounded intelligence. Such results do give important information; for example, they can tell you that trying to find a polynomial-time algorithm for an NP-hard problem is probably a waste of time, or they can tell you that finding a complete axiomatization for a particular domain is impossible, or they can give useful information about the features which cause high complexity. However, without some additional empirical evidence the conclusion that you will not be able to solve the problems that naturally occur in a particular domain via deductive reasoning is unwarranted. Furthermore, it is quite possible that additional domain-dependent structure can be uncovered which can make deductive reasoning in that domain quite efficient.

Complexity—Default Reasoning

The system of default reasoning developed in Chapter 5 depends not only on the idea of direct inference but also on non-monotonic reasoning.

---

[14]As pointed out by Henry Kautz [personal communication, 1989] one has to be careful about procedures which can prove satisfiability versus those which can prove unsatisfiability, as it is the latter which is required for deduction. That is, just because a procedure can determine satisfiability rapidly (on average) does not mean that it can determine unsatisfiability rapidly. However, Goldberg et al.'s results pertain to a *decision* procedure for satisfiability; i.e., the procedure checks both satisfiability and unsatisfiability.

The non-monotonic reasoning is of a form similar to default reasoning
in default logic (Reiter [114]). It sanctions certain assumptions on the
condition that they are consistent with what is known. Checking for
consistency is an uncomputable task. Hence, our system of default reasoning (along with other consistency-based systems of non-monotonic
reasoning) poses a much more difficult complexity problem. In deductive reasoning you only need to find a single deduction of the assertion
that interests you. As argued above, it is not unreasonable to assume
that methods can be developed which will find the needed deductions
within reasonable resource constraints. However, these arguments do
not carry over to the non-monotonic case.

In any reasonable logical system of default reasoning, deductive reasoning must take precedence. That is, if an agent can deduce an assertion from the knowledge that he has accepted as being true, then this
deduction must take precedence over any default reasoning which may
lead him to conclude the contrary, the reason being that deductive reasoning from true facts cannot lead to false conclusions whereas default
reasoning can.[15]

One way of looking at logical systems of default reasoning is as suppositional reasoning. Such reasoning is used in deductive systems based
on natural deduction (Kalish and Montague [57]). Natural deduction
proofs use the device of making suppositions, or assumptions, which are
later discharged (i.e., proved to be valid). Defaults, or non-deductive
jumps (Perlis [103]), can be viewed as being suppositions which are
never discharged. Reiter's default logic [114] in particular is amenable
to this point of view, as one of his initial intuitions about defaults was
that they were ways of making assumptions that extend a logical theory. One can then view interacting defaults as being competing deductive proofs each generated from different sets of suppositions (and

---

[15]This brings up a subtle point related to our earlier call for transparent semantics.
Deductive reasoning in a logic is sound *with respect to the semantics of the logic*. It is
relative to those semantics that truth and falsehood are evaluated. It is quite possible
to construct a logic with semantics that are very far removed from our own intuitions
about our environment. In such a logic inferences which defy our intuitions may well
be sound deductive inferences. That is, relative to those semantics these inferences
cannot be false, but relative to our intuitions they may well be. Ultimately our
willingness to accept deductive inferences as being infallible depends on our conviction
that the semantics are an accurate model of some aspect of our environment. I have
argued above that the semantics of first-order logic satisfy this constraint, as does
its extension to include a notion of proportion.

the agent's knowledge). Preference criteria between different proofs can then be developed which are based on preferences between the different sets of suppositions. One natural preference is for proofs based on fewer suppositions (one must use a subset criterion, not cardinality). From this point of view there is no need to perform a consistency check *before* using a default. For example, say that by default the supposition Bird(Tweety) → Fly(Tweety) can be made, and that Bird(Tweety) and ¬Fly(Tweety) are both provable from the agent's knowledge. There will be a proof, using the supposition, of the assertion Fly(Tweety), but there will also be a proof of the opposite assertion ¬Fly(Tweety) *which will not use any suppositions.*[16]

If the above process of generating different suppositional proofs is allowed to run, pruning old proofs as new preferred proofs are found until it attains equilibrium (i.e., until no more proofs are be generated or defeated), one ends up with something similar to an extension generated via a fixed point construction. One can then accept the conclusions present in the limit equilibrium as being as justifiable as the suppositions (defaults) they depend on.

The problem here is that the logical analysis of such reasoning revolves around the properties of the final equilibrium state, and, unlike deductive reasoning, no definite conclusions about what will be present at equilibrium can be reached by a resource bounded agent.[17] A number of writers (e.g., Etherington [26], Pollock [108]) have suggested that if an agent is only able to allocate a finite quantity of computation to a particular piece of default reasoning, then he should simply use the best conclusions that he is able to generate with those resources. In other words, they are recommending a "time-out" computational policy: use the best conclusions you have at the moment time runs out. Indeed this seems to be an eminently reasonable policy, and is supported by introspection on our own reasoning. For example, because of time pressures we often act on conclusions which later consideration demonstrates were not the best. Yet we may have been in a much worse situation if we had failed to act altogether. However, "reasonableness" does not constitute an analysis. What is needed are some definite results which can char-

---

[16] More detailed systems which use approximately these ideas of competing proofs (more generally, competing arguments) have been developed by Pollock [107] and Loui [85].

[17] Except in those rare cases where, due to restrictions on what we can express as knowledge, we can generate all possible proofs quickly.

acterize the effect of "time-out" computations. Why would an agent be justified in using his best time-out conclusions?[18]

It is not clear what kind of tools could be used to give answers to these questions, although logical approaches have been attempted (e.g., Elgot-Drapkin and Perlis [25]), as well as decision theoretic approaches (e.g., Horvitz [53], Etzioni [28]). Work on models of non-logically omniscient agents may also provide some results (e.g. Levesque [77], Fagin and Halpern [29], Moses [95]). However, it is clear that we are still a long way from resolving these issues.

Despite this problem we can still defend a logical analysis of default reasoning. First, the characterization of the final equilibrium state offered by such an analysis will be an important component in the analysis of real-time default reasoning. Characterizations of the state to which unlimited computation takes you can give some idea of the value of extra computation, and of the risk of curtailing computation. And second, the characterization of equilibrium states offered by such logical analysis gives far more information than other approaches to non-deductive reasoning, e.g., procedural or heuristic approaches. The mere fact that the precision of the logical analysis allows one to easily identify its inadequacies is a strong point in its favor.

Inconsistency and Belief Revision

The other area besides complexity that seems to pose a difficulty for any logic-based analysis of knowledge are the problems arising from inconsistent knowledge or beliefs.

Logic, or any other formalism, will not determine what is and what is not true. Logic determines the consequences of believing certain things to be true; logic is concerned with arguments, not truth. It provides an analysis of arguments which are in some formal sense justifiable, e.g., valid arguments which are sound with respect to the formal semantics. But it does not tell you what things you should believe to be true in the first place.

This observation throws a different light on the common complaints about the effect of inconsistency on logic. There have been various arguments that an agent's beliefs will often be logically inconsistent, either

---

[18]One thing that can be noted is that the risk of error in taking the best time-out conclusion may not be significantly greater than the risk of error inherent in default reasoning itself. But we will not know this without analysis.

because of reflection (Perlis [103]) or because of such considerations as the lottery paradox (Kyburg [65]). Even if you don't feel that an agent will always be in an inconsistent state, it is fairly clear that an agent will *sometimes* be in an inconsistent state, simply because it may take some time for an agent to realize that a new belief conflicts with one of his already held beliefs.

It is often claimed that logic is useless in the face of inconsistency because anything can be deduced from an inconsistent knowledge base (e.g., Hewitt [49]). There are a couple of rejoinders to this claim. First, in a practical sense even if an agent is reasoning by using deduction on a set of explicitly represented beliefs, his reasoning processes will not be paralyzed by an inconsistent set of beliefs. Take for example the following propositional knowledge base:

$$KB = \{ \quad A \to B \quad B \to C$$
$$A$$
$$D \qquad \neg D \quad \}.$$

This knowledge base is inconsistent because of the presence of both D and its negation. Consider a proof of C. C can be proved from A and the two implications. Since the knowledge base is inconsistent we can also prove $\neg C$. However, a proof of $\neg C$ must use the inconsistent part of the knowledge base: a proof of $\neg C$ must contain both D and $\neg D$. The proof of $\neg C$ must use parts of the knowledge base which are not connected to C (i.e., there are no sentences in the knowledge base which contain both C and D). In fact, it is not difficult to see that under a basic set of support strategy (which is a fundamental strategy for resolution theorem provers) a proof for $\neg C$ *will not be found*. Thus if an agent uses some elementary considerations of relevance in his search for deductions, an inconsistency in one part of his knowledge will not paralyze all of his deductive reasoning.

There is, however, a more fundamental refutation to the inconsistency argument, a refutation which does not depend on implementation issues. In detecting an inconsistency logic *is giving you the most information that any formalism can*. It is telling you that all of your beliefs cannot be true. In fact, logic may even be able to identify a subset of your beliefs which contain the inconsistency. This will be the set of formulas that were used in the deductions of a sentence and its negation.

Because logic cannot tell you what is true, it can provide no guidance

in correcting your beliefs. That is, it cannot tell you which of your
beliefs is false (unless they are logical falsehoods), just that at least
one of them must be. To guide the revision of beliefs we need other
mechanisms. Some attack has been made on this front, e.g., keeping
track of justifications for one's beliefs (Doyle [21], de Kleer [17]), or
theories which guide the revision so as to minimize changes (Gärdenfors
[34], Levi [80]). Again much work remains to be done in this area.
However, it is *logic* which allows you to detect inconsistency and to
realize when your beliefs need to be revised. And as noted, in purely
practical terms inconsistency in one part of your knowledge does not
have to affect deductive reasoning in other parts.

One last point should be made about the formalisms developed in this
work, a point which has to do with belief revision. As has been pointed
out by Israel [55], the processes involved in belief revision comprise a
large portion of what makes up non-monotonic reasoning. The formalism for non-monotonic default reasoning presented here is not concerned
with the dynamic effects of new information on an agent's beliefs. Instead it deals with default reasoning from a static set of beliefs, i.e.,
the manner in which an agent can draw plausible conclusions from his
current set of beliefs. Such reasoning is non-monotonic under simple
expansions to the agent's beliefs,[19] and the effect of such expansions on
the agent's default conclusions can be analyzed within the formalism.
However, we will not deal with more complex changes to an agent's beliefs, like contractions or revisions (see [34] for a good introduction to
these notions). In other words, we restrict our attention to the notions
of default reasoning that have been studied in AI.

---

[19]Simple expansions are the additions of new beliefs which do not contradict
any current deductively derived beliefs, although they might contradict some of the
agent's default conclusions.

Appendix—Probability Theory

The probability theory we will use in this book is very simple. Most important for the reader, is to understand the formal definition and axioms of a probability function. Here we present a brief introduction to these notions for those readers who perhaps have not seen much probability theory recently.

A *probability function* is a real valued function: it maps some domain to the reals. Such functions are sometimes called measures, as in probability measure, or distributions, as in probability distributions. The term distribution seems particular to the study of probability theory, but the term measure comes from the study of measure theory: probability functions are a special type of set measure. The feature of probability functions which differentiates them from ordinary functions is that they can only be defined over domains with a special structure. This turns out to be not much of a limitation, however, as from any domain we can always construct a structured domain suitable for defining a probability function.

There are four fairly standard interpretations of the domains over which probability functions can be defined (Kyburg [66]). First, we can take the domain to be a collection of propositions such as the proposition that it will rain tomorrow. Second, we can take the domain to be a collection of sentences, typically of a formal language. This may be more suitable for those who find the concept of a proposition somewhat nebulous. Third, we can take the domain to be a collection of events such as the event of it raining tomorrow. Fourth, we can take the domain to consist of a collection of sets.

The key point is that all of these domains can possess a certain structure: they can be closed under some notion of negation and union. And in order for them to be suitable domains for a probability function, they must possess this structure. In a domain of propositions we include the negation of every proposition, e.g., it will not rain tomorrow, and the union of every pair of propositions, e.g., either it will rain tomorrow or the next day (or both). Similarly for a domain of events. In a domain of sentences we can close the sentences under the logical connectives negation ¬ and disjunction ∨. In a domain of sets we can close the collection under the operations of union and complementation with respect to a universal set. The universal set contains all of the individuals present in all of the other sets.

Work on probability in mathematics has used the fourth, set-theoretic view of probability functions, and this is the view we will use in this book. It is not difficult to see that this involves no loss of generality: what every is true of set-theoretic probabilities has an analogue for the other interpretations.

The modern set-theoretic view of probabilities was set out by Kolmogorov, and probability functions are often described as functions which satisfy the Kolmogorov axioms.[20]

A collection of sets that has sufficient structure to serve as a domain for a probability function is known as a field of set.

DEFINITION 1 (FIELD OF SETS)
A collection of sets $\mathcal{F}$ is *field of sets* if it satisfies the following conditions:

1. $\mathcal{F}$ contains a universal set V such that every member of $\mathcal{F}$ is a subset of V.

2. If H is a member of $\mathcal{F}$, then $\overline{H}$ is a member of $\mathcal{F}$, where $\overline{H}$ is the complement of H with respect to V.

3. If H and E are members of $\mathcal{F}$, then $H \cup E$ is a member of $\mathcal{F}$.

To obtain the full generality that is necessary in many applications, we can require the field $\mathcal{F}$ to be a *sigma-field*. A sigma-field is a field that is closed under *countable* unions. That is, if $H_1, \ldots, H_n, \ldots$ is an infinite (but countable) collection of sets all in $\mathcal{F}$, then $\bigcup_{i=1}^{\infty} H_i$ is in $\mathcal{F}$. Note that if $\mathcal{F}$ is a field containing only a finite number of sets, then it is automatically a sigma-field (all but a finite number of the H_i will be identical).

For example, we can generate a field of sets from any reasonably sized collection of sets.[21] We simply take the universal set to be the union over all of the sets, and we close the collection under complementation and union. This produces the smallest field of sets that contains the original collection; it is the field of sets generated by that collection. If we further close our collection under countable unions we will obtain a

---

[20] A translation of Kolmogorov's presentation is contained in [60]. This elegant presentation is still one of the clearest introductions to probability theory available.

[21] By reasonably sized we mean to exclude such collections as the collection of *all* sets. Such extremely large collections can lead to paradoxes: is the set of all sets a member of the set of all sets?

sigma-field. Another example of a field of sets comes from the power set 2^S of a set S. The power set of S contains all subsets of S, including the trivial subsets the empty set and S itself. A power set is always a field of sets, with the original set S acting as the universal set.

Once we have a field or sigma-field of sets over which we can define our probability function, the probability function is determined by three simple axioms.

DEFINITION 2 (PROBABILITY FUNCTIONS)
A probability function P is a real-valued function defined over a field or sigma-field of sets $\mathcal{F}$ which satisfies the following axioms:

Total Probability. $P(V) = 1$, where V is the universal set.

Positivity. $P(H) \geq 0$, for every $H \in \mathcal{F}$.

Additivity. If $H \cap E$ is empty, then $P(H \cup E) = P(H) + P(E)$.

Again to obtain full generality we can require that P be sigma-additive (as long as $\mathcal{F}$ is a sigma-field). This amounts to the following extra condition:

Sigma-additivity. If $H_1, \ldots, H_n, \ldots$ is a countable collection of sets in $\mathcal{F}$ such that for every $j \geq 2$, $\left(\bigcup_{i<j} H_i \right) \cap H_j$ is empty, then

$$P\left(\bigcup_{i=1}^{\infty} H_i \right) = \sum_{i=1}^{\infty} P(H_i)$$

The additivity of the probability function over all finite collections of disjoint sets is a simple consequence of its additivity over pairs of disjoints sets. Sigma-additivity is simply a generalization of this property to countable collections of sets. Note that if $\mathcal{F}$ contains only a finite number of sets, it will be a sigma-field and any probability function defined over it will be sigma-additive. This a result of the trivial reduction of sigma-additivity to finite-additivity when only a finite collection of disjoint sets can be formed.

In sum, probability functions are real-valued functions[22] defined over sigma-fields of sets that satisfy three simple axioms. Their behavior can, however, be quite complex as it is the result of the interplay between the field structure of the domain, the structure of the real numbers, and the structure of the probability function itself.

---

[22]More abstract probability functions that are not real-valued have been investigated (e.g., Koopman [64], Aleliunas [3]).

2 Propositional Probabilities

2.1 Probabilities over Formulas

Propositional probabilities are probabilities assigned to particular propositions or assertions. In a logical framework it is natural to represent these propositions as formulas of a logic. If we then wish to assign probabilities to these propositions, we can look for mechanisms that will assign probabilities to the formulas of the logic. That is, we can place our probabilities over the objects we use to represent our propositions: the formulas of a logic. The simplest type of logic, which usually forms a part of more complex logics, is propositional logic. It is easy to demonstrate how probabilities can be placed over the formulas of a propositional logic.

Propositional logics consist of a set of atomic propositional letters and a set of logical connectives. For example, we may have the set of letters $\{A_1, A_2\}$ and the connectives $\{\neg$ (negation), $\wedge$ (conjunction), $\vee$ (disjunction), $\rightarrow$ (implication)$\}$. The atomic letters are the simplest formulas of the logic, and we can use the logical connectives to generate more complex formulas; e.g., $A_1 \wedge A_2$ is a complex formula. The entire set of formulas of the language is the closure of the atomic letters under application of the connectives. To each formula we can assign a truth value, **true** or **false**. These truth values are assigned by first choosing a set of truth values for the atomic letters. The truth values of the more complex formulas is then evaluated by applying the standard truth functions for the connectives; e.g., $A_1 \wedge A_2$ will be **true** if and only if both A_1 and A_2 are. Thus the truth value of all formulas is completely determined by the initial assignments to the atomic letters. Such an initial assignment is called a truth valuation of the language. If a formula, α, is assigned **true** by every truth valuation we call α a *tautology*.

With this standard notion of truth values attached to the formulas we can group the formulas into equivalence classes. We place two formulas α and β in the same equivalence class if their truth value is identical under all possible truth valuations.[1] For example, the pair of formulas $\{A_1 \wedge A_1, A_1\}$ are in the same equivalence class, as are the pair

---

[1] Equivalently, α and β are in the same equivalence class iff $(\alpha \rightarrow \beta) \wedge (\beta \rightarrow \alpha)$ is a tautology.

$\{A_1 \rightarrow A_2, \neg A_1 \lor A_2\}$.

The logical connectives act as operators over the set of equivalence classes defining an algebraic structure known as a Boolean algebra. Using $[\alpha]$ to denote the equivalence class that the formula α is a member of, the logical connectives over the equivalence classes are simply defined by $\neg[\alpha] = [\neg\alpha]$, $[\alpha] \land [\beta] = [\alpha \land \beta]$, etc. Negation becomes complementation, conjunction becomes meet, and disjunction becomes join in the Boolean algebra. The Boolean algebra also contains a partial order defined as $[\alpha] \leq [\beta]$ iff every truth valuation which assigns **true** to α assigns **true** to β.[2] Under this partial order there is a unique greatest element, the equivalence class of tautologies, and a unique smallest element, the equivalence class of unsatisfiable formulas (the negations of tautologies).

The Boolean algebra generated by the equivalence classes has sufficient structure to define a probability function over it. Using [1] to denote the greatest element in the algebra and [0] to denote the smallest element, a probability function μ over the algebra is a function from the elements of the algebra to the unit real interval [0,1] which satisfies the following conditions:

1. $\mu([1]) = 1$,

2. If $[\alpha \land \beta] = [0]$, then $\mu([\alpha \lor \beta]) = \mu([\alpha]) + \mu([\beta])$.

It is not difficult to see that such a function is identical in its behavior to a probability function defined over a field of subsets. In this case the operator $\lor$ behaves in the same manner as set union, and $\neg$ behaves as complementation.[3]

With a probability function in place over the Boolean algebra associated with the language,[4] it is easy to assign probabilities to the formulas of the language. We simply set the probability of a formula α to be equal to $\mu([\alpha])$. With this definition it can be shown that the probability of a tautology is always one, and that the probability of a disjoint disjunction

---

[2] Equivalently, $[\alpha] \leq [\beta]$ iff $\alpha \rightarrow \beta$ is a tautology.

[3] In a formal sense probability functions defined over Boolean algebras can be redefined as probability functions defined over sigma-fields of subsets: Stone's representation theorem demonstrates that every Boolean algebra is isomorphic to a sigma-field of subsets [7]. (But not every sigma-field of subsets is isomorphic to a Boolean algebra; i.e., probability functions defined over fields of subsets are strictly more general than functions over Boolean algebras).

[4] This Boolean algebra is usually called the Lindenbaum-Tarski algebra of the language.

$\alpha \lor \beta$ is equal to the sum of probabilities of the disjuncts.[5] Furthermore, it can be shown that the probabilities of the formulas are a generalization of the normal binary truth values, with probability one acting as the truth value **true**, probability zero acting as the truth value **false**, and intermediate probabilities acting as intermediate truth values. This means that the traditional deductive use of knowledge can be modeled by probability assignments.

For example, if one has some knowledge base of formulas that are regarded as being true, one can use these formulas to deduce new, equally valid, formulas. These new formulas are entailed by the knowledge base. In terms of truth valuations this means that any truth valuation which assigns **true** to the formulas of the knowledge base will also assign **true** to the entailed formulas. From the probabilistic point of view any probability function which assigns probability one to the formulas of the knowledge base will assign probability one to the entailed formulas. The probability functions are a generalization since one can also assign a non-extreme probability to a formula, something beyond the capabilities of binary truth valuations. These non-extreme probabilities can also be used in reasoning. For example, if we have that the probabilities of lung-cancer(John) and skin-cancer(John) are both greater than 0.9, it can be shown, via the above two conditions which define the probability function, that the probability of lung-cancer(John) $\land$ skin-cancer(John) must be greater than 0.8. Furthermore, assuming that lung-cancer $\lor$ skin-cancer $\rightarrow$ cancer it can also be shown that the probability of cancer(John) is greater than 0.9. As we will show later, it is possible to construct a logic whose deductive proof theory is capable of generating such inferences via its ability to reason with the probabilities.

When we turn to first-order languages we add the complication of quantification. However, first-order languages also contain a propositional subset: those formulas which are quantifier free. There are various methods that have been developed for extending a probability function over the propositional sublanguage, defined in the manner outlined above, to a probability function over the entire first-order language. Typically these approaches involve extending the first-order language to include terms or names for all of the objects in the domain. In the ex-

---

[5] We call a disjunction $\alpha \lor \beta$ disjoint if the probability of $\alpha \land \beta$ is zero.

tended language probabilities can be assigned to quantified formulas via a limit or supremum operation. For example, Gaifman [33][6] defines the probability of a quantified formula as

$$\mu([\exists x.\phi(x)]) = \sup\Big\{\mu\big([\bigvee_{i=1}^{n} \phi(a_i)]\big)\Big| \{a_1,\ldots,a_n\} \subset \mathcal{D}\Big\},$$

where $\mathcal{D}$ is the domain of discourse for the first-order language, and the supremum is taken over all finite subsets $\{a_1,\ldots,a_n\}$ of $\mathcal{D}$. In other words, the probability of a quantified formula becomes a limit defined over the probabilities of its possible instantiations.

These extensions are designed to preserve the "logic" of the language. That is, the extreme values of probability continue to act as a truth valuation over the quantified language preserving the behavior of the quantifiers. Hence, standard first-order entailment is preserved under the probabilistic interpretation.

Although these methods for assigning probabilities to the formulas of a logic have led to some interesting philosophical alternatives to truth assignments, they fail to address some of the main concerns of AI.

These methods can be viewed as providing an alternative semantics for logics, a semantics based on probability functions instead of truth valuations.[7] However, the manner in which the probabilities are placed over the formulas leads to a separation between the probabilities and the formulas of the language itself. That is, the probabilities are defined over the language, but the language itself has not been extended. Hence, one cannot make reference to the probabilities in the language. The probabilities are at the semantic level and there is no access to them at the syntactic level.

It is reasonable to suppose that an agent may have probabilistic constraints on his beliefs. For example, he may think that the assertion represented by the formula α is as equally probable as the assertion represented by β. If he learns some new information which causes him to

---

[6] Other approaches to defining probabilities over first-order languages include Carnap [11], Scott and Krauss [120], Field [32], van Fraassen [130], and Morgan [94].

[7] It is not necessary to use a primitive notion of a truth valuation in the construction of a probability function as we did. Instead families of probability functions can be used directly and the standard notions of truth valuations and entailment can be defined from them. Thus one can demonstrate that probabilities offer an alternative and completely independent semantics. See LeBlanc [75], for more on the probabilistic approach to semantics.

increase his degree of belief in α, he may reason that his degree of belief in β should also increase. If we wish to model this kind of reasoning we need languages which are capable of expressing and reasoning with probabilistic constraints. That is, we need a language which not only can express the assertions which form the agent's beliefs, but which is also capable of expressing the agent's probabilistic constraints on those beliefs. The methods outlined above do not provide this capability; they make no attempt to extend the expressiveness of the language.

Early work on probability logics in AI has suffered from similar problems. Nilsson's probability logic [98] is an example, even though it uses a slightly different notion of a probability distribution over truth valuations or possible worlds. Nilsson demonstrated some interesting linear algebraic properties of propositional probabilities, but did not develop a unified language for assertions and probabilities over those assertions. The probabilities and the language remain separate with the probability values being manipulated via matrix computations. As we will see below, however, his notion of a probability distribution over truth valuations or possible worlds is an essential step towards the solution of this problem. Similar comments hold for work done by Bundy [10]. In Bundy's work the probability values are manipulated separately from the language by maintaining a model of the distribution, an incidence vector. Besides the poor integration between reasoning with assertions in the language and reasoning with the probabilistic constraints over the language, both systems were quite limited in the forms of probabilistic information they could represent and the types of probabilistic reasoning they could perform.

2.2 Probabilities over Possible Worlds

There is an alternative approach to assigning probabilities to the formulas of a logical language which is more amenable to the development of a unified language for assertions and probabilistic constraints on those assertions. One can place a distribution over a field of sets of interpretations or truth valuations of the language. These different interpretations can be viewed as being different possible worlds. Each possible world assigns a truth value to all of the formulas of the language, and the set of formulas which are assigned **true** varies from world to world. If a formula is assigned **true** at a particular possible world we say that the world *satisfies* the formula.

With a probability distribution over a field of sets of possible worlds in place, we can assign a probability to every formula of the language. The probability of a formula becomes the probability of the set of possible worlds that satisfy the formula.

For example, consider the simple propositional language consisting of the letters A and B. There are four possible worlds or truth valuations (using σ to denote the truth valuation):

1. $A^\sigma = $ **true** and $B^\sigma = $ **true**.

2. $A^\sigma = $ **true** and $B^\sigma = $ **false**.

3. $A^\sigma = $ **false** and $B^\sigma = $ **true**.

4. $A^\sigma = $ **false** and $B^\sigma = $ **false**.

Say we place a uniform probability distribution over the power set of this set of worlds so that each singleton set has probability $1/4$. Under this probability function the probability of the formula $A \vee \neg B$ will be equal to $3/4$. This formula is satisfied by the set of worlds $\{1, 2, 4\}$ which has probability $3/4$, as it is the disjoint union of three singleton sets. Similarly,the formula A will have probability $1/2$, and the formula $A \wedge B$ will have probability $1/4$.

When we use logical languages in the standard manner, we do not specify the truth value (or probabilities) of every formula of the language. Instead we make some set of assertions in the language and then we search for the logical consequences of these assertions. In essence, we are placing a set of constraints on the set of possible worlds; i.e., we are constraining the set of possible worlds to contain only those worlds which satisfy the assertions that we have made. When we search for the deductive consequences of our assertions we are searching for additional formulas which are satisfied in this constrained set of possible worlds.

We can use the same concept when we deal with probabilities. Instead of specifying the probability of each possible world we can instead specify certain probabilistic constraints on the probability distribution over the possible worlds. For example, if we specify that the probabilities of both A and B are greater than $3/4$, then we can conclude that the probability of $A \wedge B$ must be greater than $1/2$. The set of worlds which satisfies A is $\{1, 2\}$, the set which satisfies B is $\{1, 3\}$, and the set which satisfies

A $\wedge$ B is $\{1\}$. The constraints specify that both $\mu(\{1,2\})$ and $\mu(\{1,3\})$ are greater than 3/4, and we also have that $\mu(\{1,2,3\}) \leq 1$. From these constraints it is easy to see that $\mu(\{1\}) > 1/2$:

$$\mu(\{1,2,3\}) = \mu(\{1,2\}) + \mu(\{1,3\}) - \mu(\{1\}).$$

That is, any probability distribution which satisfies our two constraints will satisfy the third assertion. We will demonstrate how a logic can be constructed which can express constraints like these and can reason to entailed probabilistic conclusions like the above.

It is not difficult to see that the possible worlds approach to probabilities is essentially equivalent to probabilities assigned directly to the formulas. For example, if α is a tautology it will be true in every possible world and will thus have probability one. Similarly, if α is unsatisfiable it will be true in the empty set of worlds and will have probability zero. If we constrain the probability distribution over the set of possible worlds so that it assigns probability one to some set of formulas, e.g., a knowledge base, then it will also assign probability one to all entailed formulas, as those formulas will be true in every world that satisfies the knowledge base. Hence, probabilities assigned to formulas via a possible worlds distribution generalize binary truth values, as do probabilities assigned via a distribution over the Boolean algebra.

The major advantage of placing probabilities over a set of possible worlds is that it preserves a standard denotational semantics: possible world semantics. This facilitates the construction of a probability logic with the power to represent and reason with the probabilities. We can construct a denotational structure which contains a set of possible worlds along with a probability distribution over that set. The possible worlds can be used to interpret (assign truth values to) traditional assertions represented as formulas of a logical language. And, through the probability function, the structure can also be used to interpret probabilistic constraints on those assertions. That is, with respect to a particular structure, an assertion like prob(A) $\geq$ 3/4 will be either true or false; i.e., the probability function in that structure will assign a probability to the set of worlds satisfying A that either will or will not be $\geq$ 3/4.

As this sample assertion suggests, to assign truth values to probabilistic assertions we need to extend our language so that it is capable of expressing such assertions. This is done by two simple steps. First, we add a probability operator which, like a modal operator, takes a formula of the language as an argument. This operator generates a term which denotes the probability of the formula; i.e., it denotes the probability of the set of possible worlds which satisfy the formula. This probability is a number and it leads naturally to the second step. We must further extend the language so that it contains numeric terms along with a set of predicates which can be used to make various assertions about these terms. For example, we can add a '<' predicate so that we can assert that one number is less than another number or that one probability is less than another probability.

A first-order logic for representing probabilities attached to formulas based on these ideas will now be presented in more detail. This logic is a modification of a logic developed by Halpern [43].

2.3   A Probability Logic for Propositional Probabilities

The logic is an extension of ordinary first-order logic, with a probability operator which can be used to denote the probability of a formula. The language is two sorted, with one sort being used to describe a particular domain, as in ordinary first-order logic. The second sort consists of the numeric terms and predicates for describing numeric relationships.

The probability operator generates numeric terms, and we may also want to have other non-probabilistic numeric terms. Probability functions are traditionally real-valued; this means that the numeric terms which denote the probabilities actually denote real numbers. To reason with these probabilities it is necessary to develop a logic which is capable of reasoning with the reals. For example, if we have the assertions prob($A \wedge B$) = 3/4 and prob($A \wedge \neg B$) = 1/4, then we want to be able to reason via the probability calculus that prob(A) = 1. To perform such reasoning we need not only the axioms of the probability calculus but also axioms which sufficiently characterize the behavior of the reals to capture the reasoning that $1/4 + 3/4 = 1$. In other words, we need to have a language in which we can perform calculations and other reasoning with the reals. It is not possible to *fully* characterize the reals in a language with only first-order quantification, without resorting to complications like set theory.[8] However, there is a technique which will

---

[8] That is, we can employ first-order logic technically and build up the reals via set

serve our purposes. We do not really need a full characterization of the reals, with all its limit properties and its transcendental numbers,[9] for capturing the kinds of reasoning about probabilities that we want.

Essentially, all we really need is to be able to do arithmetic computations and reasoning about order. With just these abilities and with sufficient computational resources we can compute arbitrarily accurate approximations for most of the useful real-valued functions, even those that are defined in terms of limits or in terms of transcendental numbers. The arithmetic and ordering behavior of the reals comes from its structure as a totally ordered field of numbers (not to be confused with a field of sets), and for our purposes it is sufficient to axiomatize this field structure in the logic.[10]

In summary, the logic that we now present has two features which distinguish it from ordinary first-order logic. First, it has a probability operator which maps formulas to numeric terms. And second, it is two sorted with one of the sorts being the reals. The syntax is extended so that we can form formulas which make various assertions about the numeric terms, including the probability terms generated by the probability operator.

2.3.1   Syntax

In the following presentation of the logic we first define the set of allowed symbols. Then rules are given which specify the strings of symbols that are the well-formed formulas. This defines the syntax of the logic. Next, the semantics are given, by first defining a propositional probability

---

theory. In this approach, however, the objects that are the reals are very complex sets: infinite sets of rational numbers (Dedekind cuts) that in turn are sets (pairs) of integers that in turn are built up from the empty set. This approach violates our desire to use logic as transparently as possible.

[9]Transcendental numbers are numbers like π which are not a root of any rational coefficient polynomial; as a result they are also necessarily irrational.

[10]A field of numbers is an algebraically structured collection of numbers closed under the operations of multiplication and addition in which every element, except for zero, has an inverse under both operations. Zero, the unit for the addition operation has no multiplicative inverse, and is its own inverse under addition. Most of the numeric structures we are used to dealing with are fields, e.g., the rationals, the reals, the complex numbers. There are also various types of finite fields, e.g., the integers modulo a prime. However, once we impose the additional requirement that the elements of the field are totally ordered, it can be shown that the field must be infinite. Furthermore, it can be shown that the field must be an extension of the rationals; i.e., it must contain an isomorphic copy of the rationals (Shoenfield [125, p. 88]).

structure and then a correspondence between truth in the probability structure and the well-formed formulas.

The letters 'n' and 'm' are used as meta-variables denoting natural numbers.

Symbols: We start with a set of function and predicate symbols.

a) For every $n \geq 0$ a set of n-ary function symbols $(f, g, h, \ldots)$. We use the convention that constant symbols are 0-ary function symbols.

b) For every $n > 0$ a set of n-ary predicate symbols $(P, Q, R, \ldots)$.

The function and predicate symbols can be of two types, object symbols and numeric symbols. The object symbols are chosen so that they are suitable for describing some domain of interest.

Also included are the distinguished symbols of the logic, i.e., those symbols which are always part of the language irrespective of the particular domain being described.

a) The binary object predicate symbol $=$.

b) The numeric constants -1, 1, and 0; the binary numeric predicate symbols $<$ and $=$;[11] and the binary numeric function symbols $+$ and $\times$.

c) The connectives $\wedge$ and $\neg$.

d) The quantifier $\forall$.

e) The sentential probability operator **prob**.

f) A set of numeric variables and a set of object variables.

We make the restriction that there is at most a countably infinite number of symbols.

Formulas: The formulas of the language are strings of symbols formed by the following recursive rules. The formulas constructed by these rules are the only formulas.

T0) A single object variable or constant is an *o-term*; a single numeric variable or constant is an *f-term*.

---

[11] Note that '$=$' is used as both a numeric and an object equality symbol. The particular type used should, however, be clear from context.

T1) If f is an n-ary object function symbol and $t_1, \ldots, t_n$ are o-terms, then $ft_1 \ldots t_n$ is an *o-term*. If $\mathbf{f}$ is an n-ary numeric function symbol and $\mathbf{t}_1, \ldots, \mathbf{t}_n$ are f-terms, then $\mathbf{ft}_1 \ldots \mathbf{t}_n$ is an *f-term*.

F1) If P is an n-ary object predicate symbol and $t_1, \ldots, t_n$ are o-terms, then $Pt_1 \ldots t_n$ is a *formula*.

F2) If $\mathbf{P}$ is an n-ary numeric predicate symbol and $\mathbf{t}_1, \ldots, \mathbf{t}_n$ are f-terms, then $\mathbf{Pt}_1 \ldots \mathbf{t}_n$ is a *formula*.

F3) If α is a formula, then so is $\neg\alpha$.

F4) If α and β are formulas, then so is $\alpha \wedge \beta$.

F5) If α is a formula and x is a variable (of either type), then $\forall x.\alpha$ is a *formula*.

T2) If α is a formula, then $\mathsf{prob}(\alpha)$ is an *f-term*.

This definition of formulas is different from the standard first-order definition; the last rule of formation allows numeric terms to be constructed from already existent formulas.

Definitional Extensions: The connectives $\vee$, $\rightarrow$ and $\equiv$, and the quantifier $\exists$ are defined in the standard manner from the given primitives. For example, $\alpha \equiv \beta$ is defined to be $\neg(\alpha \wedge \neg\beta) \wedge \neg(\neg\alpha \wedge \beta)$. We will write the function symbols $+$ and $\times$ in the more readable infix form using standard conventions of precedence, and brackets where necessary to disambiguate (the prefix form used in the definition is unambiguous). We will use minus, '$-$', as a function, both binary and unary. That is, $x - y$ will abbreviate $x + (-1 \times y)$ and $-x$ will abbreviate $-1 \times x$. And we will write multiple quantified variables together, e.g., $\forall xy.\alpha$ will abbreviate $\forall x.\forall y.\alpha$. It is also convenient to introduce the following abbreviations to express inequalities between numeric terms.

DEFINITION 3

a) $x \leq y =_{df} (x < y) \vee (x = y)$ b) $x \in [y, z] =_{df} y \leq x \wedge x \leq z$
c) $x \geq y =_{df} \neg(x < y)$ d) $x > y =_{df} y < x$

Another useful definition is an abbreviation for probability one, or certainty.

DEFINITION 4 (CERTAINTY)

$$\mathsf{cert}(\alpha) =_{df} \mathsf{prob}(\alpha) = 1$$

We also need to extend our language to include conditional probability terms.

DEFINITION 5 (AXIOM OF CONDITIONAL PROBABILITIES)

$$\mathsf{prob}(\beta) \neq 0 \rightarrow \mathsf{prob}(\alpha|\beta) \times \mathsf{prob}(\beta) = \mathsf{prob}(\alpha \wedge \beta)$$
$$\wedge \qquad \mathsf{prob}(\beta) = 0 \rightarrow \mathsf{prob}(\alpha|\beta) = 0.$$

The important feature of this definition is that conditional probabilities are defined to be equal to zero if the conditioning formula has zero probability. Normally such conditional probabilities remain undefined, but in a logical language there is no way of duplicating this. In the syntax we have no access to the denotation of the terms; hence, we have no way of determining in the syntax if a probability term is equal to zero. If we wish to generate conditional probability terms in the syntax we must make provision for those terms formed by conditioning on formulas with zero probability. We have chosen here to make these terms equal to zero.

With this definition we can always rewrite a formula containing a conditional probability term into an equivalent formula containing only standard probability terms. With this observation it can be demonstrated that any formula of the extended language, containing conditional probability terms, will be provable from a proof theory augmented by the above definitional axiom if and only if its equivalent formula in the extended language is provable from the unaugmented proof theory.[12] These results allow us to use conditional probability terms in our language and at the same time not worry about them in the formal development of the language.

We will also freely extend our language to include constants denoting any non-transcendental real number, i.e., any number which is the root of a rational coefficient polynomial. We can capture the behavior of this constant by adding a defining axiom. For example, if we wished to add

---

[12] See Shoenfield [125, p. 59] for a description of how definitional extensions like this one can be used to rewrite formulas in the extended language to equivalent formulas of the unextended language, and a proof that such extensions do not change the proof-theoretic properties of the language.

the new constant '0.5' and have it behave in the proper manner (e.g., we want $0.5 + 0.5 = 1$ to be valid in the extended language) we could add the new constant along with the axiom $0.5 \times (1+1) = 1$. Similarly, we could add the constant $\sqrt{2}$ by adding the axiom $\sqrt{2} \times \sqrt{2} = (1+1)$. As with the division function it can be shown that such extensions of the language do not change its proof-theoretic properties [125]. That is, we can always rewrite the formulas containing the new constants to equivalent formulas containing just the initial constants -1, 1 and 0. Hence, we can use such additional constants freely in our examples while still being able to ignore them in our discussion of proof-theoretic issues.

Finally, we will use two special formula symbols *true* and *false*. These are formulas which always have the truth values **true** and **false**. One can regard these formulas as being abbreviations for any tautology and its negation, e.g., $\alpha \vee \neg\alpha$ and $\alpha \wedge \neg\alpha$.

2.3.2 Semantics

Definition 6 (Propositional Probability Structures)
We define the following structure which we use to interpret the formulas of our language for propositional probabilities.

$$M = \langle \mathcal{O}, S, \vartheta, \mu \rangle$$

Where:

a) $\mathcal{O}$ is a set of individuals representing objects of the domain that one wishes to describe in the logic. $\mathcal{O}$ corresponds to the domain of discourse in the ordinary usage of first-order logic.

b) S is a set of states or possible worlds.

c) ϑ is a function that associates an interpretation of the language with each world. For every $s \in S$, $\vartheta(s)$ is an interpretation that assigns to every object predicate symbol a relation of the right arity in $\mathcal{O}$. It also assigns to every object function symbol a function of the right arity over $\mathcal{O}$. For example, it maps the 0-ary functions symbols, the constants, to particular individuals in $\mathcal{O}$. For simplicity, we require that the object function symbols be *rigid*. That is, while the denotations of the predicate symbols can vary from world to world, the function symbols remain fixed: they have the same interpretation in every world. The numeric predicate and function symbols are mapped by ϑ to relations and functions over the reals. Again we require that these symbols be rigid. Hence, the only symbols whose interpretation depends on the world are the object predicate symbols.[13] We also require that the distinguished function and predicate symbols of the language be interpreted in a special manner by ϑ. The numeric constants -1, 1, and 0 must be interpreted as the reals negative one, one, and zero; the functions '$+$' and '$\times$' must be interpreted as the ordinary real addition and multiplication functions; and the numeric predicates '$=$' and '$<$' must be interpreted as equality and less than under the normal ordering of the reals. Finally, we require that the object equality predicate symbol '$=$' be interpreted as ordinary equality over the domain of objects. Hence, the object equality predicate symbol is one object predicate symbol that is required to be rigid.

d) μ is a discrete probability function on S. That is, μ is a function that maps the elements of S to the real interval $[0,1]$ such that $\sum_{s \in S} \mu(s) = 1$. This function defines a probability distribution over the subsets of S by the following device: for every $A \subseteq S$ we define $\mu(A) = \sum_{s \in A} \mu(s)$.[14] With a discrete probability function every subset of S will have a probability, but also that all except a denumerable number of worlds in S will have zero probability.

2.3.3   The Interpretation of the Formulas

A truth valuation is defined over the formulas using the interpretation assigned to each world by ϑ. This interpretation provides a truth value for the atomic formulas of the language, and the rest of the formulas are assigned a truth value inductively. In addition to the interpretation function we also need a variable assignment function. This function maps each variable to a particular individual from the proper domain;

---

[13] We will deal with non-rigid terms in Chapter 4.

[14] This is perhaps the simplest way of defining the probability function that we require, and was used by Halpern. This insures that every subset of S has a probability, even if S is uncountably infinite. Often, measures (which are generalizations of probability functions) over uncountable sets are only defined over a restricted field of subsets, not over the set of all subsets. For example, Lebesgue measure over the reals is defined over the field of Borel sets not over all sets of reals. An alternative approach, used in [5], is to fix a field of subsets of S that includes the subsets which we need to assign probabilities to. This collection of subsets then becomes a part of the semantic structure.

i.e., an individual object is assigned to each object variable and a real number is assigned to every numeric variable. In sum, the truth value assigned to a formula will depend on three items: the semantic structure or model M (which determines the probability distribution μ, the interpretation function ϑ, and the domain of objects $\mathcal{O}$); the current world s; and the variable assignment function v. We now give the inductive specification of the truth assignment, writing $(M, s, v) \models \alpha$ if the formula α is assigned a truth value **true** by the triple and writing $t^{(M,v)}$ for the individual denoted by the term t in the triple (since all of the function symbols are rigid, the terms are independent of the current world).

T0) If x is a variable (of either type), then $x^{(M,v)} = v(x)$; i.e, the variable assignment determines the interpretation of the variables.

T1) If f is an n-ary function symbol (of either type) and $t_1, \ldots, t_n$ are terms of the same type, then

$$(ft_1 \ldots t_n)^{(M,v)} = f^{\vartheta}(t_1^{(M,v)} \ldots t_n^{(M,v)}).$$

F1) If P is an n-ary predicate symbol (of either type) and $t_1, \ldots, t_n$ are terms of the same type, then

$$(M, s, v) \models Pt_1 \ldots t_n \quad \text{iff} \quad \langle t_1^{(M,v)}, \ldots, t_n^{(M,v)} \rangle \in P^{\vartheta(s)}.$$

In addition, if P is a numeric predicate symbol then $P^{\vartheta(s)} = P^{\vartheta(s')}$ for all $s, s' \in S$. That is, the numeric predicates are rigid.

F1=) If s and t are terms of the same type, then

$$(M, v) \models (s = t) \quad \text{iff} \quad s^{(M,v)} = t^{(M,v)}.$$

F2) For every formula α,

$$(M, s, v) \models (\neg \alpha) \quad \text{iff} \quad (M, s, v) \not\models \alpha.$$

F3) For every pair of formulas α and β,

$$(M, s, v) \models (\alpha \wedge \beta) \quad \text{iff} \quad (M, s, v) \models \alpha \quad \text{and} \quad (M, s, v) \models \beta.$$

F4a) For every formula α and object variable x,

$$(M, s, v) \models \forall x.\alpha \quad \text{iff} \quad (M, s, v[x/o]) \models \alpha \quad \text{for all } o \in \mathcal{O},$$

where $v[x/o]$ is the variable assignment function identical to v except that it maps the variable x to the individual o.

F4b) For every formula α and numeric variable x,

$$(M, s, v) \models \forall x.\alpha \qquad \text{iff} \qquad (M, s, v[x/r]) \models \alpha \quad \text{for all } r \in \mathbb{R},$$

where $v[x/r]$ is the variable assignment function identical to v except that it maps the variable x to the real number r.

T2) For every formula α, the f-term created by the probability operator $\mathsf{prob}(\alpha)$ is given the interpretation

$$\big(\mathsf{prob}(\alpha)\big)^{(M,v)} = \mu\big\{s' \in S : (M, s', v) \models \alpha)\big\}.$$

The interpretation of the formulas is fairly standard: the denotations of the variables are determined by the variable assignment function v; the predicate symbols are determined by the interpretation function associated with the current world $\vartheta(s)$; the function symbols are determined by the interpretation function ϑ, independently of the current world; the logical connectives are standard; and the universal quantifier runs the variable through all possible instantiations over the proper domain. The only wrinkle is clause **T2**. This gives the promised interpretation to the probability operator; it maps a formula to a term denoting the probability of the set of worlds which satisfy that formula.

We now present some examples of knowledge representation in this language to give a better feel for the logic and its expressiveness.

2.4   Examples of Representation

It must be remembered that assertions of propositional probability are most naturally viewed as being assertions about some agent's degree of belief. Therefore, our logic is best suited for representing assertions about the degrees of belief an agent may have in various propositions.[15] The model of belief that results is very similar to standard Hintikka-style models of belief (Halpern and Moses [46]). Since an agent typically has incomplete information about his world, the model posits a collection of possible worlds. Even though each of these worlds represents a different description of the real world, as far as the agent is concerned any one of

---

[15] The logic can also be viewed as a language for representing and reasoning with uncertainty, i.e., as a language for describing general probabilistic constraints on propositions. This view may be more suitable in situations where it is not important to be explicit about the agent, e.g., the "agent" might be a medical diagnosis program.

them could be the correct description. In our probabilistic model this picture is more refined: not only is there a collection of possible worlds but also a probability distribution over them. This models the agent believing some worlds as being more likely to be correct descriptions of the real world than others. The agent's degree of belief in a particular proposition is then determined by how likely he thinks it to be that the set of possible worlds that satisfy the proposition contains a correct description of the real world. We will return to the relationship between our logic and standard logics of belief in section 2.8.

EXAMPLE 1 (AN AGENT'S DEGREES OF BELIEF)

1. *"John probably has some type of cancer."*

$$\mathsf{prob}\big(\exists x.\mathsf{has\text{-}cancer\text{-}type}(\mathsf{John}, x)\big) > 0.5.$$

This formula says that in the agent's subjective state the probability of the set of worlds that satisfy $\exists x.\mathsf{has\text{-}cancer\text{-}type}(\mathsf{John}, x)$ is greater than 0.5.[16] The agent's domain of discourse includes a set of individuals which are types of cancer, and in each of the satisfying worlds one of these individuals lies in the has-cancer-type relation with the individual denoted by the constant John. Since all function symbols, including the constants which are 0-ary functions, have the same denotation in every world, the individual denoted by the constant John remains fixed from world to world. Also, this formula makes no commitment about the particular type of cancer that John has. There could be a different x in each satisfying world. Hence, for any particular type of cancer the probability that John has that type could be very small. Finally, we can note that this formula is satisfied by many different structures, each of which may have a different probability distribution over the worlds. That is, the actual probability of the set of satisfying worlds of this formula could be any number, as long as it is greater

---

[16] It should be noted that since we make no restrictions on the probability distribution in our semantic structure, it is quite possible that this formula is satisfied in a *numeric* minority of worlds. What is important here is not the number of satisfying worlds but the probability of the set of satisfying worlds. If each world had an equal probability then probabilistic majority would correspond to numeric majority. The problem with this is that numeric majority makes no sense when we move to an infinite number of worlds, nor does assigning an equal probability to every world.

than 0.5. This is an example of an assertion in our language generating a constraint on the probability distribution over the set of possible worlds, instead of *determining* that distribution.

2. *"It is more likely that John has lung cancer than any other type of cancer."*

$$\forall x.\text{cancer-type}(x) \land x \neq \text{lung}$$
$$\rightarrow \text{prob}\big(\text{has-cancer-type}(\text{John}, \text{lung})\big)$$
$$> \text{prob}\big(\text{has-cancer-type}(\text{John}, x)\big).$$

This formula asserts that the probability of the set of worlds where the individual denoted by the constant John has the cancer type denoted by the constant lung is strictly greater than the set of worlds where John has any other particular type of cancer. Note that in this example the quantification of x occurs outside of the probability context. So by the time we interpret the probability operator the variable x has already been given a particular assignment. The outermost universal quantification runs through all possible assignments to x. All those x which satisfy the antecedent of the implication must satisfy the probabilistic constraint in the consequent.

This formula can be contrasted with the following two formulas, where quantification occurs inside of the probability operator.

- $\text{prob}\big(\text{has-cancer-type}(\text{John}, \text{lung})\big)$
  $\geq \text{prob}\big(\forall x.\text{has-cancer-type}(\text{John}, x)\big).$

- $\text{prob}\big(\text{has-cancer-type}(\text{John}, \text{lung})\big)$
  $\leq \text{prob}\big(\exists x.\text{has-cancer-type}(\text{John}, x)\big).$

Both of these formulas are valid in the propositional probability structures. That is, they are true under all variable assignment functions in all worlds of every propositional probability structure. They are unlike the original formula which is contingent, i.e., true in some probability structures and false in others. The first formula asserts that the probability of the set of worlds where John has lung cancer is greater than the set of worlds where he has every type of cancer. It is easy to see that the set of worlds where John has lung cancer must be a superset of the set of worlds where he has every type of cancer, since in those worlds he must also have lung cancer. From the definition of a probability function the probability of a set must be greater than or equal to the probability of any of its subsets. Hence, the formula must be true in every propositional probability structure. The reasoning behind the second assertion is similar, and is left as an exercise for the reader.

There is one problem, however, with our representation of the original assertion. The previous example did not depend on a particular world for its interpretation, but this example does: the antecedent is dependent on the current world. That is, the set of types of cancers (the satisfying instantiations of x in the antecedent) may vary from world to world. Hence, it is possible that this formula could be satisfied in some worlds and not in others. Consider a structure where John had skin cancer in every world except one, and in that world lung cancer was the *only* type of cancer; in such a structure the formula would be satisfied at this exceptional world simply because the antecedent is false in that world, but the formula would be false at every other world.

We can avoid this difficulty by placing the entire formula inside of a prob operator, i.e., by asserting something about the agent's degree of belief in this formula. For example, if we place the formula inside of a cert operator we would be asserting that the agent's degree of belief in the formula is one. This would mean that the agent believes that this formula is true at every world he considers to have non-zero probability.

3. *"It is more than twice as likely that John has skin cancer than lung cancer."*

$$\text{prob}\big(\text{has-cancer-type}(\text{John}, \text{skin})\big)$$
$$> 2 \times \text{prob}\big(\text{has-cancer-type}(\text{John}, \text{lung})\big).$$

This example demonstrates that we can make assertions about the relationship between the agent's degrees of belief in various propositions which go beyond simple ordering, and still not make any commitments to the particular values of the probabilities.

4. *"The probability that John has cancer lies in the interval 0.6 to*
   0.95."

   $$\text{prob}\big(\exists x.\text{has-cancer-type}(\text{John}, x)\big) \in [0.6, 0.95].$$

We can assert that the agent's degrees belief satisfy interval constraints. Dempster-Shafer belief functions (Shafer [124]) are closely
related to interval constraints on probabilities (see, e.g., Kyburg
[73], Fagin and Halpern [30]).

EXAMPLE 2 (CONDITIONAL PROBABILITIES)

1. One way in which an agent who has probabilistic degrees of belief
   can modify his beliefs is by conditioning on new evidence. We can
   represent the effects of conditioning through the use of conditional
   probabilities. Consider the formula

   $$\forall x.\text{prob}\big(\text{bird}(x)\big) > 0 \rightarrow \text{prob}\big(\text{fly}(x)|\text{bird}(x)\big) > 0.75.$$

This formula says that in the agent's current state of beliefs, for
every individual x whom the agent believes might be a bird, if
the agent was to modify his beliefs by conditioning solely on the
evidence that x was in fact a bird then the agent's new beliefs would
include a high degree of belief in x being a flier. Note, however,
that this formula does not say what the agent's beliefs will be if he
further conditions on more information about the individual x. For
example, this formula does not imply that $\text{prob}\big(\text{fly}(x)|\text{bird}(x) \wedge$
$\text{penguin}(x)\big) > 0.75$.
     One problem with this description of the agent's prior beliefs
(i.e., prior to learning about any particular birds) is that the
agent cannot believe in the existence of non-flying birds in his
prior state. That is, if this formula is true of the agent's beliefs,
then $\text{cert}\big(\exists x.\text{bird}(x) \wedge \neg\text{fly}(x)\big)$ cannot also be true of his beliefs.
Any individual that satisfies the existential will satisfy

   $$\text{prob}\big(\text{bird}(x)\big) > 0 \wedge \text{prob}\big(\text{fly}(x)|\text{bird}(x)\big) = 0;$$

i.e., any individual that satisfies the existential will falsify the universal.

Geffner and Pearl [36] use universally quantified conditional probabilities like this formula in their system of default reasoning. In their system the agent's prior beliefs are described by a background context which contains universally quantified formulas of this type. Assertions about particular individuals are not allowed in the background context, as such assertions can easily contradict the universal assertions that are present. When reasoning about particular individuals the agent moves to a posterior set of beliefs by conditioning on information specific to these individuals. For example, to reason about the bird Tweety the agent will condition his background context (prior beliefs) with the formula bird(Tweety). As our example demonstrates, the agent's posterior beliefs will assign a high degree of belief to fly(Tweety). If the agent subsequently learns that Tweety is a penguin, then when he conditions on this new information his degree of belief in fly(Tweety) will change. This is an interesting probabilistic approach to default reasoning, but the problem we have pointed out with the existential raises questions about the naturalness of the background context. Why should the agent not be allowed to believe in his background context that non-flying birds exist? Why should there be a division between information about particular individuals and general information? It seems reasonable to assume that general information is obtained by some form of induction from information about particular individuals. If this is true, then where did the information about particular cases go? It had to be present to infer the general information in the background context, yet it is somehow removed when the background context is constructed. In Chapter 5 we will develop an alternative probabilistic approach to default reasoning, an approach that does not require the artificial construction of a background context.

Another limitation of conditioning on new evidence is that the agent cannot condition on new evidence that he is certain is false. For example, if the agent's degree of belief in $\neg bird(T)$ was one, i.e., $cert(\neg bird(T))$, then he could not condition on the new evidence $bird(T)$. Conditioning will not work if the new evidence is directly contradicted by the agent's current beliefs. This is why we need the antecedent $prob(bird(x)) > 0$ in the formula.

Cheeseman [13] has claimed that universally quantified formulas like this example, where the quantifier occurs outside of the probability operator, can be used to represent statistical assertions, in this case the assertion "More than 75% of all birds fly." We will examine the validity of this claim in Section 2.5.

2. Another possible use of conditional probabilities is to represent some of the nuances of conditional statements (see Nute [99] for an introduction to conditionals). For example, consider the proposition "It is likely that John will succeed if he works hard." Two possible representations of an agent believing this proposition are:

   (a) $\text{prob}\big(\text{succeed}(\text{John})|\text{work-hard}(\text{John})\big) > c$

   (b) $\text{prob}\big(\text{work-hard}(\text{John}) \rightarrow \text{succeed}(\text{John})\big) > c,$

   where c is a numeric constant that is used to denote a degree of belief that is strictly greater than 0.5 but is otherwise indeterminate.

   The material implication (b) is true of an agent who has a high degree of belief that John will succeed if he works hard, but it is also true of an agent who has a high degree of belief that John will not work hard: it is equivalent to the formula $\neg\text{work-hard}(\text{John}) \lor \text{succeed}(\text{John})$, and hence the agent will always have a higher degree of belief in the implication than in the formula $\neg\text{work-hard}(\text{John})$.

   The representation as a conditional probability (a) comes closer to representing the connection between John's work habits and his success. It is not affected by the agent's degree of belief in $\neg\text{work-hard}(\text{John})$, unless the agent's degree of belief in this assertion is one. Note, however, that by our definition of conditional probabilities if $\text{prob}\big(\text{succeed}(\text{John})|\text{work-hard}(\text{John})\big) > 0$ is true of the agent's beliefs then so is $\text{prob}\big(\neg\text{work-hard}(\text{John})\big) < 1$.

   A classical example of conditional statements is the pair of assertions "If a match is struck, it will light" and "If a wet match is struck, it will not light". When represented as a pair of material implications these two statements are contradictory; however, they are not contradictory as conditional probabilities. That is, it is not inconsistent to assert the pair of formulas $\text{prob}\big(\text{light}(\text{m})|\text{match}(\text{m}) \land \text{struck}(\text{m})\big) > c$ and $\text{prob}\big(\text{light}(\text{m})|\text{match}(\text{m}) \land \text{struck}(\text{m}) \land \text{wet}(\text{m})\big) < 1 - c$.

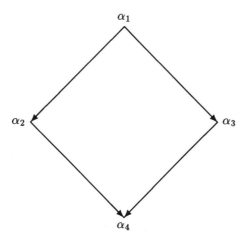

Figure 2.1
A Bayes Network

If, however, the agent was *certain* that a match would light when struck, i.e., $\text{prob}\big(\text{light}(\text{m})|\text{match}(\text{m}) \wedge \text{struck}(\text{m})\big) = 1$, then the second conditional probability would be inconsistent: a probability of one cannot be altered by conditioning. In this case it seems reasonable to represent these statements as formulas with degree of belief less than one, but this may not be reasonable for all conditional statements. The extent to which conditional probabilities can capture conditional statements is an interesting question for future research.

EXAMPLE 3 (INDEPENDENCE AND BAYESIAN NETS)

1. *"The propositions α and β are independent given δ."*

$$\text{prob}(\alpha \wedge \beta|\delta) = \text{prob}(\alpha|\delta) \times \text{prob}(\beta|\delta)$$

This example demonstrates that the language can express the canonical three place independence relation developed by Pearl [101].

2. Consider the Bayes net in Figure 2.1. A Bayes net gives a graphical device for specifying a product form for the joint distribution of

the propositions α_i (Pearl [100]). In this case the distribution represented by the Bayes net in the figure could also be specified in our language by the formula,

$$\mathsf{prob}(\alpha_1 \wedge \alpha_2 \wedge \alpha_3 \wedge \alpha_4)$$
$$= \mathsf{prob}(\alpha_4|\alpha_3 \wedge \alpha_2) \times \mathsf{prob}(\alpha_3|\alpha_1)$$
$$\times \mathsf{prob}(\alpha_2|\alpha_1) \times \mathsf{prob}(\alpha_1).$$

In addition to the structural decomposition, Bayes nets must provide a quantification of the link probabilities. These probabilities are conditional probabilities that encode the strength of the dependencies in the net. We can specify these link probabilities with some additional formulas. For example, we could specify the set of link probabilities $\{\mathsf{prob}(\alpha_1) = 0.5, \mathsf{prob}(\alpha_2|\alpha_1) = 0.75, \mathsf{prob}(\alpha_3|\alpha_1) = 0.4, \mathsf{prob}(\alpha_4|\alpha_2 \wedge \alpha_3) = 0.3\}$.

The advantage of our language is that it gives a declarative representation of the net. The structure embedded in the net is represented in a form that can be used for many different purposes. For example, there is the possibility of automatically compiling Bayes net structures from their declarative representation. In addition, the declarative representation can be easily changed to accommodate new information. When we present a proof theory for our language we will demonstrate how the inferences supported by the Bayes net structure can be captured in our logic.

2.5   Representing Statistical Probabilities

We have pointed out in chapter 1 that there is a difference between propositional probabilities, which can be used to represent an agent's subjective degree of belief in a particular assertion, and statistical probabilities which are objective statements of proportion. We have also claimed that this difference will show itself in the different formal semantics of the probability logics suitable for representing the two types of probabilities. Having presented the details of our logic for propositional probabilities, we are now in a position to demonstrate that it is not naturally suited for representing statistical assertions, e.g., the assertion "More than 75% of all birds fly."[17]

---

[17]There are technical ways of representing such assertions in the logic for propositional probabilities (see Abadi and Halpern [1]). Alternatively, one can encode set

The seemingly most plausible way to represent this statement in the propositional probability logic is to consider a probabilistic generalization of the universal sentence $\forall x.\mathtt{bird(x)} \to \mathtt{fly(x)}$. The universal in 1/0 first-order logic says that all birds fly, so perhaps if we attach a probability of > 0.9 to it we will get what we need. Unfortunately, this does not work. If we also wish to assign a high probability to the assertion that non-flying birds exist, this universal will be forced to have a probability close to zero. That is, the probability of this universal must be $1 - \mathtt{prob}\big(\exists x.\mathtt{bird(x)} \wedge \neg\mathtt{fly(x)}\big)$. Hence, if one believes to a degree greater than 0.1 that a non-flying bird exists, then the probability of the universal must be < 0.9.

If we examine this in terms of our semantic structure we can see that this behavior makes sense in terms of possible worlds. It seems quite reasonable that an agent would want to believe that $\exists x.\mathtt{bird(x)} \wedge \neg\mathtt{fly(x)}$ is true in most of the worlds he believes possible. The universal $\forall x.\mathtt{bird(x)} \to \mathtt{fly(x)}$ is false in every one of these worlds. However, it also seems quite reasonable that the agent may want to believe that "More than 75% of all birds fly" is also true in most of the worlds he believes possible. Hence, these two assertions cannot have the same semantics. We cannot use the universal quantifier in any obvious manner to represent statistical assertions, nor does resort to the existential quantifier help.

It has been suggested by Cheeseman [13] that formulas of conditional probability, where a universal quantifier appears outside of the probability operator, can be used to represent statistical assertions. In particular, he claims that we can represent our assertion about birds by the formula:

$$\forall x.\mathtt{prob}\big(\mathtt{bird(x)}\big) > 0 \to \mathtt{prob}\big(\mathtt{fly(x)}|\mathtt{bird(x)}\big) > 0.9.$$

Furthermore, he makes the claim that the universally quantified variable when it is outside of the probability operator acts as a *random* designator.

This claim demonstrates a confusion between probabilities acting as degrees of belief and probabilities acting as statistical measures. As we pointed out in Example 2.1 this formula is most naturally interpreted

theory in the logic and build up sufficient mathematics inside the language to represent statements of this form. However, neither of these approaches gives a "natural" representation of the statistical assertions. In particular, the semantics attached to these encodings fail to give a transparent representation of the notion of proportions.

as describing the effects of conditioning on the agent's beliefs, not as an assertion about the proportion of birds that fly. To make this clearer consider the following collection of assertions:

1. More than 75% of all birds fly.

2. Opus is a penguin.

3. Penguins are birds.

4. Penguins do not fly.

It seems quite reasonable that an agent may be certain of all of the assertions, i.e., the agent's current subjective state may assign probability one to all of these assertions. If this was the case and if we could represent the statistical assertion as claimed by Cheeseman, we would have the following representation.

1. $\forall x.\mathrm{prob}\big(\mathrm{fly}(x)|\mathrm{bird}(x)\big) > 0.75$.

2. $\mathrm{cert}\big(\mathrm{penguin}(\mathrm{Opus})\big)$.

3. $\mathrm{cert}\big(\forall x.\mathrm{penguin}(x) \rightarrow \mathrm{bird}(x)\big)$.

4. $\mathrm{cert}\big(\forall x.\mathrm{penguin}(x) \rightarrow \neg\mathrm{fly}(x)\big)$.

By the semantics of cert we have that the sets of worlds in which items 2, 3 and 4 are true all have probability one. A simple consequence of the probability axioms is that their intersection, where these formulas are all true, also has probability one. Since every world is closed under logical consequence, we have that $\mathrm{cert}(\mathrm{bird}(\mathrm{Opus}))$ and $\mathrm{cert}(\neg\mathrm{fly}(\mathrm{Opus}))$ are logical consequences of these formulas. Therefore, if the agent is certain of items 2, 3 and 4, he will also have the conditional belief $\mathrm{prob}\big(\mathrm{fly}(\mathrm{Opus})|\mathrm{bird}(\mathrm{Opus})\big) = 0$. But now we have a contradiction, as item 1 implies that $\mathrm{prob}\big(\mathrm{fly}(\mathrm{Opus})|\mathrm{bird}(\mathrm{Opus})\big) > 0.75$. Hence, it is impossible for the agent to be in a subjective state where he has these four beliefs simultaneously. Note that this contradiction does not depend on the agent being certain of these beliefs. We still get a contradiction even if he only has a high degree of belief in these assertions.

Clearly this is unreasonable, as the statistical assertion about birds does not contradict an assertion about any particular bird; it is perfectly reasonable for an agent to have a high degree of belief in all four of these assertions. As a result we must reject Cheeseman's claim that this is a suitable representation of statistical assertions. In Chapter 3 we will see how statistical assertions can be represented in a logic with a new type of variable binding operator which makes the variable act as a random designator. These four assertions can be consistently represented using variables acting as random designators. The semantics of the variables acting in this manner is completely different from the semantics of universally quantified variables. This demonstrates that Cheeseman's claim that universally quantified variables outside of the probability operator act as random designators is also incorrect.

Even though it fails to provide a representation for the statistical information, the formula $\forall x.\text{prob}(\text{fly}(x)|\text{bird}(x)) > 0.75$ is a possible mechanism for describing how statistical information might affect an agent's beliefs, as we have described in Example 2.1. (And perhaps this is really what Cheeseman intended). Although this is an interesting method for *using* statistical information it does not provide a *declarative representation* for such information. The statistical information is never explicitly represented; instead, what is represented is a specification of the agent's initial state of beliefs or background context as determined by external statistical information. There is no possibility of using the statistical information for other purposes, as is provided by a declarative representation such as that presented in Chapter 3. Furthermore, there are other more cogent mechanisms for representing the influence of statistical information on an agent's beliefs. We will present a very general mechanism in Chapter 5 that does not sacrifice the declarative representation of the statistical information.

The problematic nature of these attempts to represent statistical information give some evidence to our claim that the propositional probability logic is not naturally suited for representing statistical assertions. The most convincing argument, however, will come in Chapter 3, when we present a probability logic specifically designed to represent statistical assertions. This logic offers a natural representation for statistical assertions through a semantic structure that is markedly different from the probability structure presented here.

2.6 Proof Theory

In this section we examine some of the proof-theoretic properties of our logic for propositional probabilities. But before presenting any results we review some important definitions.

DEFINITION 7 (SATISFACTION AND ENTAILMENT)

A triple consisting of a propositional probability structure M, a current
world s, and a variable assignment v, *satisfies* a formula α, written
$(M, s, v) \models \alpha$, if α is assigned the truth value **true** by the triple. We
say that α is *satisfiable* if it is satisfied by some triple. A triple *satisfies*
a set of formulas Φ if $(M, s, v) \models \beta$ for all $\beta \in \Phi$. We write $M \models \alpha$ if
$(M, s, v) \models \alpha$ for all worlds s in M and all variable assignments v. We
say that a formula α is *valid* for propositional probability structures if
$M \models \alpha$ for all propositional probability structures M. Finally, we say
that a formula β *entails* a formula α, or that α is a *logical consequence*
of β, if every triple which satisfies β also satisfies α, written as $\beta \models \alpha$.[18]

DEFINITION 8 (FREEDOM AND BONDAGE)

An occurrence of a variable x in a formula α is *bound* if it occurs in a
subformula of α of the form $\forall x.\beta$; otherwise it is *free*. For example, the
first occurrence of x is free in $P(x) \wedge \forall x.R(x)$ while the second occurrence
is bound. We use the notation $\alpha(x/t)$ to denote the new formula which
results from the formula α when all *free* occurrences of x are replaced
by the term t. Blind application of this replacement rule can, however,
cause problems. For example, if α is $\exists y.x = 2 \times y$, and t is $y + 1$, then
$\alpha(x/t)$ becomes $\exists y.y + 1 = 2 \times y$. The first formula α asserted that
x was even, but the new formula $\alpha(x/t)$ makes a completely different
assertion: that y is equal to 1. The difficulty is that the variable y in y+1
has become bound, thus altering the meaning of the formula. We want
substitution to preserve meaning; hence, we say t is *free for* x in α if
for every variable y in t, no subformula of α of the form $\forall y.\beta$ contains a
free occurrence of x.[19] Substitution of the free occurrences of a variable
by a term that is free for that variable never causes a shift in meaning.

A proof theory for a language consists of a set of axioms and a collection of rules of inference. The axioms are formulas of the language
and we may have an infinite collection of axioms specified through an
axiom schema. If axiom schema are used, however, we require that the

---

[18] It is easy to see that the valid formulas are entailed by any formula: valid formulas
are satisfied by every triple.

[19] This is, of course, the same issue as the requirement for an "occurs check" in
unification. Also note that if t and α have no variables in common then t is free for
any x in α.

total set of axioms specified be recursive. That is, there must be an effective procedure for deciding if an arbitrary formula is an axiom, i.e., a member of this set. The rules of inference take some usually small set of formulas and generate a new formula. The axioms and the new formulas generated through the rules of inference are the formulas deducible from the proof theory.

DEFINITION 9 (DEDUCIBLE FORMULAS)
The closure of the set of axioms under applications of the rules of inference is the set of formulas *deducible* from the proof theory. If a formula of the language is in this set it is called *deducible* from the proof theory. If we have a particular proof theory PT and α is deducible from PT we write $PT \vdash \alpha$. Usually it is clear which proof theory is under discussion, and in this case we write simply $\vdash \alpha$.

The basic requirement for a proof theory is that it be *sound*.

DEFINITION 10 (SOUNDNESS)
A proof theory is *sound* if all of the formulas deducible from it are valid.

Another property often looked for in a proof theory is that it be complete.

DEFINITION 11 (COMPLETENESS)
A proof theory is *complete* if all valid formulas are deducible from it.

In AI we are often interested in the formulas entailed by a set of formulas, e.g., the formulas entailed by a knowledge base. It is easy to show that for every language which extends propositional logic, as does first-order logic and as does our language for propositional probabilities, β entails α iff $\beta \to \alpha$ is valid. If our set of formulas Φ is finite, it can be written as a single formula ϕ which consists of all of the formulas of Φ conjoined together (i.e., joined with the connective '$\wedge$'). This conjunction is satisfied by exactly the same set of triples as is Φ. Hence, ϕ entails α iff Φ does, and we can check for entailment by checking for the validity of $\phi \to \alpha$. If we can deduce this formula from a sound proof theory, then we will have a demonstration of its validity.

Another important syntactic concept is that of consistency.

DEFINITION 12 (CONSISTENT FORMULAS)
A formula α is *consistent* with a proof theory iff $\neg\alpha$ is not deducible.

One reason that consistency is important is the following theorem.

THEOREM 13 A proof theory is complete iff every formula consistent with it is satisfiable.

Proof: ($\Leftarrow$) If β is valid then we have that every triple satisfies β, and hence that no triple satisfies $\neg\beta$. If by hypothesis this means that $\neg\beta$ is not consistent, then by definition it means that β is deducible.

($\Rightarrow$) If β is consistent and the proof theory is complete it means that $\neg\beta$ is not valid. Hence, by definition β must be satisfiable. ∎

We now present a proof theory for our language. It consists of a set of axioms which can be naturally divided into three parts. There is a set of axioms for doing first-order reasoning. These axioms can be any standard axiomatization of first-order logic with equality. Here we use an axiomatization from Bell and Machover [7]. The second set of axioms is for doing reasoning about the numeric terms. We do not attempt to capture the full behavior of these real valued terms. Instead we use the axioms of a totally ordered field to capture a large part of their behavior. We obtain our collection of field axioms from Shoenfield [125]. The final set of axioms is for reasoning about the probability operator.

2.6.1   An Axiom System

We use α, β and δ to denote formulas of the language.

First-order Axioms

PC1a) $\alpha \to \beta \to \alpha$.

PC1b) $(\alpha \to \beta \to \delta) \to (\alpha \to \beta) \to \alpha \to \delta$.

PC1c) $(\neg\alpha \to \beta) \to (\neg\alpha \to \neg\beta) \to \alpha$.

PC2) $\forall x.(\alpha \to \beta) \to \forall x.\alpha \to \forall x.\beta$.

PC3) $\forall x.\alpha \to \alpha(x/t)$,
        where t is any term, of the same type as x, free for x in α, and
        $\alpha(x/t)$ is the result of replacing all free occurrences of x in α by t.

EQ1) $t = t$,
        where t is any term.

EQ2) $t_1{=}t_{n+1} \to \cdots \to t_n{=}t_{2n} \to ft_1 \ldots t_n{=}ft_{n+1} \ldots t_{2n}$,
where f is any n-ary function symbol and $t_1, \ldots, t_{2n}$ are terms of
a compatible type.

EQ3) $t_1{=}t_{n+1} \to \cdots \to t_n{=}t_{2n} \to Pt_1 \ldots t_n{\to}Pt_{n+1} \ldots t_{2n}$,
where P is any n-ary predicate symbol and $t_1, \ldots, t_{2n}$ are terms of
the same type.

Axioms **PC1a–b** are axioms which can generate all propositional tautologies, and axioms **EQ1–3** are axioms for reasoning with equality.

Field Axioms   Here all variables are numeric variables and they are
all universally quantified, unless the existential quantifier is explicitly
used.

F1) $x + (y + z) = (x + y) + z$.

F2) $x + 0 = x$.

F3) $x + (-1 \times x) = 0$.

F4) $x + y = y + x$.

F5) $x \times (y \times z) = (x \times y) \times z$.

F6) $x \times 1 = x$.

F7) $x \neq 0 \to \exists y.(y \times x = 1)$.

F8) $x \times y = y \times x$.

F9) $x \times (y + z) = (x \times y) + (x \times z)$.

F10) $\neg(1 = 0)$.

F11) $\neg(x < x)$.

F12) $x < y \to (y < z \to x < z)$.

F13) $x < y \lor x = y \lor y < x$.

F14) $x < y \to x + z < y + z$.

F15) $0 < x \to (0 < y \to 0 < x \times y)$.

Probability Axioms

Prob1) $\text{prob}(\alpha) \geq 0$.

Prob2) $\text{prob}(\alpha) + \text{prob}(\neg\alpha) = 1$.

Prob3) $\text{prob}(\alpha \wedge \beta) + \text{prob}(\alpha \wedge \neg\beta) = \text{prob}(\alpha)$.

These three axioms serve to axiomatize the standard behavior of probability functions: they are positive (**Prob1**), the probability of the set of all possible worlds is 1 (**Prob2**), and the probability of the union of two disjoint sets of possible worlds is equal to the sum of the probabilities of the two sets (**Prob3**).

Prob4) $\alpha \rightarrow \text{prob}(\alpha) = 1$,

if all user defined predicate symbols in α occur inside of a probability operator. The user defined predicate symbols include all object predicates, except for equality '=', and may also include some numeric predicate symbols.

Prob5) $\forall x.\text{prob}(\alpha) = 1 \rightarrow \text{prob}(\forall x.\alpha) = 1$.

These last two axioms are explained in the proof of soundness.

Rules of Inference

MP) From α and $\alpha \rightarrow \beta$ infer β (Modus Ponens).

UG) From α infer $\forall x.\alpha$ (Universal Generalization).

PE) From $\alpha \equiv \beta$ infer $\text{prob}(\alpha) = \text{prob}(\beta)$ (Probability of Equivalents). The first two rules of inference are standard rules of FOL. For the last, $\alpha \equiv \beta$ means that every world which satisfies α satisfies β and vice versa. Since the set of satisfying worlds is the same, it is clear that the probability must be the same.

2.6.2   Soundness

THEOREM 14 The proof theory is sound with respect to propositional probability structures.

Proof: A proof theory can be shown to be sound if we can show that all instances of its axioms are valid and that its rules of inference preserve validity; i.e., when operating on valid formulas the rules of inference produce new valid formulas.

The first-order axioms are all valid, for the same reasons they are valid for ordinary first-order structures. The field axioms are also clearly valid: the reals satisfy all of these axioms. The first three probability axioms can be seen to follow from the behavior of probability functions. For example, for **Prob3** it is easy to see that the set of satisfying worlds for α can be broken up into two disjoint subsets: those which satisfy β and those which do not. The probability of the union of two disjoint sets is the sum of their individual probabilities. Similarly, the rules of inference can be seen to preserve validity. The interesting cases are axiom **Prob4** and **Prob5**.

Axiom **Prob4** says that a formula like

$$\text{Tweety} = \text{Oscar} \wedge \text{prob}\big(\text{bird}(\text{Oscar})\big) = 0.75$$
$$\rightarrow \quad \text{cert}\big(\text{Tweety} = \text{Oscar} \wedge \text{prob}\big(\text{bird}(\text{Oscar})\big) = 0.75\big),$$

is valid, but a formula like

$$\text{bird}(\text{Tweety}) \wedge \text{prob}\big(\text{bird}(\text{Oscar})\big) = 0.75$$
$$\rightarrow \quad \text{cert}\big(\text{bird}(\text{Tweety}) \wedge \text{prob}\big(\text{bird}(\text{Oscar})\big) = 0.75\big),$$

is not. The second contains an object predicate that is outside of any probability operator, whereas the first only has an equality predicate outside of the probability operator. The reason that the instances of this axiom are valid lies in the fact that all of the symbols except for the object predicates are rigid. Let (M, s, v) be any triple. If the triple does not satisfy the antecedent, then it must satisfy the implication. If the triple does satisfy the antecedent, then since all of the non-rigid symbols of the antecedent are inside of a probability operator, the antecedent is independent of the current world s. Hence, if it is satisfied by s it is satisfied by every world in the probability structure, and the probability of the set of satisfying worlds must be one. Therefore, the triple satisfies the consequent, and thus the implication.

Prob5 is a probabilistic analogue of the famous Barcan formula in modal logic. It says that the universal quantifier can be taken inside of a certainty operator ($\text{prob}(\circ) = 1$). Since each world has the same domain over which quantification occurs, the antecedent, $\forall x.\text{cert}(\alpha)$, says that for every individual in that domain, α is true of it in a set of worlds with probability one. This means that α is true of every individual in every world of non-zero probability. Hence, $\forall x.\alpha$ must be true in every world of non-zero probability, and we get the truth of the consequent. It should be noted that this axiom would not be valid if the probability was less than one. Probability one, the cert operator, is isomorphic to standard belief operators in modal logics, as we will discuss in Section 2.8. ∎

2.6.3 Completeness

THEOREM 15 (ABADI AND HALPERN [1])
A complete proof theory for the propositional probability logic does not exist.

One can show that the set of valid formulas for the logic is not a recursively enumerable set. This fact makes the theorem immediate. If we had a complete proof theory we could run the rules of inference on the recursive set of axioms and generate all of the valid formulas. In other words, a complete proof theory would provide a recursive enumeration of the valid formulas, contradicting the fact that this set is not recursively enumerable.[20]

This means that the proof theory we have given here has no "special" status. It can capture a certain amount of deductive reasoning in this logic but not all of it. We can always find valid formulas which are not deducible from the proof theory. These formulas can be added to the axioms to extend the proof theory, but even such extended proof theories will not be able to deduce all valid formulas. There are, however, some reasons for choosing this particular incomplete proof theory.

First, it captures a great deal of useful reasoning about probabilities, as will be demonstrated in the examples presented in the next section. The proof theory is powerful enough to capture the probabilistic reasoning found in most AI formalisms, including Nilsson's probabilistic entailment and Pearl's Bayesian networks. In fact, it is considerably more powerful than either of these formalisms. The second reason is less empirical. It has been shown that a minor extension of this proof theory is complete for an important special case: the case when the domain is bounded in size [43].

---

[20]It should be noted, however, that this incompleteness result depends critically on the fact that the probabilities are real-valued. If we are content with the non-standard notion of field-valued probabilities, which are sufficient to do many of the calculations and much of the reasoning that we want, it is not clear that deduction in the logic will still be this intractable.

This result is of mainly theoretical interest, as it does not seem to add much to our ability to implement some form of reasoning based on this logic. However, as pointed out in chapter 1, it is the logic's ability to transparently represent knowledge that has the most utility for us. We can analyze legitimate uses of this knowledge by analyzing the formalism. For example, most of the theorems presented will be proved directly from the semantics rather than from the proof theory. The proof theory as it stands, however, gives some interesting insights into the types of reasoning that the formalism is capable of, and provides an abstract specification by which we can measure various forms of automated reasoning. For example, we may have a particular algorithm which performs some form of reasoning with the probabilistic constraints on our degrees of belief. We could then ask if it produces inferences that are sanctioned by the proof theory, and we could examine ways of extending the reasoning by looking at aspects of the proof theory that are not captured by the algorithm.

Completeness for Finite Structures

An extension of the proof theory can be shown to be complete for bounded domains, and in this section we outline the extensions required. The reader who is interested in these proof-theoretic issues is encouraged to consult Abadi and Halpern [1] for details about the complexity of validity, and Halpern [43] for details of the completeness proof.

The extension concerns some technical axioms which extend the field axioms. (They were excluded as they do not seem to play an important role in practical reasoning). The axioms given here are satisfied by any ordered field, of which the reals are but one example. This means that certain formulas valid for the reals will not be derivable from these axioms, because they are not valid for an arbitrary ordered field. Since the proof theory is sound, one can only derive formulas from the axioms which are true in *all* structures which satisfy them. By admitting more different satisfying structures (i.e., more different fields besides the reals) we are cutting down on the valid formulas that can be derived. In particular, there are two sets of axioms expressible in our language that are valid of the reals and are not derivable from the field axioms.

The reals are a special type of field, called a *real-closed field*. The name refers to the fact that the roots of certain polynomials are always real numbers; i.e., the reals are closed under factorizations of these polynomials. The first are quadratic polynomials: the square root of every positive real is also a real. This can be represented in our language by the axiom

RCF1) $\forall x.0 < x \rightarrow \exists y.(y \times y = x)$.

The second closure property is that for every odd ordered polynomial, at least one root is a real number. This can be represented by the recursive set of axioms, for every odd n,

RCF2$_n$) $\forall y_1 \cdots y_n.y_n \neq 0 \rightarrow \exists x.(y_n \times \underbrace{x \times \cdots \times x}_{n \text{ times}} + \cdots + y_1 \times x + y_0 = 0)$.

With these additional sets of axioms it can be shown that for domains $\mathcal{O}$ of bounded size, i.e., $\|\mathcal{O}\| \leq N$ for some N, our proof theory is complete for a slightly more restricted language.

We can specify that our domain $\mathcal{O}$ is bounded in size, $\|\mathcal{O}\| \leq N$ for some N, by the following axiom (where all of the variables are *object* variables):

FIN$_N$) $\exists x_1 \ldots x_N \forall y.(y = x_1 \vee \cdots \vee y = x_N)$.

This axiom says that everything is equal to one or more of x_1 to x_N.

If we add the sets of axioms **RCF1** and **RCF2$_n$** (for all odd n) to the rest of the field axioms and a **FIN$_N$** axiom for some N, and we restrict our language so that we don't allow any user defined *numeric* functions or predicates, then the following theorem can be proved.

THEOREM 16 (HALPERN [43])
The proof theory extended by adding these extra axioms is complete for the restricted language.

That is, the extended proof theory can deduce all formulas which can be written in the restricted language that are valid for propositional probability structures where the domain is bounded in size.

2.7   Examples of Reasoning

EXAMPLE 4 (NUMERIC AND EQUALITY REASONING)
We give a few examples to convince the reader that the field axioms along with the axioms for equality are sufficient to do all of our normal

algebraic manipulations and reasoning with numbers. From here on we will refer to such manipulations as simply "numeric reasoning." Similarly, the equality axioms are sufficient to deduce that equals can be freely substituted for each other in any formula. Of course, the equality axioms are sufficient for the ordinary first-order formulas; however, the fact that terms are rigid in our logic allows us to also substitute equals inside the modal-like probability operator.

1. If $t_1 = t_2$ then $t_1 + s = t_2 + s$. That is, we can add an equal quantity to both sides of an equality. In the following we indicate on the right the instance of the axiom or rule of inference used.

$t_1 = t_2$	Hypothesis
$s = s$	EQ1
$t_1 = t_2 \rightarrow s = s \rightarrow t_1 + s = t_2 + s$	EQ2
$s = s \rightarrow t_1 + s = t_2 + s$	MP
$t_1 + s = t_2 + s$	MP

2. A standard first-order result demonstrates that our equality axioms allow us to freely substitute equal terms for each other in any first-order formula, i.e., those formulas without the probability operator. This result can be proved by induction of the length of the formulas. For example, if we have the first-order formula $\forall x.\alpha$ which contains the term t that does not contain x, then we can prove that $s = t \rightarrow (\forall x.\alpha \equiv \forall x.\alpha(t/s))$ is valid for any term s which is free for t in α. (In particular, this means that x cannot occur free in s). By the induction assumption $s = t \rightarrow (\alpha \equiv \alpha(s/t))$ is valid; and from universal generalization we have the validity of $\forall x.(s = t \rightarrow (\alpha \equiv \alpha(s/t)))$. Since x does not appear free in $s = t$ we can, using first-order reasoning and **PC2** in particular, deduce the validity of $s = t \rightarrow (\forall x.\alpha \equiv \forall x.\alpha(t/s))$ as required.

   In order to deal with the full set of formulas of our language, i.e., those which may contain the probability operator, we can use **Prob4**. From **Prob4** we can infer $\mathsf{prob}(s = t) = 1$ from $s = t$. Using probabilistic tautologies (examples of which are given below), we can then infer that $\mathsf{prob}(\alpha) = \mathsf{prob}(\alpha \wedge s = t)$. That is, we can take the equalities inside of the probability operator. Once the equality is inside the probability operator we can use our inductive result to substitute $\alpha(t/s)$ for its equivalent α. That is, since $(s = t \wedge \alpha) \equiv (s = t \wedge \alpha(s/t))$ we can use rule **PE** to deduce that $\mathsf{prob}(s = t \wedge \alpha) = \mathsf{prob}\big(s = t \wedge \alpha(s/t)\big)$. Hence, we end up with a chain of equalities $\mathsf{prob}(\alpha) = \mathsf{prob}(s = t \wedge \alpha) = \mathsf{prob}\big(s = t \wedge \alpha(s/t)\big) = \mathsf{prob}\big(\alpha(s/t)\big)$, the last coming from the fact that $\mathsf{prob}(s = t) = 1$. The equality axioms allow us to deduce the required $\mathsf{prob}(\alpha) = \mathsf{prob}\big(\alpha(s/t)\big)$, demonstrating that equals can also be substituted inside of the probability operator.

Hence, in our semantics the modal nature of the probability operator does not affect substitution of equals. This is a result of the fact that equality is rigid and that all terms are rigid. That is, if $s = t$ then the equality is true in all possible worlds, so $\mathsf{prob}(s = t) = 1$ as given by **Prob4**.

3. $0 < t \rightarrow s < s + t$.

$0 < t \rightarrow 0 + s < t + s$	F14
$0 < t \rightarrow s < t + s$	F2 and Substitution of Equals
$t + s = s + t$	F4
$0 < t \rightarrow s < s + t$	Sub. Eq.

EXAMPLE 5 (PROBABILISTIC TAUTOLOGIES)
The proof theory is powerful enough to capture common examples of probabilistic reasoning.

1. $\mathsf{prob}(true) = 1$.

$\mathsf{prob}(\alpha \wedge \neg\alpha) + \mathsf{prob}(\alpha \wedge \alpha) = \mathsf{prob}(\alpha)$	Prob3
$\mathsf{prob}(false) = \mathsf{prob}(\alpha \wedge \neg\alpha)$	PE
$\mathsf{prob}(\alpha \wedge \alpha) = \mathsf{prob}(\alpha)$	PE
$\mathsf{prob}(false) + \mathsf{prob}(\alpha) = \mathsf{prob}(\alpha)$	Sub. Eq.
$\mathsf{prob}(false) = 0$	Numeric Reasoning
$\mathsf{prob}(false) + \mathsf{prob}(\neg false) = 1$	Prob2
$\mathsf{prob}(true) = 1$	Num. Rea. and PE

2. $\mathsf{prob}(\alpha \vee \beta) = \mathsf{prob}(\alpha) + \mathsf{prob}(\beta) - \mathsf{prob}(\alpha \wedge \beta)$.

$\mathsf{prob}(\alpha \vee \beta) = \mathsf{prob}\big((\alpha \vee \beta) \wedge \alpha\big) + \mathsf{prob}\big((\alpha \vee \beta) \wedge \neg\alpha\big)$	Prob3

$$\text{prob}(\alpha \vee \beta) = \text{prob}(\alpha) + \text{prob}(\beta \wedge \neg\alpha) \qquad \text{PE}$$

$$\text{prob}(\beta \wedge \neg\alpha) = \text{prob}(\beta) - \text{prob}(\beta \wedge \alpha) \qquad \text{Prob3}$$

$$\text{prob}(\alpha \vee \beta) = \text{prob}(\alpha) + \text{prob}(\beta) - \text{prob}(\beta \wedge \alpha) \qquad \text{Sub. Eq.}$$

3. $\text{prob}(\alpha \wedge \beta) \leq \text{prob}(\alpha)$.

4. We say that the formulas $\alpha_1, \dots \alpha_n$ are mutually exclusive if for every $i \neq j$, $\text{prob}(\neg(\alpha_i \wedge \alpha_j)) = 0$. If they are mutually exclusive then

$$\text{prob}(\alpha_1 \vee \cdots \vee \alpha_n) = \text{prob}(\alpha_1) + \cdots + \text{prob}(\alpha_n).$$

5. $\text{prob}(\alpha) = 1 \rightarrow \text{prob}(\alpha \wedge \beta) = \text{prob}(\beta)$.

6. $\text{prob}(\alpha) = 1 \rightarrow \text{prob}(\alpha \vee \beta) = 1$.

EXAMPLE 6 (BAYESIAN REASONING)
Bayes's rule and Bayesian reasoning which results from the rule are also captured by the proof theory.

1. $\text{prob}(\alpha) \neq 0 \wedge \text{prob}(\beta) \neq 0 \rightarrow \text{prob}(\alpha|\beta) = \dfrac{\text{prob}(\beta|\alpha) \times \text{prob}(\alpha)}{\text{prob}(\beta)}$.
   This result (Bayes's Rule) can be proved via a simple application of the definitions and some numeric reasoning.

2. We have already demonstrated how Bayesian networks can be represented declaratively by formulas of our language (Example 3).

   The declarative representation we gave for the Bayes net in Figure 2.1 was

$$\text{prob}(\alpha_1 \wedge \alpha_2 \wedge \alpha_3 \wedge \alpha_4)$$
$$= \text{prob}(\alpha_4|\alpha_3 \wedge \alpha_2) \times \text{prob}(\alpha_3|\alpha_1)$$
$$\times \text{prob}(\alpha_2|\alpha_1) \times \text{prob}(\alpha_1).$$

It can be proved from our proof theory that this formula entails every formula of the same form in which any number of the propositions α_i are uniformly negated. For example, the formula

$$\text{prob}(\alpha_1 \wedge \neg\alpha_2 \wedge \alpha_3 \wedge \neg\alpha_4)$$
$$= \text{prob}(\neg\alpha_4|\alpha_3 \wedge \neg\alpha_2) \times \text{prob}(\alpha_3|\alpha_1)$$
$$\times \text{prob}(\neg\alpha_2|\alpha_1) \times \text{prob}(\alpha_1)$$

is deducible from the previous formula.

This means that the behavior of the Bayes net is captured by
the first formula. That is, the fact that the product decomposition
holds for every truth assignment to the propositions is captured
by the proof theory.

We can also represent the quantification of the link probabilities in the net by additional formulas. These probabilities are the
conditional probabilities that encode the strength of the depen-
dencies in the net. For example, we could specify the set of link
probabilities $\{\mathsf{prob}(\alpha_1) = 0.5, \mathsf{prob}(\alpha_2|\alpha_1) = 0.75, \mathsf{prob}(\alpha_3|\alpha_1) = 0.4, \mathsf{prob}(\alpha_4|\alpha_2 \wedge \alpha_3) = 0.3\}$. With these additional formulas we
can determine the probabilities of any of the individual variables
given an instantiation of some of the other variables, e.g., the val-
ues of terms like $\mathsf{prob}(\alpha_1|\alpha_2 \wedge \neg\alpha_4)$. These probabilities are en-
tailed by the product decomposition and by the link probabilities.
Furthermore, our proof theory is powerful enough to deduce these
entailments. The entailed values come from probabilistic reasoning and numeric calculations, and our probability and field axioms
are sufficient to capture the finite computations involved.

Of course the proof theory has none of the computational advantages of propagation and local computation in the Bayes net. But
it does provide a specification for a class of valid inferences which
includes this kind of reasoning. It also captures a wide variety of
other types of reasoning, including qualitative probabilistic reasoning, numeric reasoning, and logical reasoning. Thus it provides a
global framework in which the specialized reasoning performed by
Bayes nets can be placed. This offers the possibility of integrating
Bayes net reasoning with more general logical and probabilistic
reasoning.

EXAMPLE 7 (PROBABILISTIC ENTAILMENT)
Nilsson [98] has developed a class of probability logics based on a similar
possible worlds approach. He has shown how the probabilities of sentences in the logic are constrained by known probabilities, i.e., by the
probabilities of a base set of sentences. For example, if $\mathsf{prob}(\alpha \wedge \beta) = 0.5$,
then the values of $\mathsf{prob}(\alpha)$ and $\mathsf{prob}(\beta)$ are both constrained to be ≥ 0.5.
Nilsson developed a method for representing the implied constraints of
the base set of sentences in a canonical manner, as a set of linear equations. These equations can be used to identify the strongest constraints

on the probability of a new sentence, i.e., the tightest bounds on its probability. These constraints are, in Nilsson's terms, probabilistic entailments.

He gave some approximate methods for calculating these entailments, as well as noting that the methods of linear programming can give exact solutions. The important point, however, is that these bounds are simply consequences of the axioms of probability. In fact, the theorem

$$\mathsf{prob}(\alpha \vee \beta) = \mathsf{prob}(\alpha) + \mathsf{prob}(\beta) - \mathsf{prob}(\alpha \wedge \beta),$$

along with the fact that probabilities are non-negative, gives the full set of constraints from which all probabilistic entailments can be derived. As we have pointed out in a previous example, this probabilistic tautology is deducible from our proof theory. Hence, it is not difficult to show that our proof theory is powerful enough to deduce all such linear probabilistic entailments. Such entailments depend only on the probability axioms and on numeric reasoning which is captured by our field axioms.[21]

For example, if the base set in Nilsson's logic is $\{\mathsf{prob}(\alpha) = 0.6,$ $\mathsf{prob}(\alpha \rightarrow \beta) = 0.8\}$, probabilistic entailment gives the conclusion $0.4 \leq \mathsf{prob}(\beta) \leq 0.8$. If we include definitional axioms for the constants 0.4, 0.6 and 0.8, we can easily deduce the same bounds from our proof theory.

2.8 Certainty and Knowledge

The probability operator has a modal character: its interpretation depends on truth over a set of possible worlds. Modal logics, with possible world semantics, have proved useful for modeling notions of knowledge and belief (Halpern and Moses [46] give a useful introduction). The basic idea behind the modal approach stems from early work by Hintikka [50], who developed a possible worlds semantics for these two notions. The probability logic developed in this chapter has a very close relationship to Hintikka-style logics of belief. In fact, it can legitimately be viewed as being a generalization of these logics.

---

[21]Fagin et al. [31] have provided a *non-quantified* logic with a complete proof theory which is capable of performing probabilistic entailment. They have also shown that in the non-quantified case such reasoning is no more difficult than propositional satisfiability; i.e., it is NP-complete.

The basic idea behind modal logics of belief is that an agent believes a formula α, if α is true in every world that the agent considers possible. The notion of "considers possible" is given an exact meaning through an accessibility relation, a standard device in modal logic. At each possible world there is some set of alternative worlds which are accessible from it: those worlds which are related to it via the accessibility relation. Hence, an agent believes a formula α, written $B\alpha$, at a particular world exactly when that formula is satisfied in all worlds accessible from that world. The intuition is that the agent is unable to determine which of the alternative accessible worlds is the "true" world. Hence, to be conservative, he only believes those formulas which are true in all of the accessible worlds, i.e., in all of the worlds he considers possible. He only believes those formulas which he is certain of. As we will see, our probability logic allows a generalization of this notion: the agent can believe a formula to a variable degree which corresponds to the probability of the set of possible worlds where the formula is satisfied. That the probability logic is in fact a generalization will be demonstrated when we show that formulas which have probability one correspond to those formulas which are believed in the KD45 logic of belief.

The semantic structure used to model an agent believing a set of assertions consists of a domain and a set possible worlds. It is identical to our probability structures, except that there is no probability distribution over the possible worlds. Instead there is an accessibility relation. Each possible world gives an interpretation of the formulas of some language. It is in this language that we represent the agent's beliefs. For example, we may have a language in which we can talk about dogs and their colors. In this language we could express formulas like brown(Fido) $\land$ dog(Fido) whose intuitive content is that Fido is a brown dog. The assertions expressible in this language are the objects of the agent's beliefs; i.e., the agent can believe or not believe various assertions expressed as formulas of the language. So in our example language the agent can have various beliefs about dogs and their colors. The expressiveness of the language determines the scope of the agent's beliefs.

To arrive at a belief logic we add modal operators to the base language, such as a belief operator, B, or a knowledge operator, K. These operators take formulas as their arguments and the resulting string is itself a formula of the belief logic. There is a key difference, however, between formulas of the base language and formulas of the belief logic.

The base language is a language which is used by the agent to express various assertions about the world. The belief language, on the other hand, need not be used directly by the agent; instead, it can be used to express various assertions *about* the agent and his beliefs. This difference also exists between languages for statistical and propositional probabilities. The agent can use a language for statistical probabilities to express statistical assertions about the world, while the language for propositional probabilities can be used to express assertions about the agent, in particular, about his degrees of belief.

2.8.1 Some Formal Details

To facilitate further discussion we give a more formal description of Hintikka-style belief logics (we will not discuss other modal notions like knowledge or common knowledge).

Syntax: The syntax of these logics is very similar to our probability logic, except that it is not two sorted: there is no numeric sort. We start off with the same kinds of object symbols. The key difference is that we have a belief operator B in place of the probability operator **prob**.

The formulas of the language are generated by the same set of formation rules, **T0–T1** and **F1–F5**. The only change is that the probability operator rule **T2** is omitted and instead we have a new formula formation rule:

F6) If α is a formula then so is $B\alpha$.

Semantics: The formulas of the belief logic can be interpreted by a structure similar to our propositional probability structures, except that the probability function is replaced by an accessibility relation. The modal-structures have the form:

$$M = \langle \mathcal{O}, S, R, \vartheta \rangle,$$

where $\mathcal{O}$, S, and ϑ are a domain of individuals, a set of possible worlds, and a world dependent interpretation function respectively, just as they were in our propositional probability structures. R is a binary relation on S; i.e., various pairs of worlds $\langle s_i, s_j \rangle$ are members of R.

The formulas of the logic are interpreted with respect to a triple, (M, s, v), consisting of a structure M, the current world s, and a variable

assignment function v. Again this is the same as the interpretation of
the formulas of our probability logic. In fact, the rules of interpretation
T0–T1 and **F1–F4b**, used for the probability logic, are all the same as
those used for belief logics. The only difference is that we do not need a
rule for interpreting the probability operator; instead we replace it with
the following rule for interpreting the belief operator:

$$(M, s, v) \models B\alpha \quad \text{iff} \quad (M, s', v) \models \alpha \text{ for all } s' \text{ such that } (s, s') \in R.$$

That is, $B\alpha$ is satisfied at the current world if and only if α is satisfied
by every world accessible from that world.

2.8.2 KD45

Beliefs are fallible. It is quite possible that an agent believes something which is false. For example, members of the flat world society
may believe that the earth is flat, contrary to all evidence, or computer
scientists may believe that $P \neq NP$ in accord with all evidence even
though it is possible that this may be false. Hence, we want our formal
model of belief to capture this property. That is, we do not want belief
in a formula to imply the truth of that formula; we do not want $B\alpha \rightarrow \alpha$
to be valid. We can define the behavior of the belief operator by placing
conditions on the accessibility relation. With different types of accessibility relations we get different modal logics. The logic that has been
considered the most appropriate for modeling belief, with its fallibility,
is the logic KD45 (a.k.a. weak S5 with consistency) (e.g., Levesque [77],
Fagin and Halpern [29]).

In KD45 we require that the accessibility relation be *serial, Euclidean*,
and *transitive*. The accessibility relation R is serial if for all $s \in S$
there is some s' such that $(s, s') \in R$. It is Euclidean if $(s, t) \in R$ and
$(s, u) \in R$ implies that $(t, u) \in R$. And it is transitive if $(s, t) \in R$ and
$(t, u) \in R$ implies that $(s, u) \in R$. These conditions do not imply that
R is reflexive; i.e., it is not necessarily the case that $(s, s) \in R$ for any
world s. Hence, the formula $B\alpha \rightarrow \alpha$ is not valid; it is quite possible for
α to be satisfied by all worlds accessible from a particular world s and
at the same time fail to be satisfied by s since s may not be accessible
from itself.

Each one of these conditions of the accessibility relation leads to the
validity of an axiom schema which serves to characterize the behavior
of the belief operator. The fact that R is serial implies that $\neg B$*false*

is valid. This comes from the fact that *false* is not satisfied in any world; hence, it cannot be satisfied in the set of worlds accessible from a particular world, as long as this is a non-empty set. When R is serial we are guaranteed that the set of accessible worlds is non-empty. R being transitive ensures that the schema $B\alpha \rightarrow BB\alpha$ is valid. If $B\alpha$ is satisfied by a particular world s, α will be satisfied by every world accessible from s. For any such world, say t, α will also be satisfied in every world accessible from t, since by transitivity all of the worlds accessible from t are already accessible from s; thus, they are satisfying worlds for α. Therefore, t will satisfy $B\alpha$ and since this is true for any t accessible from s, s will satisfy $BB\alpha$. Finally, R being Euclidean means that the schema $\neg B\alpha \rightarrow B\neg B\alpha$ is valid. If s satisfies $\neg B\alpha$ then there must be some world u accessible from s such that u does not satisfy α. By the Euclidean property, for every world t accessible from s we must have that u is accessible from t. Hence, every world accessible from s satisfies $\neg B\alpha$, and s itself must satisfy $B\neg B\alpha$.

KD45, then, specifies a belief logic in which an agent can have false beliefs; i.e., $B\alpha$ and $\neg\alpha$ can be satisfied in the same world. Also the agent's beliefs are closed under positive and negative introspection: if the agent believes something he believes that he believes it, and if the agent does not believe something he believes that he does not believe it.

We can supply a proof theory for KD45 belief logics where there is a single domain of discourse for all possible worlds. The proof theory embodies the above axiom schemata which force the accessibility relation to have the three required properties. The proof theory consists of two sets of axioms, first-order and modal, and three rules of inference.

First-Order Axioms   All of the axioms of first-order logic with equality, e.g., as given in Section 2.6.

KD45 Modal Axioms

K) $(B\alpha \land B(\alpha \rightarrow \beta)) \rightarrow B\beta$.

D) $\neg Bfalse$.

4) $B\alpha \rightarrow BB\alpha$.

5) $\neg B\alpha \rightarrow B\neg B\alpha$.

BF) $\forall x.(B\alpha) \rightarrow B(\forall x.\alpha)$.

This is the Barcan formula, and it is valid only when each world has the same domain of discourse.

Rules of Inference

MP) From α and $\alpha \rightarrow \beta$ infer β (Modus Ponens).

UG) From α infer $\forall x.\alpha$ (Universal Generalization).

N) From α infer $B\alpha$ (Necessitation).

It is easy to show that the proof theory is sound with respect to the modal structures, defined above, in which the accessibility relation is serial, Euclidean, and transitive. Furthermore, from the canonical model construction for normal modal predicate logics[22] given by Hughes and Cresswell [54, p. 176], it is equally easy to show that the proof theory is also complete.[23] Hence, a formula is valid if and only if it can be deduced from the proof theory.

2.8.3 Probabilistic View of KD45

A number of writers in philosophy have demonstrated relationships between probabilities and various modal logics (e.g., Morgan [93,92]). These works have demonstrated that many modal logics can be given probabilistic semantics, in the sense that the standard notions of validity and entailment can be defined in terms of probability functions over the formulas of the logic. As we pointed out in Section 2.1, such semantics do not extend the language to allow one to reason with the probabilities. The main point of these works is, however, quite clear; formulas assigned probability one under some probability assignment behave just like formulas which are true in all accessible worlds under some belief structure. In the context of extended languages where one can make reference to the probabilities Halpern [44] has demonstrated that in the propositional case there is an equivalence between formulas that have probability one and formulas that are true in all accessible worlds. Here we extend his results to the quantified case.

---

[22] A modal logic is called normal if it contains all valid propositional formulas, the axiom schema **K**, and the rules of inference **MP** and **N** [54].

[23] The construction given by Hughes and Cresswell is for function-free languages, i.e., languages in which the only terms are variables. However, their construction also works for languages in which the functions are rigid, as is the case with our language.

Consider the sublanguage of our propositional probability language where the only probability statements are $\mathsf{cert}(\alpha)$; i.e., we do not have any intermediate probabilities. We can construct this sublanguage by starting off with object variables and functions, generating object terms, forming atomic formulas using the object predicates and terms, and then closing off under application of cert, $\neg$, $\wedge$, and $\forall x$, where x is any object variable. Hence, we do not have any numeric assertions, like $1 + 0 = 1$ or $0 < 1$, in our sublanguage. We can denote that the probability of a formula is equal to 1 by writing $\mathsf{cert}(\alpha)$ and that it is less than 1 by writing $\neg\mathsf{cert}(\alpha)$. Nesting of probability operators is allowed, so we can also say things like $\mathsf{cert}\big(\neg\mathsf{cert}(\alpha)\big)$, and we can have quantification using object variables. For example, formulas like $\forall x.\mathsf{cert}(\alpha)$, $\mathsf{cert}(\alpha) \wedge \beta$, and $\mathsf{cert}(\alpha) \vee \mathsf{cert}(\exists x.\beta)$ are all part of our sublanguage.

We will call this "certainty" sublanguage $\mathcal{L}^{\mathrm{cert}}$, and the ordinary KD45 belief language $\mathcal{L}^B$. Given a formula of $\mathcal{L}^{\mathrm{cert}}$ we can translate it to a formula of $\mathcal{L}^B$ by the simple device of replacing every certainty operator cert by a belief operator B. Similarly, we can do the translation the other way around. If α is a formula of $\mathcal{L}^{\mathrm{cert}}$, we indicate its translation by α^B. Similarly if α is a formula of $\mathcal{L}^B$, its translation will be denoted by α^{cert}.

As a final bit of notation, let us call the proof theory presented above KD45, and let KD45^{cert} be used to indicate the same proof theory where every instance of the belief operator has been replaced by the certainty operator. Also we will call the proof theory we have already developed for our propositional probability language AXPROB.

We can now present the main theorem of this section, which shows the strong relationship between formulas of quantified KD45 and formulas of the propositional probability logic which have probability one.

THEOREM 17 KD45^{cert} is a sound and complete axiomatization for our sublanguage $\mathcal{L}^{\mathrm{cert}}$.

Proof: We can prove soundness by showing that all instances of the axioms of KD45^{cert} are provable from AXPROB. We have already established that AXPROB is sound with respect to propositional probability structures, and these are the same structures used to interpret the formulas of our sublanguage $\mathcal{L}^{\mathrm{cert}}$. This will show that all of the axioms are sound. Then we show that the rules of inference preserve validity;

hence, every formula that can be deduced from the proof theory must
be valid, and the proof theory is sound.

First-order axioms All these axioms are already part of AXPROB.

$\mathbf{K}^{\text{cert}}$ $\big(\text{cert}(\alpha) \wedge \text{cert}(\alpha \to \beta)\big) \to \text{cert}(\beta)$: Using probabilistic tautologies
one can easily prove $\text{prob}(\alpha \wedge \neg\beta) = 0$ from $\text{prob}(\alpha \to \beta) = 1$.
From this, and the assumption that $\text{prob}(\alpha) = 1$, one can show
that $\text{prob}(\alpha \wedge \beta) = 1$ by using axiom **Prob3**. We showed in our
examples that $\text{prob}(\beta) \geq \text{prob}(\alpha \wedge \beta)$; hence, we get that $\text{cert}(\beta)$
as required.

$\mathbf{D}^{\text{cert}}$, $\mathbf{4}^{\text{cert}}$, $\mathbf{5}^{\text{cert}}$, $\mathbf{BF}^{\text{cert}}$ The proof of these axioms from AXPROB is
immediate (using axiom **Prob4**).

Rules Modus ponens and universal generalization are part of AXPROB.
Since the other rules are sound, by induction, α is only deducible
without necessitation if it is valid. This means that it is provably
equivalent to *true*. Therefore, we get $\text{cert}(\alpha)$ by rule **PE**. That is,
the conclusion of $\mathbf{N}^{\text{cert}}$ is valid.

To show completeness we use a simple construction due to Halpern
[44]. By Theorem 13 it suffices to show that if α is consistent with
KD45^{cert}, then it is satisfiable. If α is consistent with KD45^{cert} its $\mathcal{L}^B$
transform, α^B, must be consistent with KD45. This follows from the
fact that any deduction of $\neg\alpha^B$ from KD45 could be transformed into a
deduction of $\neg\alpha$ from KD45^{cert}. Since KD45 is complete for $\mathcal{L}^B$ there
exists a triple which satisfies α^B.

LEMMA 18 If a formula of $\mathcal{L}^B$, β, is satisfiable, it is satisfied by a triple
(M', s, v) such that the set of worlds accessible from s is at most countably infinite.

Proof: Say that β is satisfied by a triple (M, s, v), $M = \langle \mathcal{O}, S, R, \vartheta \rangle$.
Let us denote the set of worlds accessible from s by $R(s)$. Define
$M' = \langle \mathcal{O}, S', R', \vartheta' \rangle$, where $S' \subseteq S$, R' is R restricted to S', and
ϑ' is ϑ restricted to S'. We define S' as follows. For every formula
$\neg B\delta$ satisfied by (M, s, v) we choose one world t from $R(s)$ such that
t satisfies $\neg\delta$. Such a world must exist by the semantic definition of
$\neg B\delta$. We let S' be the set which consists of all such worlds, t, along
with s. It is easy to check by induction that for all formulas $\alpha \in \mathcal{L}^B$,

$(M', s, v) \models \alpha$ iff $(M, s, v) \models \alpha$. For example, if α is of the form $B\phi$, then if $(M, s, v) \models \alpha$, $(M, t, v) \models \phi$ for all $t \in R(s)$. Since $R'(s) \subseteq R(s)$ we must have $(M', t', v) \models \phi$ for all $t' \in R'(s)$, and thus $(M', s, v) \models \alpha$. In the opposite direction, if $(M, s, v) \not\models \alpha$ then, by our construction, there exists a world $t \in R'(s)$ such that $(M, t, v) \models \neg\phi$. Hence, we have that $(M', s, v) \not\models \alpha$.

Thus we have that (M', s, v) satisfies β. There are at most a countable number of formulas of the form $\neg B\delta$, and thus at most a countable number of worlds in S'.[24] ∎

Let us denote a triple which satisfies α^B by (M, s, v) where we choose, by the lemma, a triple where there are at most a countably infinite number of worlds accessible from s. Let $M = \langle \mathcal{O}, S, R, \vartheta \rangle$, and let $R(s)$ be the set of worlds accessible from s. We can now define a propositional probability structure $P = \langle \mathcal{O}, S', \mu, \vartheta' \rangle$, where $S' = R(s) \cup \{s\}$, and ϑ' is ϑ restricted to S'. To define μ we choose some enumeration of the worlds in $R(s)$, say $\langle t_1, t_2, \ldots \rangle$, and choose a sequence of numbers $\langle n_1, n_2, \ldots \rangle$ of equal length which sums to one. If $R(s)$ is countably infinite we simply choose a suitable infinite sequence which sums to one. We then let $\mu(t_i) = n_i$. Note that if s is accessible from itself, i.e., $s \in R(s)$, we have that $\mu(s) > 0$, otherwise we have that $\mu(s) = 0$. We can show by induction that for every formula $\beta \in \mathcal{L}^{\text{cert}}$ and all worlds $t \in S'$ we have that $(P, t, v) \models \beta$ iff $(M, t, v) \models \beta^B$. For example, if β is of the form $\text{cert}(\delta)$ we have that $(P, t, v) \models \text{cert}(\delta)$ iff $(P, t', v) \models \delta$ for all $t' \in R(s)$, by our construction. This is true (by induction) iff $(M, t', v) \models \delta^B$ for all $t' \in R(s)$; i.e., iff $(M, s, v) \models B(\delta^B)$. Now we have two cases: (1) $t = s$, in which case we get that $(M, t, v) \models B(\delta^B)$ and this means that $(M, t, v) \models (\text{cert}(\delta))^B$ as required; or (2) $t \neq s$ in which case we have, by the transitivity of belief structures, that $(M, s, v) \models BB(\delta^B)$ and hence that $(M, t, v) \models B(\delta^B)$, since $t \in R(s)$. Again we get that $(M, t, v) \models (\text{cert}(\delta))^B$.

The consequence is that $(P, s, v) \models \alpha$; hence, α is satisfiable. ∎

COROLLARY 19 A formula $\alpha \in \mathcal{L}^{\text{cert}}$ is valid in our propositional probability structures iff α^B is valid in KD45 belief structures.

Proof: By completeness, if α is valid it is provable from KD45^{cert}. This

---

[24] S' may well be finite. A single world t selected as a member of the *set* S' may be selected many times for different formulas $\neg B\delta$.

proof can be transformed into a proof of α^B in KD45; hence, α^B is valid. The opposite direction is identical. ■

This corollary says that the logical behavior of beliefs in a KD45 logic is the same as the behavior of those beliefs that the agent assigns probability one to. The sets of valid formulas are isomorphic and entailment is preserved under the translation. Our proof of soundness also showed the following corollary.

COROLLARY 20 The proof theory for the propositional probability language subsumes KD45^{cert}. That is, if α is deducible from KD45^{cert} it is deducible from the proof theory developed in Section 2.6. Hence, the proof theory we have developed subsumes KD45 reasoning about beliefs.

This result proves our claim that the logic for propositional probabilities is a generalization of ordinary Hintikka-style logics of belief. The modal logic of belief KD45 captures those beliefs that the agent is certain of, i.e., those beliefs to which the agent assigns probability one. Our logic for propositional probabilities allows the modeling of a far wider range of degrees of commitment on the part of the agent. Furthermore, because of this quantitative notion of degree of belief it is capable of expressing a range of qualitative relationships between the agent's beliefs. For example, it can represent the situation where the agent has a greater degree of belief in one assertion than in another. It is also capable of representing some forms of conditional beliefs.

KD45 allows false beliefs. That is, the agent could believe α in a particular world, yet that world could fail to satisfy α. A similar situation can occur with our propositional probability logic. In this case the agent could assign certainty to a proposition α while at the same time α could be false at various worlds. That is, it is quite possible that $\neg \alpha \wedge \text{cert}(\alpha)$ could be satisfied in a particular world. The only restriction is that these worlds must have probability zero. This demonstrates that the probability distribution over the worlds has nothing to do with what is true in the real world. The distribution has to do with what the agent believes to be the case. It is quite possible that the agent's beliefs are described by a structure which assigns zero probability to the actual world. Hence, certainty is no guarantee of truth, it simply expresses that the agent has no doubts.

3 Statistical Probabilities

3.1 Probability Measures of Sets

Probabilities defined over sets of individuals model statistical probabilities. Such probabilities do not refer to the properties of particular individuals in the set, but rather they refer to properties of the set as a whole. For example, when we say that most birds fly we are making a statement about the relative measure of the set of individuals that fly among the set of individuals that are birds; we are not making an assertion about any particular bird. Hence, to develop a logic for representing statistical probabilities we need a mechanism for referring to various sets of individuals and for assigning probabilities to these sets.

3.1.1 λ-abstraction

In first-order languages n-ary predicate symbols denote sets of n-ary vectors of individuals. However, the use of such symbols in first-order logic is quite constrained; e.g., a predicate symbol by itself is not a legal formula. We must use predicate symbols in conjunction with the correct number of terms. For example, if P is a monadic predicate symbol, it will denote a set of individuals and syntactically it must be used in conjunction with a term, as in the formula P(t). Similarly, if Q is a binary predicate symbol, it will denote a set of pairs of individuals and it must be used in conjunction with two terms, as in the formula $Q(t_1, t_2)$. Free use of predicate symbols, i.e., the use of these symbols as if they were ordinary terms, places one into the realm of second-order logic, which is much more difficult to work with.

Even if we could use bare predicate symbols in our language we still would not be able to refer to all of the different sets of individuals that we need to: we also need to refer to those sets that are implicitly generated by the formation of complex formulas. For example, with the predicate symbols bird and fly we can generate formulas like $bird(t) \land fly(t)$ which says that t is a member of the intersection of the sets denoted by bird and fly; i.e., it is a flying bird. This formula is making implicit reference to the intersection of the sets denoted by the predicate symbols. More subtle examples occur when we use quantifiers. Say that ancestor is a binary predicate where ancestor(t,s) asserts that t is an ancestor of **s**, then we can make implicit reference to the set of individuals that are the ancestors of all individuals: $\forall \mathsf{y}.\mathsf{ancestor}(\mathsf{t}, \mathsf{y})$ says that the individual denoted by **t** is a member of this set. Or we could implicitly refer to the set of individuals that are an ancestor of some individual: $\exists \mathsf{y}.\mathsf{ancestor}(\mathsf{t}, \mathsf{y})$.

We can gain the ability to refer directly to such sets by using ideas from lambda abstraction (see, e.g., Dowty et al. [20]). Before discussing this concept, let us briefly review the manner in which first-order languages are interpreted. First-order structures for interpreting these languages are of the form $M = \langle \mathcal{O}, \vartheta \rangle$, where $\mathcal{O}$ is a set of individuals, the domain of discourse, and ϑ is an interpretation function which maps all the function symbols to functions over $\mathcal{O}$ and all of the n-ary predicate symbols to n-ary relations over $\mathcal{O}$ (equivalently, the n-ary predicate symbols are mapped to subsets of $\mathcal{O}^n$, the n-ary direct product of $\mathcal{O}$). First-order formulas are interpreted with respect to a pair (M, v) consisting of a first-order structure M and a variable assignment function v. The variable assignment function maps each variable to a particular domain individual. Under this pair an atomic formula like $\mathsf{Q}(\mathsf{t}_1, \mathsf{t}_2)$ will be assigned the truth value **true**, written $(M, v) \models \mathsf{Q}(\mathsf{t}_1, \mathsf{t}_2)$, if and only if the pair of individuals denoted by $\langle \mathsf{t}_1, \mathsf{t}_2 \rangle$ is a member of the set of pairs denoted by the binary predicate symbol Q. Here the denotation of the terms t_1 and t_2 is determined by the interpretation function ϑ and, if the terms contain any variables, the variable assignment function v. Complex formulas are assigned a truth value using the standard rules for interpreting the logical connectives. With the presence of a variable assignment function it does not matter if the formulas have free variables (variables unbound by any quantifier). For example, the formula $\mathsf{P}(\mathbf{x})$ will be true under (M, v) if and only if $v(\mathbf{x})$ is a member of the set denoted by P. This separation into structure and variable assignment function allows a clean treatment of quantification. Quantified formulas are true if the formula in the scope of the quantifier is true under some range of different variable assignment functions, with the structure being held constant. For example, $(M, v) \models \forall \mathbf{x}.\mathsf{P}(\mathbf{x})$ if and only if $(M, v') \models \mathsf{P}(\mathbf{x})$ for all variable assignment functions v' that differ from v only in their mapping of $\mathbf{x}$. The structure M remains constant throughout.

We often use a relatively informal notion of a set defined by some statement. For example, we may define the set of odd numbers as $\{n :$

n is not divisible by 2}, or the set of NFL players as $\{x : x$ is an active player for an NFL club}. In these examples we have defined a set by using a statement which characterizes the members of that set. The statement contains a variable being used as a placeholder: any individual that makes the statement true when substituted for x is a member of the set. Lambda abstraction formalizes this notion of set definition "by a statement" in the context of logical languages. If we have a formula of our formal language we can assert that this formula defines a set of individuals by simply specifying which of its variables are acting as placeholders. The set of individuals defined in this manner is identified by looking at all instantiations of the placeholder variables that make the formula true. This can be accomplished at the semantic level by simply varying the variable assignment function, just as we did when interpreting quantified variables. At the syntactic level we can denote the placeholder variables by using a lambda abstraction operator λ.

For example, if we have the first-order formula dog(x), we can form the lambda abstraction λx.dog(x). This specifies that the variable x is the placeholder, and it denotes or defines the set of *satisfying instantiations* of the variable x. In this case the set of satisfying instantiations is identical to the set denoted by the predicate symbol dog; i.e., the lambda abstraction denotes the set of dogs. Similarly, the lambda abstraction λx.dog(x) ∧ large(x) denotes the intersection of the sets denoted by the predicate symbols dog and large; i.e., it denotes the set of large dogs. We can also specify more than one variable as a placeholder, in which case we are defining a set of vectors of individuals. For example λxy.son(x, y) specifies the set of pairs of individuals that are the satisfying instantiations of x and y in son(x, y), i.e., the set of pairs that stand in the son relation. We can have other variables besides the placeholder variables in the formula. For example, λx.∃y.ancestor(x, y) specifies the set of individuals that have at least one descendent.

We can define the interpretation of the lambda terms more formally as follows. Under the pair (M, v) the lambda abstraction $\lambda x.\alpha$ denotes the set

$$\{ o : o \in \mathcal{O} \quad \text{and} \quad (M, v[x/o]) \models \alpha \},$$

where $v[x/o]$ denotes the variable assignment function that is identical to v except that it maps the variable x to the individual o.

The variables specified as placeholders by the lambda abstraction need not depend in any way on the variables actually present in the formula. For example, we can specify the lambda abstraction $\lambda\mathbf{x}.(\forall\mathbf{x}.P(\mathbf{x}))$. If we use our formal interpretation to examine the set of satisfying instantiations of $\mathbf{x}$ in this formula we find that this set is either all of the domain or the empty set. By our definition, the set denoted by this abstraction is $\{o : (M, v[\mathbf{x}/o]) \models \forall\mathbf{x}.P(\mathbf{x})\}$. Recursively determining if any particular $(M, v[\mathbf{x}/o])$ satisfies this formula we find that

$$(M, v[\mathbf{x}/o]) \models \forall\mathbf{x}.P(\mathbf{x}) \quad \text{iff} \quad (M, v') \models P(\mathbf{x}),$$

for all v' that differ from $v[\mathbf{x}/o]$ in their mapping of $\mathbf{x}$. It is easy to see that the particular o chosen at the first stage makes no difference when we apply the recursive interpretation of $\forall\mathbf{x}.P(\mathbf{x})$: the formula is satisfied by every pair $(M, v[\mathbf{x}/o])$ or by none. What has happened here is that although $\mathbf{x}$ appears in the formula $\forall\mathbf{x}.P(\mathbf{x})$ it does not appear free. It is only the free occurrences of the placeholder variables that have a role in determining the set of satisfying instantiations.

In addition, the formula can have free variables other than the placeholder variables, e.g., the abstraction $\lambda\mathbf{x}.\texttt{ancestor}(\mathbf{x}, \mathbf{y})$. Under the pair (M, v), this abstraction will denote the set of individuals that are ancestors of $v(\mathbf{y})$, i.e., ancestors of the individual denoted by $\mathbf{y}$ under the current variable assignment function.

Although we will not use the lambda operator directly, we will use the "placeholder variable" idea from lambda abstraction to solve our first problem: that of referring to various sets of individuals. Now we turn to the second problem, that of specifying the probabilities of these different sets.

3.1.2   Probabilities over the Domain

Typically statements of statistical probability make assertions about the proportion of individuals from a particular set that are members of some other set, e.g., the proportion of elephants that are gray. As we have discussed, probabilities are a generalization of simple proportion, proportions being equivalent to uniform probability distributions over finite spaces. If we place a probability distribution over the domain of discourse (i.e., the set of all individuals $\mathcal{O}$) we will be able to assign probabilities to various sets of individuals using this distribution.

The approach of placing a distribution over the domain of discourse has received scant attention in previous studies, unlike the approach of placing a distribution over the formulas of the language, discussed in the previous chapter. The idea has been used before by Keisler [59] to develop a logic for representing mathematical probability notions, and by Åqvist et al. [4] to develop a logic for representing adverbs of frequency. However, to my knowledge this idea had never been applied to the problem of representing statistical information.

Using the ideas described in the previous section we can use formulas with placeholder variables to denote a wide variety of sets of individuals or vectors of individuals. Furthermore, we can place a probability distribution over the domain of discourse that has the property that every set of individuals definable by a formula will have a probability under that distribution.[1] By using a probability operator in our language, we can generate terms which denote the probability of the set of individuals defined by the formula to which the operator has been applied. This is very similar to the operation of the propositional probability operator used in the previous chapter. The only difference here is that the statistical probability operator must also specify the set of placeholder variables. Additionally, more than one placeholder variable may be specified. If a tuple of variables is used, the probability operator will denote the probability of a set of *vectors* of individuals. Therefore, not only do we need a probability distribution over $\mathcal{O}$, we also need for every n a probability distribution over the product space $\mathcal{O}^n$ which consists of all n-ary vectors of individuals from $\mathcal{O}$.

The probabilities assigned to these sets are taken with respect to a probability distribution defined over the domain of discourse $\mathcal{O}$. That is, the probability of a set of individuals defined in this manner corresponds to the proportion of *all* individuals that are members of that set. If we want to refer to, e.g., the proportion of birds that fly, we need something more. Here we are referring to the proportion of the set of *birds* that are members of the set of flying individuals, not to the proportion of all individuals (birds and non-birds) that are flying birds. Fortunately, we can refer to such probabilities quite easily by using conditional probabilities. If we divide the probability measure of the set of flying birds (i.e., the proportion of all individuals that are flying birds) by the probability

---

[1] Probability distributions do not have to assign a probability to every set; i.e., the probability function does not have to be defined on every set. Those sets on which the probability function (measure) is undefined are called nonmeasurable sets. See Fagin and Halpern [30] for further discussion of nonmeasurable sets and an interesting application to Dempster-Shafer belief functions.

measure of the set of birds, we will get the relative measure of flying birds among birds, as required.

The terms denoting the probabilities of various sets of individuals are numeric terms; they denote particular real numbers under each possible probability distribution. Using a two-sorted language with numeric predicates and functions we can make complex qualitative assertions about these probabilities, just as we were able to make complex assertions about our propositional probabilities.

We now turn to a presentation of our language for statistical probabilities, which is simply a formalization of these ideas.

3.2 A Probability Logic for Statistical Probabilities

3.2.1 Syntax

The syntax of our logic is much like the propositional probability logic we developed in Chapter 2. In particular, we start off with a set of user defined symbols and a set of distinguished symbols that are always part of the language. There are only two changes. First, we do not have the propositional probability operator prob; instead we have a variable binding statistical probability operator. We will use square brackets, '[' and ']', around its formula argument and a subscripted set of placeholder variables to indicate the application of this operator. Second, we allow an extra set of user defined function symbols which we call *measuring functions*. These are functions which map individual objects, or vectors of individual objects, to numbers. For example, we may wish to discuss the weight of various people using a weight function. This function would be a measuring function: it maps individual objects, in this case people, to numbers, in this case the number that represents their weight in some convenient unit.[2]

---

[2]These measuring functions are very similar to Hayes's [48] quality spaces. In particular, we could have defined weight to be a function from individuals to an abstract numeric quantity of weight and further defined kilograms, pounds, etc. as numeric functions from the abstract numeric quantities to numbers which give the weight in these particular units. The only difference is that we are assuming that the abstract quantities are real numbers, although we make no commitment as to what particular numbers they are. Hayes, on the other hand, simply assumes that the abstract quantities are closed under addition. Furthermore, we use the name "measuring function" instead of "measure function" that was used by Hayes. This avoids possible confusion with the mathematical concept of a measure function, of

These measuring functions are known in statistics and probability theory as *random variables*. A random variable is a function from some space over which a probability distribution is defined to the reals, just like our measuring functions. Hence, if we want a general logic for representing statistical information, we need such functions. We avoid the name "random variable," however, because it is rather misleading in the context of logics where variables are quite different from functions. The reason that these functions are called *random* variables in statistics and probability theory is that they induce a probability distribution over the reals. Say that weight is a measuring function and that μ is a probability distribution over $\mathcal{O}$. That is, μ assigns a probability to every subset of $\mathcal{O}$. The function weight maps $\mathcal{O}$ to the reals $I\!\!R$, and it induces the following probability distribution, $\mu_{I\!\!R}$, over $I\!\!R$:

$$\mu_{I\!\!R}(\mathcal{B}) = \mu\big(\texttt{weight}^{-1}(\mathcal{B})\big),$$

where $\mathcal{B}$ is a Borel set, $\mathcal{B} \subseteq I\!\!R$, and $\texttt{weight}^{-1}$ is the inverse map of weight; i.e., $\texttt{weight}^{-1}(\mathcal{B}) = \{o : \texttt{weight}(o) \in \mathcal{B}\}$. That is, the probability of a set of real numbers is equal to the probability of its inverse image under the probability distribution over $\mathcal{O}$. When it is said that weight is normally distributed this means that the distribution over the reals induced by the measuring function is, or is approximated by, a normal distribution.[3]

The propositional probability logic of Chapter 2 did not include measuring functions. It is not reasonable to assume that such functions are constant across different possible worlds; i.e., they are not rigid. For example, an individual's weight may vary from world to world, even if the individual does not. Hence, we omitted such functions to avoid the complexities of non-rigid terms. However, for the statistical probability logic presented here, there is no set of possible worlds; so we do not have to deal with the rigidity of terms.

Formulas: We have the same rules, **T0–T1** and **F1–F5**, for the formation of well formed formulas that were used in our propositional probability logic. The only change is that rule **T2** is replaced by:

---

which probability functions are instances.

[3] If we have only a finite number of individuals in $\mathcal{O}$ the distribution induced over the reals can only be approximated by a continuous distribution like the normal distribution.

T2) If α is a formula and $\vec{x}$ is a vector of n *object* variables $\langle x_1, \ldots, x_n \rangle$, then $[\alpha]_{\vec{x}}$ is an *f-term*.

This rule is quite similar to the rule that we used for our propositional probability operator: it takes an existent formula and generates a new numeric term. The key difference is that the statistical probability operator is a variable binding operator. In addition to the formula that it is applied to, it requires a vector of object variables $\vec{x}$. These are the variables that will be used in defining the set of satisfying instantiations; i.e., they are the placeholder variables. As with lambda abstraction there is no necessary relationship between the set of variables in the formula α and the variables in $\vec{x}$. For example, not all of the variables of α need appear in $\vec{x}$.

Definitional Extensions: We include the same set of definitional extensions to our language that we used in Chapter 2. So we have an extended set of logical connectives, the existential quantifier, an extended set of inequality predicates, and extra numeric constants.

We also define conditional probabilities in a very similar manner:

DEFINITION 21 (AXIOM OF CONDITIONAL PROBABILITIES)

$$[\beta]_{\vec{x}} \neq 0 \rightarrow [\alpha|\beta]_{\vec{x}} \times [\beta]_{\vec{x}} = [\alpha \wedge \beta]_{\vec{x}}$$
$$\wedge \quad [\beta]_{\vec{x}} = 0 \rightarrow [\alpha|\beta]_{\vec{x}} = 0.$$

The important thing to notice here is that the set of variables $\vec{x}$ remains constant throughout. Also, as with the propositional conditional probabilities defined in Chapter 2, our statistical conditional probabilities have the property that if the conditioning formula has probability zero then the conditional probability will be equal to zero.

3.2.2   Semantics

DEFINITION 22 (STATISTICAL PROBABILITY STRUCTURES)
We define the following structure which we use to interpret the formulas of our statistical probability language.

$$M = \langle \mathcal{O}, \vartheta, \mu \rangle$$

Where:

a) $\mathcal{O}$ is a set of individuals representing objects of the domain that one wishes to describe in the logic.

b) ϑ is an interpretation function for the symbols of the language. It assigns to every object predicate symbol a relation of the right arity in $\mathcal{O}$ and to every object function symbol a function of the right arity over $\mathcal{O}$. The numeric predicate and function symbols are mapped by ϑ to relations and functions over $\mathbb{R}$. The measuring function symbols are mapped to functions of the right arity from $\mathcal{O}$ to $\mathbb{R}$. And the distinguished function and predicate symbols of the language are interpreted in the same special manner by ϑ as they were in the propositional probability structures.

c) μ is a discrete probability function on $\mathcal{O}$. That is, μ is a function that maps the elements of $\mathcal{O}$ to the real interval $[0,1]$ such that $\sum_{o \in \mathcal{O}} \mu(o) = 1$. This function defines a probability distribution over the subsets of $\mathcal{O}$: for every $A \subseteq \mathcal{O}$, $\mu(A) = \sum_{o \in A} \mu(o)$.[4]

So we see that there are two essential differences between the propositional probability structures and the statistical probability structures. First, we do not have a set of possible worlds: there is only one fixed interpretation function ϑ. And, most importantly, we have a probability distribution over the domain of discourse $\mathcal{O}$, instead of over a set of possible worlds.

3.2.3 The Interpretation of the Formulas

When we turn to the interpretation of the formulas things are again very similar to the propositional probability logic. However, we no longer need a current world to interpret the formulas. The interpretation of the formulas depends only on a statistical probability structure M and a variable assignment function v. We write $(M, v) \models \alpha$ if the formula α is assigned the truth value **true** by the pair. Except for the omission of the current world most of the rules of interpretation remain identical to those used for the propositional probability language. In particular, rules **T0–T1**, and **F1–F4b** are the same. The only change is in the interpretation of the probability operator.

---

[4] We note that as in the propositional probability structures every subset of $\mathcal{O}$ will have a probability regardless of how large $\mathcal{O}$ is. The only restriction is that at most a countable number of objects in $\mathcal{O}$ will have non-zero probability.

T2) For every formula α, the f-term created by the probability operator
$[\alpha]_{\vec{x}}$ is given the interpretation

$$([\alpha]_{\vec{x}})^{(M,v)} = \mu^n\{\vec{a} : (M, v[\vec{x}/\vec{a}]) \models \alpha\}.$$

Here $\vec{x}$ and $\vec{a}$ are n-ary vectors of object variables and individual objects respectively. We use the notation $v[\vec{x}/\vec{a}]$ to denote a
new variable assignment function which differs from v only in that
$v(x_i) = a_i$ (for $i = 1, \ldots, n$). And μ^n represents the n-fold product
measure formed from μ.

Product measures are a standard technique for extending a measure
to the product space. Starting with our probability function (a special
type of measure) defined on $\mathcal{O}$ we can define, for any n, a probability
function on the product domain $\mathcal{O}^n$. We let $\mu^n(\langle o_1, \ldots, o_n \rangle) = \mu(o_1) \times
\cdots \times \mu(o_n)$ for every $\langle o_1, \ldots, o_n \rangle \in \mathcal{O}^n$. Then for any set $A \subseteq \mathcal{O}^n$ we
let $\mu^n(A) = \sum_{\langle o_1,\ldots,o_n\rangle \in A} \mu^n(\langle o_1, \ldots, o_n \rangle)$. It is not difficult to show
that the functions μ^n defined in this manner are in fact probability
functions over $\mathcal{O}^n$. We will discuss the effect of using product measures
in Section 3.2.5.

Inspection of this rule should convince the reader that it gives the
promised interpretation of the statistical probability terms. Each one
of these terms denotes the probability of the set of satisfying instantiations of the variables $\vec{x}$. Since the probability function is a real-valued
function we see that the probability terms do in fact denote particular
real numbers.

3.2.4 Random Selection

As we have discussed above, we can think of the statistical probability
terms as representing the probability measure of the set of satisfying
instantiations of the variables cited by the probability operator. Under
this interpretation a formula like $[\mathtt{Bird(x)}]_{\mathbf{x}} > 0.5$ asserts that the measure of the set of birds in the domain is greater than 0.5. The variable
$\mathbf{x}$ cited by the probability operator acts simply as a placeholder under
this interpretation.

There is, however, an alternative interpretation, one which attaches a
meaning to the variables. If we have a random selection process which
selects individuals from the domain in accord with their probability, i.e.,
if the probability that any particular individual o is selected is $\mu(o)$,

then we can view the variables as being *random designators*. Under this interpretation the formula $[\text{Bird}(x)]_x > 0.5$ asserts that the probability that a randomly selected domain individual will be a bird is greater than 0.5. Now the variable x can be interpreted as "denoting" a randomly selected bird; it is a random designator. Note that in the formal sense of denoting the variable x does not denote anything. That is, it does not represent any particular domain individual. The domain contains no "randomly selected" individuals; the notion of random selection is simply a convenient meta-logical notion.

3.2.5 Product Measures

One of the key features of the way in which we interpret our statistical probability terms is that we use a product measure μ^n to obtain the probability of a set of n-ary vectors. This choice ensures that the probability terms behave in a reasonable manner.

In particular, with product measures the interpretation of a random designator does not affect the interpretation of any other random designator; distinct variables cited in the probability operator behave in an independent manner. This is similar to the independence of distinct universally quantified variables in first-order logic. For example, the sentence $\forall xy.P(x) \wedge Q(y)$ can be decomposed into two independent sentences, $\forall x.P(x)$ and $\forall y.Q(y)$; since y and x are distinct quantified variables their interpretations do not affect each other. Similarly, we do not want the interpretation of one random designator to affect the interpretation of another.

With this independence of interpretation we have that the probability terms are unaffected by tautologies, e.g., $[P(x) \wedge (R(y) \vee \neg R(y))]_{\langle x,y \rangle} = [P(x)]_x$. And similarly, the terms are unaffected by extraneous variables, e.g., $[P(x)]_{\langle x,y \rangle} = [P(x)]_x$, or by permutations of the order in which the variables are cited, e.g., $[R(x,y)]_{\langle x,y \rangle} = [R(x,y)]_{\langle y,x \rangle}$. These equivalences all result from the independence of the interpretation of the variable y from the interpretation of the variable x.

It should be noted that the use of product measures does not entail the kinds of independence assumptions commonly found in probabilistic inference engines (e.g., the independence assumptions of the Prospector system [23], see Johnson [56]). It is equivalent to the assumption that the random selection process that gives the interpretation of a particular random designator is independent of the selection process for any distinct random designator.[5] The product measure does not, however, make any presumptions concerning the independence of formulas which contain the same set of probability variables. That is, in general, $[\alpha \wedge \beta]_{\vec{x}} \neq [\alpha]_{\vec{x}} \times [\beta]_{\vec{x}}$.

The probabilistic knowledge that we wish to express in the statistical probability logic normally makes some claim of correlation between the properties possessed by the same object (or tuple of objects); for example, correlation between the properties of being a bird and being able to fly. In this example the correlation can be expressed by the probability term $[\texttt{Fly(x)}|\texttt{Bird(x)}]_{\mathbf{x}}$, where the same variable appears throughout. This probability term expresses the proportion of flying birds among the birds. It can be contrasted with the probability term $[\texttt{Fly(y)}|\texttt{Bird(x)}]_{\langle \mathbf{x,y} \rangle}$. In this term the variables are distinct, and its semantic meaning is that we have chosen pairs of objects and are expressing the proportion of pairs in which the first object is a bird and the second object can fly among the pairs in which the first object is a bird irrespective of the properties of the second object. Since we are referring to two different randomly selected objects, there is no reason for there to be any correlation between their properties.

Correlations between the properties of a *particular* collection of objects can be expressed through the use of n-ary predicates. For example, the probability term

$$\left[\big(\texttt{man(x)} \wedge \texttt{woman(y)}\big) \vee \big(\texttt{woman(x)} \wedge \texttt{man(y)}\big) \big| \texttt{married(x,y)} \right]_{\langle \mathbf{x,y} \rangle}$$

is not, in general, equal to the product of any simpler probability terms.

In sum, the product measure interpretation ensures that the probability terms behave in a coherent manner. The logic would become extremely unwieldy if, e.g., the order of the variables affected the value of the probability terms. We can also note that the manner in which we interpret the probability terms implies that the random designators act simply as placeholders; we can rename the placeholder variables without affecting the meaning of the assertion. That is, the probability terms are invariant under variable name changes, e.g., $[\texttt{P(x)}]_{\mathbf{x}} = [\texttt{P(y)}]_{\mathbf{y}}$.

---

[5] We will discuss the implications of this assumption further in Section 3.6.

3.3 Examples of Representation

EXAMPLE 8 (NOTIONS OF TYPICALITY)

1. *"Most birds can fly."*

$$[\mathtt{fly(x)}|\mathtt{bird(x)}]_\mathbf{x} > 0.5,$$

where '> 0.5' is the least presumptive reading of 'Most'. Alternatively, this could be read as "a bird selected at random is more likely to be a flying bird than not."

2. *"In most zoos the elephants usually like the zoo-keepers."*

$$\left[\left[\mathtt{like(x,y)}\middle|\begin{matrix}\mathtt{elephant(x)} \land \mathtt{at(x,z)}\\ \land\, \mathtt{zookeeper(y)} \land \mathtt{at(y,z)}\end{matrix}\right]_{\langle x,y\rangle} > 0.5\middle|\mathtt{zoo(z)}\right]_\mathbf{z} > 0.5$$

This formula asserts that most zoos z have a certain statistical property. This property is that most of the elephants like most of the zoo-keepers at the zoo; i.e., most pairs consisting of an elephant and a zoo-keeper are in the likes relation.

EXAMPLE 9 (FUNCTIONAL PROBABILISTIC RELATIONS)

1. *"Heavier birds are less likely to be able to fly."*

$$\forall r.[\mathtt{weight(x)} > r|\mathtt{bird(x)}]_\mathbf{x} > 0 \land [\mathtt{weight(x)} < r|\mathtt{bird(x)}]_\mathbf{x} > 0$$
$$\rightarrow [\mathtt{fly(x)}|\mathtt{bird(x)} \land \mathtt{weight(x)} < r]_\mathbf{x}$$
$$> [\mathtt{fly(x)}|\mathtt{bird(x)} \land \mathtt{weight(x)} > r]_\mathbf{x}$$

That is, for every number r as long are there are some birds with weight greater than r and some birds with weight less than r, there will be a higher proportion of flying birds among the birds lighter than r than among the birds heavier than r.

2. *"The probability of finding a given type of animal at a zoo is functionally dependent on the expense of acquiring and maintaining that type of animal."*

$$\forall \mathtt{x}.\mathtt{animal\text{-}type(x)} \rightarrow [\mathtt{at(x,y)}|\mathtt{zoo(y)}]_\mathbf{y} = f(\mathtt{expense(x)}),$$

where expense is a measuring function symbol and f is a numeric function symbol that denotes the function defining the dependency.

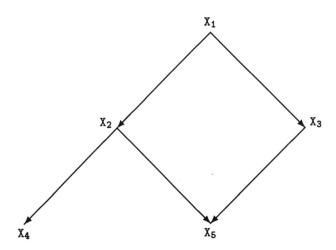

Figure 3.1
A Bayes Network with Multi-valued Variables

We could also assert that **expense** can be calculated from other information, e.g.,

$$\forall x.\texttt{expense}(x) = \texttt{weight}(x) \times 100 + \texttt{initial-cost}(x).$$

Although we may not know exactly what the functional dependency is, we could represent various things that we do know about it. For example, we may know that f is non-decreasing. This could be asserted in the language with the following formula:

$$\forall r_1 r_2 . r_1 > r_2 \rightarrow f(r_1) > f(r_2).$$

EXAMPLE 10 (MULTI-VALUED BAYES NETS)
    In Chapter 2 we gave an example of representing a Bayes net with propositional (binary valued) nodes, using the propositional probability logic. Here we give an example of a Bayes net which has multi-valued nodes. That is, each node in the net can take on some finite set of different values. In this case the independences encoded in the network represent independence over all possible values of the nodes.
    The Bayes net in Figure 3.1 has multi-valued nodes X_i. We can represent the independence conditions encoded by this net with the following

formula.

$$\forall z_1 z_2 z_3 z_4 z_5.$$
$$[X_1(x) = z_1 \wedge X_2(x) = z_2 \wedge X_3(x) = z_3 \wedge X_4(x) = z_4 \wedge X_5(x) = z_5]_x$$
$$= [X_1(x){=}z_1]_x \times [X_2(x){=}z_2|X_1(x){=}z_1]_x \times [X_3(x){=}z_3|X_1(x){=}z_1]_x$$
$$\times [X_4(x){=}z_4|X_2(x){=}z_2]_x \times [X_5(x){=}z_5|X_2(x){=}z_2 \wedge X_3(x){=}z_3]_x$$

Here the nodes X_i are considered to be functions. The formula asserts that for every particular set of X_i values (i.e., for every instantiation of the z_i variables), the measure of the set of individuals x which possess those X_i values is given by a product of simpler probabilities.[6] The net gives a graphical encoding of this assertion.

In multi-valued Bayes nets the links are quantified by a matrix of conditional probabilities: one conditional probability for every different set of values taken on by the nodes. For example, to quantify the links to X_5 we need a conditional probability for every triple of values taken on by X_2, X_3, and X_5. If they all take on two different values, say c_1 and c_2, we would need conditional probabilities like $[X_5(x) = c_1|X_2(x) = c_1 \wedge X_3(x) = c_1]_x$ and $[X_5(x) = c_1|X_2(x) = c_1 \wedge X_3(x) = c_2]_x$. It is easy to see that these conditional probabilities can also be specified declaratively as formulas of our language.

One point that is important to note, however, is that the Bayes nets that can be represented in the statistical probability language are different in content from the nets that can be represented in the propositional probability language: the type of probabilities involved are different. The Bayes net in Figure 3.1 represents a product decomposition of *statistical* probabilities.

EXAMPLE 11 (STATISTICAL NOTIONS)

1. *"A sequence of ten tosses of a fair coin will land heads with a frequency between 45–55% with greater than 95% probability."*

   [frequency-heads(x) $\in$ (0.45, 0.55)|sequence-10-tosses(x)]$_x$
   > 0.95.

   Here the domain contains a set sequence-10-tosses(x). Each member of this set represents a sequence of ten tosses of a fair coin. We also have a measuring function frequency-heads that

---

[6]Both sides of the equality will be zero whenever the denotation of any of the z_i's is outside of the range of the corresponding X_i function.

maps each sequence of tosses to a number in the closed interval [0,1] representing the relative frequency of heads in that sequence.

2. *"The height of adult males (humans) is normally distributed with mean 177cm and standard deviation 13cm."*

$$\forall r_1 r_2.[\texttt{height}(z) \in (r_1, r_2)|\texttt{adult-male}(z)]_z \\ = normal(r_1, r_2, 177, 13)$$

Here *normal* is a numeric function which, given an interval of real numbers (r_1, r_2), a mean, and a standard deviation, returns the integral of a normal distribution with specified mean and standard deviation over the given interval.

3.4   Proof Theory

We now present a proof theory for the statistical probability language. It is very similar to the proof theory that was developed for propositional probabilities in the previous chapter: only the probability axioms differ. However, there are complications which arise from the variable binding property of the statistical probability operator.

3.4.1   Substitution

When the probability operator is applied to a formula α all of the variables $x_i \in \vec{x}$ which are cited as random designators by the operator become bound in α. That is, their semantic interpretation is altered, as specified by the rule of interpretation for the operator. This creates a difficulty when dealing with formulas containing other quantifiers, a difficulty similar to the difficulty arising from nested quantifiers in ordinary first-order logic.

One of the rules of inference in first-order logic allows terms to be substituted for the variable bound by the universal quantifier. For example, in first-order logic it is valid to infer the sentence $\texttt{man(Socrates)} \rightarrow \texttt{mortal(Socrates)}$ from the sentence $\forall \texttt{x.man(x)} \rightarrow \texttt{mortal(x)}$. Here the term $\texttt{Socrates}$ has been substituted for the bound variable $\texttt{x}$. When first-order quantifiers are nested, care must be used to avoid invalid conclusions. For example, in the formula $\forall \texttt{x.P(x)} \rightarrow \exists \texttt{x.Q(x)}$ a term $\texttt{t}$ substituted for the first (universally) quantified $\texttt{x}$ cannot be substituted for the second $\texttt{x}$; the second $\texttt{x}$ is in the scope of a distinct quantifier.

Such a substitution would lead to the erroneous conclusion $P(t) \rightarrow Q(t)$. In general, terms can only be substituted for the free occurrences of a variable.

Another difficulty arises from the fact that the term t may itself contain variables (especially in this language, where the probability terms can contain arbitrary formulas). When such a term is substituted into a formula its variables may be accidently captured by other quantifiers in the formula. For example, in the formula $\forall x.\exists y.P(x) \wedge Q(y)$, if the term $f(y)$ is substituted for the variable x, the formula $\exists y.P(f(y)) \wedge Q(y)$ results, where the y in $f(y)$ has been captured by the existential quantifier. This formula cannot be validly inferred from the previous formula. In general, only terms free for a variable can be substituted for that variable (Definition 8).

Since the probability terms bind variables, these two difficulties arise in the interaction of the probability terms with the ordinary quantifiers $\forall$ and $\exists$. These difficulties are dealt with, as in first-order logic, by definitions which specify when a given variable is free in a given formula. Substitution of terms for variables is then defined in such a way that only free variables are affected. The problem of accidental capture is overcome by developing rules for renaming quantified variables. These rules transform formulas to new formulas which are identical in their semantic meaning and in which there is no possibility of accidently capturing any of the variables in the term to be substituted in.

The standard first-order treatment of substitution can be extended to handle the variables that are bound by the probability terms, and we cite the theorems which demonstrate that the behavior of substitution in our language is a natural extension of its behavior in first-order logic. The proofs of the theorems cited are straightforward extensions of the proofs used in first-order logic, so we have omitted them.[7]

As usual we start with the notion of free and bound occurrences of variables in formulas. In our language, just as in first-order logic, a particular occurrence is free if and only if it is not bound. However, not only are the universally quantified variables bound, but also the random designators which appear inside of the probability operator.

DEFINITION 23 (BOUND PROBABILITY VARIABLES)
If $\alpha = [\beta]_{\vec{x}}$, and $x \in \vec{x}$ (i.e., $x = x_i$ for some i), then every occurrence

---

[7] The proofs are presented in full detail in Bacchus [5].

of x in α is *bound* in α. Otherwise, a given occurrence of x in α is *free* in α iff that occurrence is free in β.

We say x is *free in* α if x has at least one free occurrence in α. The *free variables* of α are all those variables which are free in α. The next theorem shows that given a fixed statistical probability structure M, the meaning of a formula or term is determined by the values of its free variables.

THEOREM 24 Let v and v' be two variable assignment functions which agree on every free variable of α. For every statistical probability structure M

$$(M, v) \models \alpha \quad \text{iff} \quad (M, v') \models \alpha \quad \text{if } \alpha \text{ is a formula,}$$

$$\alpha^{(M,v)} = \alpha^{(M,v')} \qquad\qquad \text{if } \alpha \text{ is a term.}$$

Furthermore, if $\alpha = [\beta]_{\vec{x}}$ we have that the set of satisfying instantiations are identical:

$$\{\vec{a} : (M, v[\vec{a}/\vec{x}]) \models \beta\} = \{\vec{a} : (M, v'[\vec{a}/\vec{x}]) \models \beta\}.$$

A formula α which has no free variables is called a *sentence* or a *closed* formula. This theorem implies that the truth value of a sentence depends only on the probability structure M and not on the variable assignment function v.

To deal with substitution when accidental capture would occur, it is necessary to rename some of the bound variables in the formula. In first-order logic this is accomplished by defining rules which generate *variants*. Variants are new formulas which contain different variable names, but preserve the semantics of the original formula. First-order logic gives rules which allow one to recursively change the names of universally quantified variables. By renaming the variables in this manner we avoid the problem of accidental capture. Since our language also has bound random designators, it is necessary to extend the notion of variants to the probability terms. For example, if we wanted to substitute the term $f(y)$ for the variable x in the formula $\forall x.P(x) \rightarrow [R(x, y)]_y > .5$, we would get $P(y) \rightarrow [R(f(y), y)]_y > .5$, in which the y has been accidentally captured by the probability operator. It is necessary to produce a variant of the original formula in which the probability term has a renamed variable, e.g., the variant $\forall x.P(x) \rightarrow [R(x, z)]_z > .5$. Substitution in the variant formula can then proceed without problem. The total set of variants of a given formula must be defined recursively since the different bound variables (universal and probabilistic) may have nested scope and the probability operators may bind a vector of variables. But for our purposes it is sufficient to simply note that among the set of variants are the following variants defined by variant probability terms.

DEFINITION 25 (VARIANT PROBABILITY TERMS)
If $[\beta]_{\vec{x}}$ is a probability term then

$$[\beta(\vec{x}/\vec{y})]_{\vec{y}},$$

is a *variant probability term*, where $\vec{y}$ is a vector of object variables of the same size as the vector $\vec{x}$, and we have that either $y_i = x_i$ (i.e., no variable name change for the i-th random designator) or y_i is a new variable which does not occur in β. Furthermore, $\beta(\vec{x}/\vec{y})$ indicates the new formula which results from substituting all free occurrences of x_i in β by y_i, for all i.

DEFINITION 26 (VARIANT FORMULAS)
If α is a formula which contains a probability term $[\beta]_{\vec{x}}$ and $[\beta']_{\vec{y}}$ is a variant of $[\beta]_{\vec{x}}$ that is free for $[\beta]_{\vec{x}}$ in α, then the new formula $\alpha([\beta]_{\vec{x}}/[\beta']_{\vec{y}})$, which is the result of substituting in the variant probability term, is a *variant* of α.

These variants are in addition to the variants defined by renaming the universally quantified variables. The important feature of variants, which is preserved by this expanded set of variants, is that they preserve meaning. This is made exact by the following theorem.

THEOREM 27 If α' is a variant of α then for every variable assignment function v and statistical probability structure M

$$(M, v) \models \alpha' \quad \text{iff} \quad (M, v) \models \alpha \quad \text{if } \alpha \text{ is a formula,}$$

$$\alpha'^{(M,v)} = \alpha^{(M,v)} \qquad \qquad \text{if } \alpha \text{ is a term.}$$

Furthermore, the underlying sets of individuals defined by two variant probability terms are identical. That is, if $[\beta]_{\vec{x}}$ and $[\beta']_{\vec{y}}$ are variant probability terms, then

$$\{\vec{a} : (M, v[\vec{x}/\vec{a}]) \models \beta\} = \{\vec{a} : (M, v[\vec{y}/\vec{a}]) \models \beta'\}.$$

This theorem allows us to instantiate universally quantified variables with any term we want. That is, if we have a formula $\forall x.\alpha$ we can uniformly substitute any term t for the free occurrences of the universally quantified x in α, generating the new formula $\alpha(x/t)$. If t has some variables of its own which would be captured by other quantifiers in α, we can replace α by one of its variants α' that has no variables in common with t. By the theorem α' has the same semantic content as α, so the replacement preserves meaning. Since α' is chosen to have no variables in common with t, we can now freely substitute t for x in α'.

For example, to instantiate the universally quantified $\mathbf{x}$ in $\forall \mathbf{x}.[P(\mathbf{x}, \mathbf{y})]_\mathbf{y}$ > 0.5 by the term $\mathbf{f}(\mathbf{y})$ we first form a variant of the formula which shares no variables with the term. In this case the variant $\forall \mathbf{x}.[P(\mathbf{x}, \mathbf{z})]_\mathbf{z} > 0.5$ will do. We can then apply universal instantiation to obtain $[P(\mathbf{f}(\mathbf{y}), \mathbf{z})]_\mathbf{z}$ > 0.5.

We can use the results of this section to prove various things about our logic. We give a simple example which also serves to give a flavor of the semantic behavior of the probability terms.

THEOREM 28 The set of subsets of $\mathcal{O}^n$ defined by the formulas of the language is a field of subsets.

Proof: Let A and B be two subsets of $\mathcal{O}^n$ defined by formulas of the language, i.e., $A = \{\vec{a} : (M, v[\vec{x}/\vec{a}]) \models \alpha\}$ and $B = \{\vec{b} : (M, v[\vec{y}/\vec{b}]) \models \beta\}$. By Definition 25, there exist two variants of $[\alpha]_{\vec{x}}$ and $[\beta]_{\vec{y}}$, $[\alpha']_{\vec{z}}$ and $[\beta']_{\vec{z}}$, formed by substituting all the variables $x_i \in \vec{x}$ in α and all the variables $y_i \in \vec{y}$ in β by a new set of variables $\langle z_1, \ldots, z_n \rangle$ which do not appear in α or β. By Theorem 27, $A' = \{\vec{c} : (M, v[\vec{z}/\vec{c}]) \models \alpha'\} = A$, and $B' = \{\vec{c} : (M, v[\vec{z}/\vec{c}]) \models \beta'\} = B$; hence, $A \cap B = A' \cap B' = \{\vec{c} : (M, v[\vec{z}/\vec{c}]) \models \beta' \wedge \alpha'\}$. That is, the intersection of A and B is definable by a formula of our language.

By the semantic definition $(M, v[\vec{x}/\vec{a}]) \models \alpha$ iff $(M, v[\vec{x}/\vec{a}]) \not\models \neg\alpha$. Thus we have for A, as defined above, $\vec{a} \in A$ iff $\vec{a} \notin \overline{A} = \{\vec{a} : (M, v[\vec{x}/\vec{a}]) \models \neg\alpha\}$. That is, the complement of A with respect to $\mathcal{O}^n$ is definable by a formula. Hence, the set of subsets of $\mathcal{O}^n$ definable by formulas is closed under intersection and complementation. Finally, if we take the term $[\alpha \vee \neg\alpha]_{\vec{x}}$ the set $A = \{\vec{a} : (M, v[\vec{x}/\vec{a}]) \models \alpha \vee \neg\alpha\}$ is equal to $\mathcal{O}^n$; i.e., the universal set is a member of the collection of sets definable by the formulas. ∎

3.4.2   An Axiom System

As with our language for propositional probabilities we have three sets of axioms and some rules of inference. The first two sets of axioms, the first-order axioms and the field axioms, are exactly the same as were given in Chapter 2 for the propositional probability language. The only change comes in the set of probability axioms, and even here there are some similarities.

Probability Axioms

P1) $\forall x_1 \ldots \forall x_n \alpha \to [\alpha]_{\vec{x}} = 1$,
where $\vec{x} = \langle x_1, \ldots, x_n \rangle$ is a vector of object variables. This axiom says that if the set of satisfying instantiations of a formula contains all the vectors of $\mathcal{O}^n$, then the probability of this set is one. This axiom captures the relationship between the universal quantifier and the statistical probability terms.

P2) $[\alpha]_{\vec{x}} \geq 0$.

P3) $[\alpha]_{\vec{x}} + [\neg\alpha]_{\vec{x}} = 1$.

P4) $[\alpha \wedge \beta]_{\vec{x}} + [\alpha \wedge \neg\beta]_{\vec{x}} = [\alpha]_{\vec{x}}$.
These three axioms express the normal behavior of probabilities: they are non-negative, the entire domain has probability one, and the probability of the union of two disjoint sets is equal to the sum of the probabilities of the two sets.

P5) $[\alpha]_{\vec{x}} = [\alpha(x_i/z)]_{\vec{x}(x_i/z)}$, where z is an object variable that does not occur in α, and $\vec{x}(x_i/z)$ is the new vector of object variables: $\langle x_1, \ldots, x_{i-1}, z, x_{i+1}, \ldots, x_n \rangle$.
This axiom captures our earlier theorem that variant probability terms are equivalent.

P6) $[\alpha \wedge \beta]_{\langle \vec{x}, \vec{y} \rangle} = [\alpha]_{\vec{x}} \times [\beta]_{\vec{y}}$,
if none of the free variables of α are in $\vec{y}$, none of the free variables of β are in $\vec{x}$ and $\vec{y}$ and $\vec{x}$ are disjoint. This axiom enforces the product measure constraint. We will demonstrate the manner in which it accomplishes this in our proof of soundness.

P7) $[\alpha]_{\vec{x}} = [\alpha]_{\pi(\vec{x})}$,
where π is any permutation of $\{1, \ldots, n\}$, and $\pi(\vec{x})$ is the permuted vector $\vec{x}$, i.e., $\pi(\vec{x}) = \langle x_{\pi(1)}, \ldots, x_{\pi(n)} \rangle$. The product measures

are invariant under permutation of the dimensions. This axiom captures that property.

Rules of Inference

MP) From α and $\alpha \rightarrow \beta$ infer β (Modus Ponens).

UG) From α infer $\forall x.\alpha$ (Universal Generalization).

3.4.3 Soundness

THEOREM 29 The proof theory is sound with respect to statistical probability structures.

Proof: We show that all instances of the axioms are sound and that the rules of inference preserve validity.

The first-order axioms are all valid, for the same reasons they are valid for ordinary first-order structures. The field axioms are also clearly valid: the reals satisfy all of these axioms. The first four probability axioms can be seen to follow from the behavior of probability functions. For example, for **P4** it is easy to see that the set of satisfying instantiations of $\vec{x}$ in α can be broken up into two disjoint subsets: those which also satisfy β and those which do not. The probability of the union of two disjoint sets is the sum of their individual probabilities.

The two probability terms in **P5** are variants of each other. Therefore, the validity of the equality follows from Theorem 27. The validity of **P6** follows from the fact that the probability measures over $\mathcal{O}^n$ are product measures. Let

- $S_{\alpha \wedge \beta} = \{\langle \vec{o}_x, \vec{o}_y \rangle : (M, v[\langle \vec{x}, \vec{y} \rangle / \langle \vec{o}_x, \vec{o}_y \rangle]) \models \alpha \wedge \beta\}$, i.e., the set of satisfying instantiations defined by the left hand side of the axiom;

- $S_\alpha = \{\vec{a} : (M, v[\vec{x}/\vec{a}]) \models \alpha\}$; and

- $S_\beta = \{\vec{b} : (M, v[\vec{y}/\vec{b}]) \models \beta\}$, i.e., the two sets of satisfying instantiations defined by the probability terms on the right-hand side.

Let $\langle \vec{a}, \vec{b} \rangle$ be any pair of vectors $\vec{a}$ from S_α and $\vec{b}$ from S_β. We have that $(M, v[\vec{x}/\vec{a}]) \models \alpha$, and since $v[\langle \vec{x}, \vec{y} \rangle / \langle \vec{a}, \vec{b} \rangle]$ agrees with $v[\vec{x}/\vec{a}]$ on every free variable of α, we have that $(M, v[\langle \vec{x}, \vec{y} \rangle / \langle \vec{a}, \vec{b} \rangle]) \models \alpha$, by Theorem 24. Similarly, $(M, v[\langle \vec{x}, \vec{y} \rangle / \langle \vec{a}, \vec{b} \rangle]) \models \beta$. Hence, $(M, v[\langle \vec{x}, \vec{y} \rangle / \langle \vec{a}, \vec{b} \rangle]) \models \alpha \wedge \beta$. Therefore, every such pair $\langle \vec{a}, \vec{b} \rangle \in S_{\alpha \wedge \beta}$. From Theorem 24 we can similarly show that for every vector $\langle \vec{o}_x, \vec{o}_y \rangle \in S_{\alpha \wedge \beta}$, $\vec{o}_x \in S_\alpha$ and $\vec{o}_y \in S_\beta$. That is, $S_{\alpha \wedge \beta}$ is precisely the set of all pairs of vectors formed from S_α and S_β: it is the direct product of the two sets, $S_{\alpha \wedge \beta} = S_\alpha \times S_\beta$. If $\vec{x}$ is a vector of n elements and $\vec{y}$ a vector of m elements, then since μ^{n+m} is a product measure we have

$$\mu^{n+m}(S_{\alpha \wedge \beta}) = \mu^n(S_\alpha) \times \mu^m(S_\beta);$$

i.e., **P6** is valid.

To see that **P7** is valid let S_α denote the set of satisfying instantiations defined by $[\alpha]_{\vec{x}}$, where $\vec{x}$ is a vector of n elements, and $\pi(S_\alpha)$ denote the set defined by $[\alpha]_{\pi(\vec{x})}$. By the product measure definition of μ^n we have

$$
\begin{aligned}
\mu^n(S_\alpha) &= \sum_{\langle o_1, \ldots, o_n \rangle \in S_\alpha} \mu(o_1) \times \cdots \times \mu(o_n) \\
&= \sum_{\langle o_{\pi(1)}, \ldots, o_{\pi(n)} \rangle \in \pi(S_\alpha)} \mu(o_{\pi(1)}) \times \cdots \times \mu(o_{\pi(n)}) \\
&= \mu^n(\pi(S_\alpha)).
\end{aligned}
$$

Therefore, **P7** is valid.

The rules of inference **MP** and **UG** preserve validity for the same reasons they do so in first-order structures. ∎

3.4.4 Completeness

THEOREM 30 (ABADI AND HALPERN [1])
A complete proof theory for the statistical probability logic does not exist.

This theorem is proved in a manner similar to the corresponding theorem for propositional probability logics, by showing that the set of valid formulas is not recursively enumerable.

Once again we have given an incomplete proof theory, and we can defend it by examples which demonstrate the range of reasoning it captures. There will always exist valid formulas that are not deducible from the proof theory, and they can be added as extra axioms to extend the proof theory. However, no extension of the proof theory will capture all valid formulas; i.e., there is no end to such extensions. Despite its incompleteness in general, the proof theory is fairly complete for finite domains. And it can capture a large class of inferences in infinite domains. The theorems below will make these statements more precise.

We can construct a restricted language by omitting the measuring functions and by disallowing any user defined *numeric* functions or predicates. Furthermore, we can extend the proof theory by including the axioms which define a real-closed field, i.e., axioms **RCF1** and **RCF2**$_n$, and which specify that the domain is bounded in size, i.e., an axiom **FIN**$_N$ for some N (these axioms were given in Section 2.6.3). For this extended proof theory and restricted language we have:

THEOREM 31 (HALPERN [43])
The extended proof theory in the restricted language is complete for statistical probability structures where the domain of discourse is bounded in size.

The complexity of the language comes from our requirement that the probability functions be *real-valued*. As we have demonstrated in the previous chapter much of our normal numeric reasoning can be captured by using just the field axioms. If we allow non-standard probability functions, which take their values in a totally ordered field instead of being restricted to the reals, we do not require any restrictions on our language or extensions of our proof theory. We have the following:

THEOREM 32 (BACCHUS [5])
The proof theory as it stands along with an axiom **FIN**$_N$ which specifies that the domain is bounded in size, is complete for the full statistical probability language in structures where we allow field-valued probability functions instead of restricting to only real-valued ones.[8]

We can further relax our requirements on the probability functions so that we no longer require them to be sigma-additive.[9] In fact, when we have field-valued probability functions it is not clear if the requirement of sigma-additivity makes any sense. That is, sigma-additivity posits conditions on the limits of infinite sums, and limits are not necessarily well defined in an arbitrarily totally ordered field: some totally ordered

---

[8]This more liberal class of structures includes the originally defined class of structures: the reals are a special type of totally ordered field.

[9]Sigma-additivity is essentially the constraint that the probability functions be well behaved in the limit. See the appendix on probability theory in Chapter 1 for more information.

fields, e.g., the rationals, are not closed under the operation of taking limits. If we require only that our probability functions be finitely-additive and field-valued, then the following theorem holds.

THEOREM 33 (BACCHUS [5])
The proof theory as it stands is complete for the full language when the domain is *countable*, if we only require finitely-additive, field-valued probability functions in our probability structures.[10]

These theorems give some evidence that the proof theory captures a large set of valid deductions, since it is complete for these special cases. Our examples we will provide further, empirical, evidence to support this conclusion.

3.5 Examples of Reasoning

Since the field axioms and axioms for equality are the same as they were for our propositional probability language, the proof theory is powerful enough to perform the same kinds of numeric reasoning that we give examples of in Chapter 2. We shall continue to refer to such reasoning as "numeric reasoning."

EXAMPLE 12 (PROBABILISTIC TAUTOLOGIES)
The proof theory captures the same types of probabilistic reasoning that are captured by our proof theory for propositional probabilities. The key difference here is that the probabilities we are dealing with are different. The propositional probability language could reason with degree of belief probabilities, while the statistical language reasons with statistical probabilities. The deductions of the first five tautologies are very similar to the deductions of the corresponding propositional probability tautologies. The propositional probability analogue of the sixth item requires the use of the "Probability of Equivalents" rule of inference (**PE**), a rule which is not needed in our statistical probability language. As an example we give a full deduction of this equality and discuss its relation with **PE**.

---

[10]If we allow non-sigma-additive probability functions we can no longer use a simple discrete probability function that was used here. Instead we have to include in the semantic structure an explicit field of subsets that is the domain of the probability function. See Bacchus [5] for details.

1. $[\alpha]_{\vec{x}} \leq 1$.

2. $[\alpha \wedge \beta]_{\vec{x}} \leq [\alpha]_{\vec{x}}$ and $[\alpha \wedge \beta]_{\vec{x}} \leq [\beta]_{\vec{x}}$.

3. $[\alpha \vee \beta]_{\vec{x}} \geq [\alpha]_{\vec{x}}$ and $[\alpha \vee \beta]_{\vec{x}} \geq [\beta]_{\vec{x}}$.

4. $[\alpha \vee \beta]_{\vec{x}} = [\alpha]_{\vec{x}} + [\beta]_{\vec{x}} - [\alpha \wedge \beta]_{\vec{x}}$.

5. $[\alpha]_{\vec{x}} + [\beta]_{\vec{x}} \geq [\alpha \vee \beta]_{\vec{x}}$.

6. $([\alpha \rightarrow \beta]_{\vec{x}} = 1 \wedge [\beta \rightarrow \alpha]_{\vec{x}} = 1) \rightarrow [\alpha]_{\vec{x}} = [\beta]_{\vec{x}}$.

   We construct a deduction of $[\alpha]_{\vec{x}} = [\beta]_{\vec{x}}$ from the hypothesis $[\alpha \rightarrow \beta]_{\vec{x}} = 1 \wedge [\beta \rightarrow \alpha]_{\vec{x}} = 1$.

$([\alpha \rightarrow \beta]_{\vec{x}} = 1 \wedge [\beta \rightarrow \alpha]_{\vec{x}} = 1) \rightarrow [\alpha \rightarrow \beta]_{\vec{x}} = 1$	First-order
$[\alpha \rightarrow \beta]_{\vec{x}} = 1 \wedge [\beta \rightarrow \alpha]_{\vec{x}} = 1$	Hyp.
$[\alpha \rightarrow \beta]_{\vec{x}} = 1$	MP
$[\neg\alpha \vee \beta]_{\vec{x}} = 1$	Defn. of '$\rightarrow$'
$[\neg\alpha]_{\vec{x}} + [\beta]_{\vec{x}} \geq [\neg\alpha \vee \beta]_{\vec{x}}$	item 5
$[\neg\alpha]_{\vec{x}} + [\beta]_{\vec{x}} \geq 1$	Sub. Eq.
$[\neg\alpha]_{\vec{x}} + [\alpha]_{\vec{x}} = 1$	P3
$[\neg\alpha]_{\vec{x}} + [\beta]_{\vec{x}} \geq [\neg\alpha]_{\vec{x}} + [\alpha]_{\vec{x}}$	Sub. Eq.
$[\neg\alpha]_{\vec{x}} - [\neg\alpha]_{\vec{x}} = 0$	F3 (field axiom)
$[\neg\alpha]_{\vec{x}} + [\beta]_{\vec{x}} - [\neg\alpha]_{\vec{x}} \geq [\neg\alpha]_{\vec{x}} + [\alpha]_{\vec{x}} - [\neg\alpha]_{\vec{x}}$	F14, MP
$[\beta]_{\vec{x}} + 0 \geq [\alpha]_{\vec{x}} + 0$	F4, Sub. Eq.
$[\beta]_{\vec{x}} \geq [\alpha]_{\vec{x}}$	F2, Sub. Eq.

   Similarly from $[\neg\beta \vee \alpha]_{\vec{x}} = 1$ we derive

   $[\alpha]_{\vec{x}} \geq [\beta]_{\vec{x}}$

   thus

$[\beta]_{\vec{x}} = [\alpha]_{\vec{x}}$	F13

   From item 6 we can prove the statistical analogue of the rule of "Probability of Equivalents" used in the propositional probability language.

7. $(\forall \vec{x}.\alpha \equiv \beta) \rightarrow ([\alpha]_{\vec{x}} = [\beta]_{\vec{x}})$.

   The validity of formulas of this form demonstrates that we can perform tautological transformations on the argument of the probability operator. For example, we can transform a probability term like $[\alpha \wedge (\alpha \rightarrow \beta)]_{\vec{x}}$ to an equivalent probability term $[\alpha \wedge \beta]_{\vec{x}}$.

In the propositional probability language we needed a rule of inference to capture the validity of this type of reasoning. With statistical probabilities, however, our axioms for the probability terms suffice. The essential reason that this is possible for statistical probabilities and not for propositional probabilities is that in our language we can quantify over individuals, but not over possible worlds. Hence, in the statistical language we can represent the assertion that two formulas are equivalent for every individual (by using the universal quantifier), but in the propositional probability language we cannot represent the assertion that two formulas are equivalent in every possible world: we cannot quantify over the possible worlds.

8. $\left([\alpha]_{\vec{x}} > 0 \wedge [\alpha \to \beta]_{\vec{x}} = 1\right) \to [\beta|\alpha]_{\vec{x}} = 1.$

The antecedent is equivalent to the assertion $[\alpha \wedge \neg\beta]_{\vec{x}} = 0$. We have that

$$\frac{[\alpha \wedge \beta]_{\vec{x}}}{[\alpha]_{\vec{x}}} = \frac{[\alpha \wedge \beta]_{\vec{x}}}{[\alpha \wedge \beta]_{\vec{x}} + [\alpha \wedge \neg\beta]_{\vec{x}}} = \frac{[\alpha \wedge \beta]_{\vec{x}}}{[\alpha \wedge \beta]_{\vec{x}}} = 1$$

EXAMPLE 13 (SUBSTITUTION OF EQUALS)
We can substitute equal terms for each other in any formula, even inside of the probability operator.

As we pointed out in Chapter 2, the equality axioms, along with the rest of our first-order axioms, are sufficient to deduce that $s = t \to (\alpha \equiv \alpha(s/t))$ for any first-order formula α. That is, we can freely substitute equal terms in first-order formulas.

To deal with the full set of formulas of our language, i.e., those which may contain the probability operator, we can use the above item 7. That is, from the validity of $s = t \to (\alpha \equiv \alpha(s/t))$ for any first-order formula α, we can use universal generalization, first-order reasoning, and item 7 to infer that $s = t \to ([\alpha]_x = [\alpha(s/t)]_x)$. This demonstrates that substitution of equals inside of the statistical probability operator does not affect the value of the probability terms. The statistical probability terms are terms just like s and t. Hence, by induction we have that $s = t \to (\alpha \equiv \alpha(s/t))$ even if s is a probability term.

This means that we can freely substitute equal terms in *any* formula of our statistical probability language. (With variable renaming when necessary).

EXAMPLE 14 (REASONING WITH DEFAULTS)
If we represent defaults as statistical assertions of majority we can
perform various types of reasoning with them.

1. If the statement "P's are typically Q's" is given the statistical in-
    terpretation that the proportion of P's that are Q's is greater than
    c, where c is some number close to 1, then the opposite conclusion,
    that "P's are typically not Q's," is necessarily false. For example,
    "Birds typically fly" contradicts "Birds typically don't fly:"

    $$\vdash \big([\texttt{fly(x)}|\texttt{bird(x)}]_x > c \wedge c > 0.5\big) \rightarrow \big([\neg\texttt{fly(x)}|\texttt{bird(x)}]_x \not> c\big).$$

    The derivation follows from axiom **P3**, the definition of conditional
    probabilities, and simple numeric reasoning.

2. Similarly, the statement "P's are Q's" implies that the statement
    "P's are typically not Q's" is false. For example, "Penguins are
    birds" implies that "Penguins are typically not birds" is false.

    $$\vdash \big(\forall\texttt{x.penguin(x)} \rightarrow \texttt{bird(x)}\big) \rightarrow \big([\neg\texttt{bird(x)}|\texttt{penguin(x)}]_x \not> c\big).$$

    The derivation follows from axioms **P1** and **P3**.

3. The knowledge that "Most ravens are black" along with "Black
    objects are not white" implies that "Most ravens are not white."

    $$\vdash \begin{pmatrix} [\texttt{black(x)}|\texttt{raven(x)}]_x > c \\ \wedge\, \forall\texttt{x.black(x)} \rightarrow \neg\texttt{white(x)} \end{pmatrix} \rightarrow [\neg\texttt{white(x)}|\texttt{raven(x)}]_x > c.$$

    From axiom **P1** it can be shown that $[\texttt{black(x)} \rightarrow \neg\texttt{white(x)}]_x$
    $= 1$. Using probabilistic tautologies, $[\neg\texttt{white(x)}|\texttt{raven(x)}]_x \geq$
    $[\texttt{black(x)}|\texttt{raven(x)}]_x$ can be derived. The conclusion then follows
    from numeric reasoning.

4. The knowledge that "Most birds fly" along with "Penguins do not
    fly" implies that "Most birds are not penguins."

    $$\vdash \begin{pmatrix} [\texttt{fly(x)}|\texttt{bird(x)}]_x > c \\ \wedge\, \forall\texttt{x.penguin(x)} \rightarrow \neg\texttt{fly(x)} \end{pmatrix} \rightarrow [\neg\texttt{penguin(x)}|\texttt{bird(x)}]_x > c.$$

EXAMPLE 15 (BAYESIAN NETWORKS AND ENTAILMENT)
The proof theory can capture the probabilistic reasoning required to
perform Bayesian network calculations and Nilsson's probabilistic entailments, just as with the propositional probabilities. The only difference here is that we are dealing with statistical probabilities. So, for

example, the base set of probability assignments in Nilsson's probability logic would be a base set of statistical probabilities.

1. $\left([\alpha]_{\vec{x}} \neq 0 \wedge [\beta]_{\vec{x}} \neq 0\right) \to [\alpha|\beta]_{\vec{x}} = \dfrac{[\beta|\alpha]_{\vec{x}} \times [\alpha]_{\vec{x}}}{[\beta]_{\vec{x}}}.$

   This is Bayes's rule for the statistical probabilities, and it can be proved via a simple application of the definitions and some numeric reasoning.

2. The calculations involved in Bayesian networks can be performed in the proof theory.

3. The bounds that are probabilistically entailed (Nilsson's probabilistic entailment [98]) by a base set of statistical probability assignments can be derived by the proof theory. For example, from the base set of statistical probabilities $\{[P(x)]_x = 0.6, [P(x) \to Q(x)]_x = 0.8\}$, we can deduce $0.4 \leq [Q(x)]_x \leq 0.8$.

3.5.1 Further Properties of the Probability Terms

The conditional probability terms possess some interesting properties that will be useful in applications of the logic. Here we give lemmas which demonstrate some of these properties. Most of the lemmas are provable from the proof theory since they only involve reasoning with the field and finite additivity properties of the probabilities. Theorem 33 demonstrates that the proof theory is complete for these properties of the probability functions. That is, the proof theory captures any valid reasoning which does not appeal to sigma-additivity or to the special properties of the reals. Therefore, there exist syntactic proofs of most of these lemmas, similar to those given in the examples above. However, here we will give semantic proofs: such proofs are much shorter and easier to understand.

The lemmas indicate that certain complex probability terms are equivalent or related to simpler terms.

LEMMA 34 If no $x_i \in \vec{x}$ which appears in $\alpha \wedge \beta$ is free in λ then

$$\models [\beta \wedge \lambda]_{\vec{x}} \neq 0 \to [\alpha|\beta \wedge \lambda]_{\vec{x}} = [\alpha|\beta]_{\vec{x}}.$$

Proof: The variables in $\vec{x}$ can be divided into two disjoint subsets $\vec{z}$ and $\vec{y}$. The subset $\vec{z}$ contains the variables that appear free in $\alpha \wedge \beta$, while $\vec{y}$ contains the variables that appear free in λ. By axiom **P6**, $[\alpha \wedge \beta \wedge \lambda]_{\vec{z}} = [\alpha \wedge \beta]_{\vec{z}} \times [\lambda]_{\vec{y}}$, and $[\beta \wedge \lambda]_{\vec{z}} = [\beta]_{\vec{z}} \times [\lambda]_{\vec{y}}$. Hence, the conditional probability $[\alpha|\beta \wedge \lambda]_{\vec{z}} = [\alpha \wedge \beta]_{\vec{z}}/[\beta]_{\vec{z}}$. Furthermore, since the variables $\vec{y}$ do not appear in $\alpha \wedge \beta$ we can add these extra random designators obtaining $[\alpha \wedge \beta]_{\vec{z}}/[\beta]_{\vec{z}} = [\alpha|\beta]_{\vec{z}}$ as required.

The fact that $[\beta \wedge \lambda]_{\vec{z}} > 0 \to [\lambda]_{\vec{y}} > 0$ allows us to cancel this term in the conditional probability. ∎

There are a couple of useful special cases of this lemma, given by the following corollary.

COROLLARY 35   1. If no $x_i \in \vec{x}$ is free in λ then

$$\models [\beta \wedge \lambda]_{\vec{x}} > 0 \to [\alpha|\beta \wedge \lambda]_{\vec{x}} = [\alpha|\beta]_{\vec{x}}.$$

2. If α and λ share no free variables then

$$\models [\lambda]_{\vec{x}} > 0 \to [\alpha|\lambda]_{\vec{x}} = [\alpha]_{\vec{x}}.$$

For example, by this lemma we have that $[Q(x)|R(x) \wedge P(y)]_{\langle x,y \rangle} = [Q(x)|R(x)]_{\langle x,y \rangle}$, but not that $[Q(x)|R(x,y) \wedge P(y)]_{\langle x,y \rangle} = [Q(x)|R(x,y)]_{\langle x,y \rangle}$.

The equality $[Q(x)|R(x) \wedge P(c)]_{\langle x,y \rangle} = [Q(x)|R(x)]_{\langle x,y \rangle}$ is an example of the special case identified by the corollary: there are no free random designators in $P(c)$.

LEMMA 36 If y does not appear free in α then

$$\models [\alpha]_{\langle \vec{x},y \rangle} = [\alpha]_{\vec{x}}.$$

Proof: We have that $[\alpha]_{\langle \vec{x},y \rangle} = [\alpha \wedge true]_{\langle \vec{x},y \rangle}$, and by axiom **P6** that $[\alpha \wedge true]_{\langle \vec{x},y \rangle} = [\alpha]_{\vec{x}} \times [true]_y$. Since $[true]_y = 1$ we have the result claimed by the lemma. ∎

So, for example, we have $[Q(x) \wedge R(x)]_{\langle x,y \rangle} = [Q(x) \wedge R(x)]_x$ and $[R(x)]_{\langle x,y \rangle} = [R(x)]_x$. And, by the definition of the conditional probability terms, $[Q(x)|R(x)]_{\langle x,y \rangle} = [Q(x)|R(x)]_x$.

LEMMA 37 $\models \forall \vec{x}.(\beta \to \lambda) \to [\alpha|\beta \wedge \lambda]_{\vec{x}} = [\alpha|\beta]_{\vec{x}}$.

Proof: If the antecedent is satisfied, then any vector of objects that instantiates the variables $\vec{x}$ and satisfies β will satisfy λ. That is, the set of satisfying instantiations of β must be a subset of the satisfying instantiations of $\beta \wedge \lambda$. Clearly, the opposite containment also holds. Hence, these two formulas have the same set of satisfying instantiations and the two probability terms must be equal. ∎

LEMMA 38 $\models \forall \vec{x}.(\alpha \rightarrow \lambda) \rightarrow [\lambda|\beta]_{\vec{x}} \geq [\alpha|\beta]_{\vec{x}}$.

Proof: In any pair (M, v) that satisfies the antecedent, the set of satisfying instantiations of $\vec{x}$ in α is a subset of the satisfying instantiations in λ. Hence, its probability must be smaller, even when we select only those satisfying instances that also satisfy β. ∎

In certain applications we will need to capture the following style of probabilistic reasoning. Say our domain consists of a set of boys $\{B_1, B_2, B_3\}$ and girls $\{G_1, G_2, G_3\}$ and that the probability distribution over the domain is uniform.[11] Furthermore, say that B_1 and B_2 are popular, i.e., more than 50% of the girls are in the likes relation with each of them. To be specific, say that G_1 and G_2 like B_1 and that G_2 and G_3 like B_2. If we form the set of all pairs of individuals $\langle x, y \rangle$ such that x is a girl and y is a *popular* boy, then we would expect that more than 50% of these pairs satisfy the likes relation. This is exactly what happens: the set of such pairs is the set

$$\{\langle G_1, B_1 \rangle, \langle G_2, B_1 \rangle, \langle G_3, B_1 \rangle, \langle G_1, B_2 \rangle, \langle G_2, B_2 \rangle, \langle G_3, B_2 \rangle\}$$

Among this set of pairs the following majority of pairs stand in the likes relation:

$$\{\langle G_1, B_1 \rangle, \langle G_2, B_1 \rangle, \langle G_2, B_2 \rangle, \langle G_3, B_2 \rangle\}$$

The following lemma is a general statement of the principle behind this example.

LEMMA 39

$$\models \quad \forall r_1 r_2 . \left[[\alpha|\beta]_{\vec{x}} \in (r_1, r_2) \wedge \beta \right]_{\langle \vec{x}, \vec{y} \rangle} > 0$$

$$\rightarrow \left[\alpha \,\middle|\, [\alpha|\beta]_{\vec{x}} \in (r_1, r_2) \wedge \beta \right]_{\langle \vec{x}, \vec{y} \rangle} \in (r_1, r_2)$$

---

[11] A probability distribution is uniform if it assigns each singleton set an equal probability.

This lemma states that if we form the set of pairs of vectors $\langle \vec{x}, \vec{y} \rangle$ such that the pair together are satisfying instantiations of β, and further, that for every $\vec{y}$ in the pair the proportion of all possible instantiations of $\vec{x}$ that stand in the relation α with it lies within the bounds (r_1, r_2), then among this set of possible pairings of instantiations of $\vec{x}$ and $\vec{y}$ the proportion that satisfy the α relation will lie within the same bounds.

Applying this lemma to the boys and girls example, we have that the antecedent is satisfied, and hence we obtain the validity of the formula

$$\left[\texttt{likes(x,y)} \middle| \begin{array}{l} ([\texttt{likes(x,y)}|\texttt{girl(x)} \wedge \texttt{boy(y)}]_{\mathbf{x}} > 0.5) \\ \wedge \texttt{girl(x)} \wedge \texttt{boy(y)} \end{array} \right]_{\langle \mathbf{x,y} \rangle} > 0.5.^{12}$$

That is, a randomly selected girl $\mathbf{x}$ has a greater than 50% chance of liking a randomly selected popular boy $\mathbf{y}$, i.e., a boy who satisfies $[\texttt{likes(x,y)}|\texttt{girl(x)} \wedge \texttt{boy(y)}]_{\mathbf{x}} > 0.5$.

Proof: Let $\vec{x}$ be an n-ary vector of variables and $\vec{y}$ an m-ary vector. Let (M, v) satisfy the antecedent of the implication. Let S_{cond} be the set of satisfying instantiations of $\langle \vec{x}, \vec{y} \rangle$ in the conditioning formula $[\alpha|\beta]_{\vec{x}} \in (r_1, r_2) \wedge \beta$. The elements of S_{cond} are $(n+m)$-ary vectors of the form $\langle \vec{a}, \vec{b} \rangle$ where $\vec{a} \in \mathcal{O}^n$ and $\vec{b} \in \mathcal{O}^m$. Let $S_{cond \wedge \alpha}$ be the subset of S_{cond} that are also satisfying instantiations of $\langle \vec{x}, \vec{y} \rangle$ in α.

Without loss of generality, we can disregard all vectors in S_{cond} that have zero probability. Since the probability functions are discrete, there can only be a countable number of vectors in S_{cond} with non-zero probability.

Consider the two sets $A = \{\vec{a} :$ there exists a $\vec{b}$ such that $\langle \vec{a}, \vec{b} \rangle \in S_{cond}\}$, and $B = \{\vec{b} :$ there exists an $\vec{a}$ such that $\langle \vec{a}, \vec{b} \rangle \in S_{cond}\}$. We can fix an enumeration of the elements in these sets. Let $\vec{a}_1, \ldots, \vec{a}_i, \ldots$ be the elements of A, and $\vec{b}_1, \ldots, \vec{b}_j, \ldots$ be the elements of B. Note, it is not necessarily the case that $\langle \vec{a}_i, \vec{b}_j \rangle \in S_{cond}$ for every i and j; however, we do have that for every $\vec{a}_i$ there is *some* $\vec{b}_j$ such that $\langle \vec{a}_i, \vec{b}_j \rangle \in S_{cond}$. Similarly for every $\vec{b}_j$ there is some $\vec{a}_i$.

---

[12]Lemma 34 can be applied to further simplify this formula to

$$\left[\texttt{likes(x,y)} \middle| \left([\texttt{likes(x,y)}|\texttt{girl(x)}]_{\mathbf{x}} > 0.5 \right) \wedge \texttt{girl(x)} \wedge \texttt{boy(y)} \right]_{\langle \mathbf{x,y} \rangle} > 0.5.$$

The conditional probability term denotes

$$\frac{\sum_{\langle \vec{a}_i, \vec{b}_j \rangle \in S_{cond \wedge \alpha}} \mu^n(\vec{a}_i) \times \mu^m(\vec{b}_j)}{\sum_{\langle \vec{a}_i, \vec{b}_j \rangle \in S_{cond}} \mu^n(\vec{a}_i) \times \mu^m(\vec{b}_j)}.$$

We can regroup the summation as

$$\frac{\sum_{\vec{b}_j \in B} \left(\mu^m(\vec{b}_j) \times \sum_{\vec{a}_i | \langle \vec{a}_i, \vec{b}_j \rangle \in S_{cond \wedge \alpha}} \mu^n(\vec{a}_i) \right)}{\sum_{\vec{b}_j \in B} \left(\mu^m(\vec{b}_j) \times \sum_{\vec{a}_i | \langle \vec{a}_i, \vec{b}_j \rangle \in S_{cond}} \mu^n(\vec{a}_i) \right)}.$$

Although $\vec{b}_j \in B$ implies that there exists an $\vec{a}_i$ such that $\langle \vec{a}_i, \vec{b}_j \rangle \in S_{cond}$, there may not be any $\vec{a}_i$ such that $\langle \vec{a}_i, \vec{b}_j \rangle \in S_{cond \wedge \alpha}$. However, in this case we can still include a term in the numerator for each $\vec{b}_j \in B$ by simply letting that term be equal to zero.

Hence, we can rewrite the denotation of the conditional probability term as a sum of the form

$$\frac{\sum_{\vec{b}_j \in B} \mu^m(\vec{b}_j) \times t_j}{\sum_{\vec{b}_j \in B} \mu^m(\vec{b}_j) \times t'_j},$$

where $t_j = \sum_{\vec{a}_i | \langle \vec{a}_i, \vec{b}_j \rangle \in S_{cond \wedge \alpha}} \mu^n(\vec{a}_i)$ and $t'_j = \sum_{\vec{a}_i | \langle \vec{a}_i, \vec{b}_j \rangle \in S_{cond}} \mu^n(\vec{a}_i)$.

Each $\vec{b}_j \in B$ has a special statistical property:

$$r_1 \leq \frac{\mu^n(\{\vec{a}_i : (M, v[\langle \vec{x}, \vec{y} \rangle / \langle \vec{a}_i, \vec{b}_j \rangle]) \models \alpha \wedge \beta\})}{\mu^n(\{\vec{a}_i : (M, v[\langle \vec{x}, \vec{y} \rangle / \langle \vec{a}_i, \vec{b}_j \rangle]) \models \beta\})} \leq r_2.$$

This follows from the fact that each $\vec{b}_j$ is a satisfying instantiation of $\vec{y}$ in $[\alpha | \beta]_{\vec{x}} \in (r_1, r_2)$. The variables in $\vec{x}$ do not appear free in this formula; therefore, by an argument similar to Lemma 34, we have that

$$(M, v[\langle \vec{x}, \vec{y} \rangle / \langle \vec{a}_i, \vec{b}_j \rangle]) \models \beta$$

iff

$$(M, v[\langle \vec{x}, \vec{y} \rangle / \langle \vec{a}_i, \vec{b}_j \rangle]) \models \beta \wedge [\alpha | \beta]_{\vec{x}} \in (r_1, r_2).$$

Similarly, for $\beta \wedge \alpha$. That is, we have that

- $\{\vec{a}_i : (M, v[\langle \vec{x}, \vec{y} \rangle / \langle \vec{a}_i, \vec{b}_j \rangle]) \models \alpha \wedge \beta\} = \{\vec{a}_i : \langle \vec{a}_i, \vec{b}_j \rangle \in S_{cond \wedge \alpha}\}$
  and that

- $\{\vec{a}_i : (M, v[\langle \vec{x}, \vec{y} \rangle / \langle \vec{a}_i, \vec{b}_j \rangle]) \models \beta\} = \{\vec{a}_i : \langle \vec{a}_i, \vec{b}_j \rangle \in S_{cond}\}.$

Therefore, each t_j and t'_j, as defined above, satisfies the relation $r_1 \leq t_j/t'_j \leq r_2$, or $r_1 t'_j \leq t_j \leq r_2 t'_j$.

Returning to the denotation of the conditional probability term we see that

$$r_1 \sum_{\vec{b}_j \in B} \mu^m(\vec{b}_j) \times t'_j \leq \sum_{\vec{b}_j \in B} \mu^m(\vec{b}_j) \times t_j \leq r_2 \sum_{\vec{b}_j \in B} \mu^m(\vec{b}_j) \times t'_j.$$

Dividing through by $\sum_{\vec{b}_j \in B} \mu^m(\vec{b}_j) \times t'_j$ we see that the conditional probability term is within the bounds (r_1, r_2) as claimed. ∎

Unlike the other lemmas, it does not seem that the proof theory is capable of deducing the validity of this formula. The reason is that it depends critically on being able to rewrite the probability of a possibly infinite set as a summation over its individual elements. It is the sigma-additivity of the probability functions that makes this legitimate. The union over the individual elements is a countable union of disjoint sets. Sigma-additivity ensures that the probability of such a set is equal to the summation of the individual probabilities. As our completeness results indicate, the proof theory is only complete for the finite additivity properties of probabilities.[13]

If we can go back to the example of pairs of girls and popular boys, we can find a simple extension of this lemma. As stated before, each boy in the pair had the property that more than 50% of the girls like him, and as a consequence more than 50% of all possible pairings of girls and popular boys satisfy the likes relation. If we further restrict the selection of boys, while not affecting the selection of girls, e.g., if we select only *tall* popular boys, it is easy to see that we will still have more than 50% of the possible pairings of girls and tall popular boys satisfying the likes relation. This generalization is expressed in the following lemma.

---

[13] This lemma is more closely related to sigma-additivity than might be indicated by the simple use of sigma-additivity in its proof. The lemma identifies a property of the probability functions that is known as "conglomerability" with respect to certain partitions of the domain (a notion due originally to de Finetti [16]). Schervish et al. [118] have shown that sigma-additive probability functions are *characterized* by conglomerability with respect to every partition of the domain.

LEMMA 40 If no $x_i \in \vec{x}$ is free in the formula δ then

$$\models \quad \forall r_1 r_2. \big[\beta \wedge \delta \wedge [\alpha|\beta]_{\vec{x}} \in (r_1, r_2)\big] > 0$$
$$\rightarrow \left[\alpha \Big| \beta \wedge \delta \wedge [\alpha|\beta]_{\vec{x}} \in (r_1, r_2)\right]_{\langle \vec{x}, \vec{y} \rangle} \in (r_1, r_2).$$

For example this lemma gives the validity of the formula

$$\left[\text{likes}(x, y) \middle| \begin{array}{l} ([\text{likes}(x, y)|\text{girl}(x) \wedge \text{boy}(y)]_x > 0.5) \\ \wedge\, \text{girl}(x) \wedge \text{boy}(y) \wedge \text{tall}(y) \end{array}\right]_{\langle x, y \rangle} > 0.5.$$

That is, as long as the boy is popular the chances of the girl liking him remain the same, even if the boy has some other some additional properties, in this case the property of being tall.

Proof: The proof is an easy extension of the proof of the previous lemma. The extra condition δ serves only to further restrict the set of instantiations of $\vec{y}$ (as its free variables appear only among the $\vec{y}$), but it does not alter the condition that for each instantiation of $\vec{y}$ the proportion of the possible instantiations of $\vec{x}$ which stand in the α relation with it lies within the given bounds. ∎

3.5.2 Representing Propositional Probabilities

In Chapter 2 we argued that the logic we developed for propositional probabilities was not suitable for representing statistical probabilities. Here we give a similar argument that our statistical probability logic is not suitable for representing propositional probabilities. This time, however, we can give a more precise demonstration of our claim, through the following lemma.

LEMMA 41 If α is a closed formula, i.e., if α has no free variables, then $[\alpha]_{\vec{x}} = 0$ or 1.

Proof: By the semantic definition, for any model and variable assignment pair (M, v)

$$([\alpha]_{\vec{x}})^{(M, v)} = \mu_n(\{\vec{a} : (M, v[\vec{x}/\vec{a}] \models \alpha\}).$$

Since α has no free variables, $v[\vec{x}/\vec{a}]$ and v agree on all the free variables of α, for any $\vec{a}$. Hence, by Theorem 24, $(M, v[\vec{x}/\vec{a}]) \models \alpha$ iff $(M, v) \models \alpha$.

Thus the above set of $\vec{a}$ is either all of $\mathcal{O}^n$ or the empty set, and for any μ_n the probability is either 0 or 1. $\blacksquare$

This lemma implies that formulas like fly(Tweety) can only be assigned probability one or zero. Hence, we cannot express a probabilistic degree of belief in such assertions using the statistical probability logic.[14]

3.6   The Selection Process

Although we can view the statistical assertions expressed in our language as statements of relative frequencies, technically they are different. When treated as statements of relative frequency a statistical assertion like $[\text{fly}(\text{x})|\text{bird}(\text{x})]_x = 0.9$ would mean that 90% of all birds fly. The logic is quite capable of being treated in this manner; all that we would require is a uniform probability distribution over the domain. That is, if every singleton set was assigned an identical probability then a statement like $[\text{bird}(\text{x})]_x = 0.9$ would mean that 90% of all the domain individuals are birds, and similarly $[\text{fly}(\text{x})|\text{bird}(\text{x})]_x = 0.9$ would mean that 90% of all the birds were flying birds.

One of the problems with uniform distributions is that they are limited to finite domains. We cannot have an infinite number of individuals all with equal and non-zero probability: the probability of the entire domain would then be infinite. Of course, we still have considerable flexibility in our probability assignments. For example, the probability distribution can be uniform over an arbitrarily large but finite subset of the domain. This means, for example, that we could have a uniform distribution over the set of birds (as long as there are only a finite number of birds), even if we do not have a uniform distribution over the entire domain.

Another problem with restricting ourselves to uniform distributions lies in our view that the variables bound by the probability operator are acting as random designators. As we discussed before, we can view probability terms like $[\alpha]_x$ as representing the probability that a randomly selected individual is a satisfying instantiation of x in α. So, for example, the probability term $[\text{fly}(\text{x})|\text{bird}(\text{x})]_x$ represents the probability that a randomly selected or randomly encountered bird would be

---

[14] There are technical ways of representing propositional probabilities in the statistical probability logic (see Abadi and Halpern [1]). However, the representation fails to give a transparent or "natural" semantics to the encoded assertions.

a flying bird. The probability distribution over the domain determines the parameters of this random selection process. That is, the probability of a domain individual o being selected by the process is equal to $\mu(o)$. Under this view of random selection there is no obvious reason for the selection process to be uniform.

Say there are ten cages $\{c_1, \ldots, c_{10}\}$ full of birds. Cages c_1 through c_9 contain ten white birds, while cage c_{10} contains 100 black birds. All the cages are in a warehouse, and the agent has no knowledge of the cages or of the distribution of the birds among the cages. His only contact with the birds is through a supply clerk. Whenever the agent orders a bird from the clerk, the clerk goes into the warehouse, chooses a cage, with any particular cage equally likely to be chosen, and chooses a bird from that cage with any bird equally likely to be chosen. The warehouse is always restocked so that the colors and numbers of birds in each cage remains unchanged. Now if the agent repeats this process, ordering birds from the clerk on many different occasions, he will find that 90% of the time he will get a white bird from the warehouse. Hence, it is not unreasonable for him to accept the statistical assertion $[\texttt{white(x)}|\texttt{bird(x)} \land \texttt{from-warehouse(x)}]_{\texttt{x}} = 0.9$ into his knowledge base. However, we, and the clerk, know that the relative frequency of white birds in the warehouse is only $90/190 \approx 47\%$. Therefore, if the domain consists of the birds in the warehouse there must be a non-uniform distribution over the set of birds for the agent's statistical assertion to be true. That is, the white birds are more likely to be selected than are the black birds.

The probability function is not intended to represent "true" relative frequencies that exist in the world; rather it is intended to model the agent's statistical knowledge of the world, the statistical knowledge that is accumulated by the agent during his interactions with his environment. If the agent encounters white birds from the warehouse 90% of the time he will constrain his model of the world so that the probability distribution matches his experience, regardless of the true relative frequencies. In fact, it is difficult to see how the agent could have access to such "true" frequencies, given that his interactions with the world are limited. For example, there are many situations where the process through which we encounter an individual is not in our control, as in the case of the process followed by the warehouse clerk. And when we turn to default reasoning based on statistical information, we will see that it is the manner in which the agent interacts with the world that is important, not the way that the world "really" is. For example, if the birds the agent encounters are white 90% of the time, the agent should be willing to assume that the probability is 0.9 that the next bird he encounters will be white, even if the real proportion of white birds among the birds is only 47%. Note, however, that the agent is not limited to his direct experiences for the collection of statistical information. He also has access to information collected by other agents. The agent may accept information from these other sources if he deems them sufficiently reliable.

The warehouse example does point out that the statistical probability logic is limited to a single probability distribution. Hence, it is limited in its ability to represent alternative selection processes. To return to the example, say that the agent is fully aware of the cages and the distribution of the birds in the cages. He cannot simultaneously assert the two formulas

- $[\text{white}(x)|\text{bird}(x) \wedge \text{from-warehouse}(x)]_x = 0.9$ and
- $[\text{white}(x)|\text{bird}(x) \wedge \text{from-warehouse}(x)]_x = 90/190$

without contradiction. However, he may be aware that a bird selected by the clerk has a 90% chance of being white, while a bird selected at random from all of the birds in the warehouse (i.e., without the intermediate selection of a cage) has only a 90/190 chance of being white. To represent this situation in our language we must take full account of what the agent knows. In this case the agent knows about the different processes by which the bird may be selected.

Hence, we can suppose that the agent admits a collection of trials into his domain of objects. These trials would be of two types: $\text{from-clerk}(x)$, those trials where the selection of the bird is performed by the clerk, and $\text{from-warehouse}(x)$, those trials where every bird in the warehouse is equally likely to be selected. Each trial has an outcome: a particular bird. This can be represented by admitting a function, say outcome, that maps trials to the bird that is the outcome of the trial. Using this function we can denote the particular bird that is the outcome of trial x by $\text{outcome}(x)$. In this expanded language it is perfectly consistent to assert the two formulas

- $[\text{white}(\text{outcome}(x))|\text{from-clerk}(x)]_x = 0.9$, and

- $[\texttt{white}(\texttt{outcome}(\texttt{x}))|\texttt{from-warehouse}(\texttt{x})]_{\texttt{x}} = 90/190$

simultaneously. The outcome function induces a new probability function over the set of birds: $\mu_{\texttt{outcome}}(\texttt{A}) = \mu\{\texttt{t} : \texttt{outcome}(\texttt{t}) \in \texttt{A}\}$, where A is a subset of the set of birds. For example, under this induced probability function the set of white birds has a probability equal to the probability of the set of trials whose outcome is a white bird. The above formulas state that among the from-clerk trials the subset that yields a white bird has probability 0.9, while among the from-warehouse trials the probability is 90/190.

4 Combining Statistical and Propositional Probabilities

4.1 Non-Rigid Terms

In the last two chapters we have developed separate languages with distinct semantics for representing the two different types of probabilities that we have identified. Both logics are capable of representing and reasoning with a wide range of quantitative and qualitative probabilistic assertions, but the meaning of the probability assertions has been radically different in each logic. Furthermore, we have argued that each logic is unsuitable for representing the type of probabilities expressible in the other.

Clearly, we would like to represent and reason with probabilistic assertions of both types; hence, it would be advantageous to have a unified language capable of dealing with both types of probabilities. As first pointed out by Halpern [43], a unified language can be constructed by combining the two languages and the semantic structures used to interpret them.

In this chapter we go through the steps required to combine the two probability logics, and give some examples of the kinds of knowledge that can be represented in the resulting logic. We do, however, have to deal with a complication along the way. Before we can combine the statistical and propositional probability languages we have to extend the propositional probability logic so that it can deal with non-rigid terms.

The propositional probability logic that we developed in Chapter 2 used the simplifying assumption that all of the terms of the language were rigid. That is, it was assumed that the denotation of the terms was constant across possible worlds. This simplified two things, (1) the instantiation rules for universal quantifiers and (2) the substitution of equals.

The instantiation rules for universal quantifiers allow one to substitute a term for a universally quantified variable wherever the variable occurs. So, for example, one could substitute the term c for the universally quantified variable x in the formula $\forall$x.P(x), producing the new formula P(c). This formula is satisfied by any structure that satisfies the original quantified formula. The instantiation of universally quantified variables is sound; it is truth preserving.

However, when we are dealing with non-rigid terms, terms whose denotation changes across possible worlds, we can no longer freely instantiate universally quantified variables. Take for example the formula
$\forall x.\text{prob}(P(x)) = 0.5$, where we are using the propositional probability
operator of Chapter 2. Semantically this formula is interpreted as asserting that

$$\text{for all } o \in \mathcal{O}, \quad \mu\{s' : (M, s', v[\mathbf{x}/o]) \models P(\mathbf{x})\} = 0.5.$$

In other words, it is asserting that for every individual object o the
probability of the set of worlds in which o has property P, is equal to
0.5. The important thing here is that although the denotation of x ranges
over all domain individuals, at the time that we interpret the probability
operator its denotation is fixed. That is, we choose an individual object
and then we evaluate the probability of the set of worlds where that fixed
individual has property P. The denotation of the quantified variable is
rigid in the scope of its quantifier.

Say that we instantiated the rigid quantified variable with a non-
rigid term. For example, let c be a term whose denotation varies from
world to world. If we allowed free instantiation of universally quantified variables by such non-rigid terms we could derive the new formula
$\text{prob}(P(c)) = 0.5$. However, it is quite possible that the probability of
the set of worlds that satisfy the formula P(c) is zero, or one, or almost
any other number between zero and one. That is, there is no reason
for $\text{prob}(P(c))$ to be equal to 0.5 as asserted by the formula. We can
simply choose an interpretation for c so that in every world it denotes
an object that is non-P, satisfying $\text{prob}(P(c)) = 0$, or we could choose
an interpretation so that in every world c denotes an object that is a
P, satisfying $\text{prob}(P(c)) = 1$. Similarly, by varying c's denotation across
the possible worlds in the right manner we can satisfy $\text{prob}(P(c)) = r$
for any number $r \in [0, 1]$ such that there is a subset of possible worlds
with probability r. The universal formula entails that $\text{prob}(P(t)) = 0.5$
for all *rigid* terms t, but entails nothing about non-rigid terms.

Hence, the instantiation of universally quantified variables with non-
rigid terms is not sound; it is not truth preserving. This means that the
axioms we had in the proof theory for the propositional probability language which allowed the instantiation of universally quantified variables
by any term must be altered to preserve their soundness in the presence
of non-rigid terms.

The second difficulty arising from non-rigid terms lies in the substitution of equals. If either of the terms s or t are non-rigid, it is quite possible that their denotations may be identical in some worlds while being different in others. That is, some worlds could satisfy s = t while others may satisfy s ≠ t. Hence, inside of the propositional probability operators we cannot freely substitute equal terms. For example, s = t does not entail $\mathsf{prob}(\mathsf{P}(\mathsf{s})) = \mathsf{prob}(\mathsf{P}(\mathsf{t}))$. The equality of the probability terms is entailed only if s = t in all worlds of non-zero probability, i.e., only if $\mathsf{cert}(\mathsf{s} = \mathsf{t})$. Again we need to change the proof theory to insure that these kinds of substitutions do not occur.

The reader may wonder, given these complications, why we should bother with non-rigid terms. Although it may be reasonable to assume that our constants act as proper names and are rigid, as we have pointed out in Chapter 3 it seems natural that certain functions, like the measuring functions, should be non-rigid. Once we allow non-rigid functions we have to deal with non-rigid terms, even if we are only applying these functions to rigid constants.

There is, however, an even more important reason for allowing and dealing with non-rigid terms. We want to construct a combined probability logic that will have statistical probabilities along with propositional ones. Even if we allowed only rigid functions, we would still have non-rigid terms in our language; they arise from the statistical probability operator. Consider, for example, the statistical probability term $[\mathsf{P}(\mathsf{x})]_\mathsf{x}$. This term denotes the probability of the set of individual objects denoted by the predicate symbol P. Since the denotation of the predicate symbols may change from world to world, this term denotes the probability of a potentially different set of objects in each world. Hence, the real number that it denotes might be different in different possible worlds even if the probability function remains constant: the term is non-rigid.[1]

Aside from the added complexity of non-rigid terms the combination of the two logics we developed in the previous chapters proceeds quite smoothly. We turn now to the details.

---

[1] We cannot make the predicate symbols rigid. If all the symbols were rigid, the same set of formulas would be true at each possible world; there would be no reason to have a set of possible worlds.

4.2   A Probability Logic for Statistical and Propositional Probabilities

To combine our two probability logics into a unified logic capable of representing both types of probabilities, we simply combine the two languages and the two semantic structures. The combined language includes rules of formation which generate both propositional probability terms and statistical probability terms, and the semantic structure used to interpret the formulas of the language includes both a probability distribution over the domain of discourse and a distribution over the set of possible worlds. We do, however, alter the semantics slightly to allow for non-rigid terms.

We now present more precisely the syntax and semantics of our combined probability logic.

4.2.1   Syntax

Symbols: We have the same set of logical symbols that were present in our previous probability logics. We have both the propositional probability operator, **prob**, and the square brackets, '[' and ']', that were used to form the statistical probability terms. Along with the distinguished symbols there is some set of user defined symbols, including the measuring functions that were used in the statistical probability language.

Formulas: Included in our rules of formula formation are the standard rules for forming first-order terms and formulas: **T0–T1** and **F1–F5**. In addition, we have the term formation rules for both statistical and propositional probabilities:

T2a)   If α is a formula, then $\mathbf{prob}(\alpha)$ is an *f-term*.

T2b)   If α is a formula and $\vec{x}$ is a vector of n object variables $\langle x_1, \ldots, x_n \rangle$, then $[\alpha]_{\vec{x}}$ is an *f-term*.

It should be noted that although the only change we have made is to include rules for both types of probability terms, the combined language is more expressive than a language that simply has both types of terms. The rules of formula formation can be applied recursively, which means that we can form propositional probability terms which contain statistical probability terms, and vice versa. That is, both types of probability operators can be nested. Later we will give some examples of what can be expressed using nested probabilities.

Definitional Extensions: We include the same set of definitional extensions that were used in the statistical and propositional probability languages. So we have an extended set of logical connectives, the existential quantifier, an extended set of inequality predicates, extra numeric constants, and a cert operator.

We also have both types of conditional probabilities.

Propositional Conditional Probabilities

$$\text{prob}(\beta) \neq 0 \rightarrow \text{prob}(\alpha|\beta) \times \text{prob}(\beta) = \text{prob}(\alpha \wedge \beta)$$
$$\wedge \quad \text{prob}(\beta) = 0 \rightarrow \text{prob}(\alpha|\beta) = 0.$$

Statistical Conditional Probabilities

$$[\beta]_{\bar{x}} \neq 0 \rightarrow [\alpha|\beta]_{\bar{x}} \times [\beta]_{\bar{x}} = [\alpha \wedge \beta]_{\bar{x}}$$
$$\wedge \quad [\beta]_{\bar{x}} = 0 \rightarrow [\alpha|\beta]_{\bar{x}} = 0.$$

4.2.2   Semantics

DEFINITION 42 (COMBINED PROBABILITY STRUCTURES)

To interpret the formulas of our combined probability logic we define the following structure.

$$M = \langle \mathcal{O}, S, \vartheta, \mu_{\mathcal{O}}, \mu_S \rangle$$

Where:

a) $\mathcal{O}$ is a set of individuals representing objects of the domain that one wishes to describe in the logic.

b) S is a set of possible worlds.

c) ϑ is a function that associates an interpretation of the language with each world. For every $s \in S$, $\vartheta(s)$ is an interpretation that assigns to every n-ary object predicate a subset of $\mathcal{O}^n$, to every n-ary object function symbol a function from $\mathcal{O}^n$ to $\mathcal{O}$, to every n-ary measuring function symbol a function from $\mathcal{O}^n$ to $I\!R$, to every n-ary numeric predicate a subset of $I\!R^n$, and to every n-ary numeric function a function from $I\!R^n$ to $I\!R$.

Unlike the propositional probability structures we do not require any of the functions to be rigid, except for the distinguished symbols. In particular, the distinguished numeric function symbols $+$, $\times$, 1, -1, and 0 are all rigid; i.e., on these symbols $\vartheta(s)$ is independent of the world s. Also, the numeric predicate symbols $<$ and $=$, and the object predicate symbol $=$ are rigid. The distinguished symbols have their normal interpretation in every world.

d) $\mu_{\mathcal{O}}$ is a discrete probability function over $\mathcal{O}$; i.e., for $A \subseteq \mathcal{O}$, $\mu_{\mathcal{O}}(A) = \sum_{o \in A} \mu_{\mathcal{O}}(o)$ and $\mu_{\mathcal{O}}(\mathcal{O}) = 1$.

e) μ_S is a discrete probability function over S; i.e., for $S' \subseteq S$, $\mu_S(S') = \sum_{s \in S'} \mu_S(s)$ and $\mu_S(S) = 1$.

As the definition demonstrates, the structure that we use to interpret the combined probability logic is a straightforward combination of the statistical and propositional probability structures, with an allowance for non-rigid terms. It should be noted that we have only one domain of individual objects, only one probability distribution over that domain, and only one probability distribution over the set of possible worlds; i.e., none of these components are dependent on the current possible world.

We note also that because the distinguished symbols 1, -1, 0, $+$, $\times$, and $=$ are rigid, numeric terms added by definition, like 0.5, are also rigid; only rigid predicates and functions enter into their definition. For example, 0.5 is defined by the axiom $0.5 \times (1+1) = 1$, all of whose symbols have an interpretation that is independent of the current possible world.

4.2.3   The Interpretation of the Formulas

We interpret the formulas of our combined probability logic using a straightforward combination of the interpretation rules we used for the statistical and propositional probability languages. In particular, rules F1–F4b, which were originally used for interpreting the propositional probability language, are the same,[2] and we have the same rules to interpret the probability terms. The only, minor, changes come in the interpretation of the terms, where we need to accommodate non-rigid terms by making their interpretation dependent on the current world.

---

[2] A minor change is needed for the rule of interpretation for the atomic formula, F1. Here the interpretation of the terms appearing in these formulas depends on the current world, unlike in the propositional probability language where the terms were all rigid.

T0) If x is a variable (of either type) then $x^{(M,s,v)} = v(x)$; the variable assignment determines the interpretation of the variables independently of the current world s.

T1) If f is an n-ary function symbol (of either type) and $t_1, \ldots, t_n$ are terms of a compatible type,[3] then

$$(ft_1 \ldots t_n)^{(M,s,v)} = f^{\vartheta(s)}(t_1^{(M,s,v)} \ldots t_n^{(M,s,v)}).$$

T2a) For every formula α, the f-term created by the propositional probability operator, $\mathsf{prob}(\alpha)$, is given the interpretation

$$\big(\mathsf{prob}(\alpha)\big)^{(M,s,v)} = \mu_S\{s' \in S : (M, s', v) \models \alpha\}.$$

T2b) For every formula α, the f-term created by the statistical probability operator, $[\alpha]_{\vec{x}}$, is given the interpretation

$$([\alpha]_{\vec{x}})^{(M,s,v)} = \mu_{\mathcal{O}}^n\{\vec{a} : (M, s, v[\vec{x}/\vec{a}]) \models \alpha\},$$

where $\vec{x}$ and $\vec{a}$ are n-ary vectors of object variables and individual objects respectively.

So we see that the statistical and propositional probability terms are given the same formal interpretation they had before.

From the syntax it is clear that both the propositional and statistical probability languages are *sub-languages* of the combined language. A useful observation that is immediate from the semantics of the combined probability language is the following:

LEMMA 43 If α is a *valid* formula of either the propositional or statistical probability sub-languages, then α is a *valid* formula of the combined probability language. Furthermore, if α is a valid formula of the combined probability language, then $\mathsf{cert}(\alpha)$ is also valid.

In particular, from this lemma we see that every statistical tautology given in Chapter 3 is certain (has propositional probability one) in every combined probability structure.

---

[3]That is, if f is a numeric function then the t_i must be f-terms, and if f is a measuring function or an object function then the t_i must be o-terms. The resulting term $ft_1 \ldots t_n$ is an f-term in the first two cases and an o-term in the last case.

4.3   Examples of Representation

EXAMPLE 16 (RIGIDITY)

1. *"The object constant* Tweety *denotes the same individual in all worlds that have non-zero probability."*

$$\exists \mathbf{x}.\mathsf{prob}(\mathbf{x} = \mathtt{Tweety}) = 1.$$

2. *"The numeric constant c is rigid across the worlds of non-zero probability."*

$$\exists x.\mathsf{prob}(x = c) = 1.$$

This is a general method for declaring a term to be rigid across the worlds of non-zero probability. It says that there exists an object that is equal to the term in a set of possible worlds that has probability one. That is, in no world of non-zero probability can this equality be violated. As we discussed above, quantified variables have a rigid denotation over the scope of the quantifier. Therefore, since the quantifier scopes the propositional probability operator the value of x remains constant across the possible worlds. Hence, since equality (of both types) is also rigid, the term is equal to the same individual in every world of non-zero probability.

It is quite possible that the equality might be violated in worlds that have zero probability, but such worlds do not affect the interpretation of the propositional probability operator. It is not difficult to prove by induction on the formulas that the interpretation of any formula α by a particular triple (M, s, v) is dependent only on s and those worlds of non-zero probability.[4]

EXAMPLE 17 (COMBINING PROBABILITY TYPES)

1. *"Most birds can fly, and Tweety is a bird who can probably fly."*

$$[\mathtt{fly}(\mathbf{x})|\mathtt{bird}(\mathbf{x})]_{\mathbf{x}} > c \wedge \mathtt{bird}(\mathtt{Tweety}) \wedge \mathsf{prob}\big(\mathtt{fly}(\mathtt{Tweety})\big) > c.$$

Here we have a "flat" combination of the two types of probabilities; i.e., there is no nesting of the different types of probabilities.

---

[4]The analogue of this in modal logics with Kripke style semantics is that the interpretation of a formula depends only on the current world s and the worlds transitively accessible from s. In the probability structures the "transitively accessible" worlds are those worlds with non-zero probability.

The truth of this formula depends on the current world: the first two conjuncts may have different truth values in different worlds.

2. *"The probability is .95 that more than 75% of all birds can fly."*

$$\text{prob}\big([\text{fly}(x)|\text{bird}(x)]_x > 0.75\big) = 0.95.$$

Here, we have assigned a degree of belief to a statistical assertion. This kind of "second-order" probability assertion is produced by classical statistical testing. For example, from various statistical tests involving random samples of birds, one may conclude with probability 0.95 that more than 75% of all birds fly.

3. *"John is more likely to succeed than the average high-school student."*

$$\text{prob}\big(\text{succeed}(\text{John})\big) > [\text{succeed}(x)|\text{highschool-student}(x)]_x.$$

Again the truth of this formula is dependent on the world in which it is interpreted. Although the term $\text{prob}\big(\text{succeed}(\text{John})\big)$ is rigid, $[\text{succeed}(x)|\text{highschool-student}(x)]_x$ is not. Hence, in some worlds its denotation may be less than the denotation of $\text{prob}\big(\text{succeed}(\text{John})\big)$, and in some worlds it may be greater.

To model an agent who may believe the above assertion[5] we could write

$$\text{cert}\left(\begin{array}{l}\text{prob}\big(\text{succeed}(\text{John})\big) \\ \quad > [\text{succeed}(x)|\text{highschool-student}(x)]_x\end{array}\right).$$

This formula, unlike the previous one, has a truth value that is independent of the world in which it is being interpreted. We could use the same device of insertion into a certainty operator to model an agent believing the assertion given in item 1.

4. *"Given that John is an accountant and that most accountants are precise, John is probably precise."*

$$\text{prob}\left(\text{precise}(\text{John})\,\middle|\,\begin{array}{l}\text{accountant}(\text{John}) \\ \wedge\,[\text{precise}(x)|\text{accountant}(x)]_x > 0.5\end{array}\right) > 0.5.$$

---

[5] When we talk about believing without quantifying the degree of belief we are equating believing with being certain. This corresponds to *full* belief; see Section 2.8 for further discussion on the relationship between certainty and belief.

Here we are forming a conditional propositional probability term with a statistical assertion as part of the conditioning formula. The formula asserts that John is precise in most of the worlds where he is an accountant and where most accountants are precise.

5. *"Most of the birds that probably fly do fly."*

$$[\texttt{fly}(\mathbf{x})|\texttt{bird}(\mathbf{x}) \wedge \texttt{prob}(\texttt{fly}(\mathbf{x})) > 0.5]_{\mathbf{x}} > 0.5.$$

Here we have nested the probability operators in the opposite direction, with the statistical probability operator outermost. In the formula the denotation of the random designator $\mathbf{x}$ has been fixed by the time the propositional probability operator is interpreted.

The formula asserts that most objects that are birds in the current world and that fly in most of the possible worlds fly in the current world. The formula is dependent on the world in which it is being interpreted. Note also that a particular object could satisfy the conditioning formula even if it is not a bird in most of the possible worlds. This results from $\texttt{bird}(\mathbf{x})$ having no propositional probability operator around it. Hence, a particular object (a particular instantiation of $\mathbf{x}$) could be a bird in the current world and a flier in most worlds without being a bird in most worlds.

An alternate encoding of this assertion is

$$[\texttt{fly}(\mathbf{x})|\texttt{bird}(\mathbf{x}) \wedge \texttt{prob}(\texttt{fly}(\mathbf{x})|\texttt{bird}(\mathbf{x})) > 0.5]_{\mathbf{x}} > 0.5.$$

This alternate formula asserts that most of the birds (in the current world) that fly in most of the worlds in which they are birds, fly (in the current world). One could view this assertion as claiming that the current world is "similar" to most other worlds with respect to flying birds.

4.4 Proof Theory

A powerful proof theory for the combined language can be produced by simply combining our axiomatizations for the propositional and statistical probability languages. The only difficulty is that we must make some adjustments for non-rigid terms.

As we pointed out in the introduction, non-rigid terms cause two types of problems, problems associated with quantification and problems associated with equality. Fortunately, our treatment of equality, using the equality axioms **EQ1–EQ3**, is already sufficient to deal with equality once we make a minor change to one of the propositional probability axioms. Quantification, on the other hand, can be dealt with by restricting universal instantiation to rigid terms only.

First, we give the collection of axioms that comprises our proof theory, and then we will discuss the manner in which non-rigid terms are treated by the proof theory.

4.4.1 An Axiom System

First-order Axioms: We have the first-order axioms **PC1–PC3** and the equality axioms **EQ1–EQ3**. The only change comes in **PC3**, the axiom for universal instantiation. The modified axiom is:

PC3) $\exists y.\mathrm{prob}(y = t) = 1 \rightarrow (\forall x.\alpha \rightarrow \alpha(x/t))$,
      provided that t is free for x in α. That is, all terms that are rigid with respect to the worlds of non-zero probability are legal instantiations of the universal.

Rigid Terms: The following axiom is useful for reasoning about the effects of rigid terms.

RGV) $\exists y.\mathrm{prob}(t = y) = 1$ for every rigid term t.
      Included among the rigid terms are the numeric constants built up from 1, 0, and -1, and both types of variables.

This axiom is sound because the denotation of rigid terms does not depend on the current world. The axiom states that there is some object in the domain that is equal to the term's denotation in every world of non-zero probability.

Field Axioms: Also included are the field axioms **F1–F15**.

Statistical Probability Axioms: The axioms for the statistical probability operator **P1–P7** are part of the axiom system.

Propositional Probability Axioms: The axioms for the propositional probability operator **Prob1–Prob5** are included, with one change to **Prob4**. The axiom is modified as follows:

Prob4) $\alpha \rightarrow \mathsf{prob}(\alpha) = 1$,

if all non-rigid function and predicate symbols in α occur inside of a propositional probability operator.

In Chapter 2 the axiom only specified that user defined predicate symbols must occur inside of the propositional probability operator. Here we have extended this restriction to include non-rigid function symbols. If the terms generated by the function symbols are no longer rigid, then a formula like $s = t$ that may be true in a given world is no longer guaranteed to be true in all worlds. However, if α contains only rigid symbols outside of the propositional probability operator, then α will be true in a given world if and only if it is true in all worlds. Any non-rigid symbols become effectively rigid once we embed them inside of the propositional probability operator, as inspection of the operator's semantics will demonstrate.

Rigid Statistical Probabilities: The propositional probability axiom **Prob5**, the probabilistic analogue of the Barcan formula, expressed the fact that the set of individual objects $\mathcal{O}$ did not vary across possible worlds. Similarly, the domain probability function $\mu_\mathcal{O}$ is invariant across possible worlds. The following axiom captures this.

RGSP) $\forall x. \exists r. \mathsf{prob}([y = x]_y = r) = 1$.

The set of domain individuals defined by the statistical probability term $[y = x]_y$ is simply the singleton set consisting of the individual denoted by x. The axiom says that for every domain individual o, i.e., for every assignment of x, there is a fixed number r that is equal to $\mu_\mathcal{O}(o)$ in every world of non-zero probability. That is, for every $o \in \mathcal{O}$, $\mu_\mathcal{O}(o)$ has a fixed value in every world s such that $\mu_S(s) > 0$.

Rules of Inference: We have the three rules of inference, modus ponens, universal generalization, and probability of equivalents.

4.4.2   Dealing with Non-Rigid Terms

The modifications that we have made are sufficient to insure that the proof theory remains sound in the presence of non-rigid terms.

We demonstrated for both the statistical and propositional probability logics how the equality axioms along with first-order reasoning were sufficient to infer the substitution of equals in all formulas. Even though the equality axioms only make mention of atomic formulas, first-order reasoning is sufficient to extend them to all first-order formulas. With the statistical logic the probability axioms were sufficient to extend them to all formulas of the statistical probability language.

With the propositional probability logic the version of axiom **Prob4** used in Chapter 2 allowed one to infer $\mathsf{prob}(s = t) = 1$ from $s = t$, since there was no restriction on function symbols being outside of the probability operator in that version. With $\mathsf{prob}(s = t) = 1$ we could take $s = t$ inside of the probability operator; i.e., probabilistic tautologies allowed one to deduce the validity of $\mathsf{prob}(s = t) = 1 \rightarrow \mathsf{prob}(s = t \wedge \alpha) = \mathsf{prob}(\alpha)$. Once inside of the probability operator we could perform standard first-order reasoning to demonstrate that substitution of equals could occur inside of the operator. The probability of equivalents rule of inference legitimized the required first-order transformations inside of the probability operator.

Although we can substitute equals inside of the statistical probability operator using the same axioms, our modified axiom **Prob4** disallows the inference $\mathsf{prob}(s = t) = 1$ from $s = t$. That is, we can no longer take equalities inside of the propositional probability operator unless we already know that these equalities have probability one. Note that if s and t are both rigid

$$s = t \rightarrow \Big(\mathsf{cert}(s = t) \rightarrow \mathsf{prob}(\alpha) = \mathsf{prob}\big(\alpha(s/t)\big) \Big)$$

is valid. In this case we can take the equality inside of the probability operator and then perform the substitution.

Universal instantiation is dealt with by our modification of axiom **PC3**. The new axiom allows the instantiation of universally quantified variables by rigid terms only. For rigid terms instantiation takes place everywhere in the formula, even inside of the propositional probability operator.

The restriction does not affect instantiation in formulas which do not contain the propositional probability operator. For example, say that we have the formula $\forall z.\mathsf{P}(z)$, and we wish to infer $\mathsf{P}(c)$. This inference is valid, since we have no propositional probability operators in $\forall z.\mathsf{P}(z)$. Since c is a term, the formula $\exists x.x = c$ is valid. Hence, we have that $\exists x.x = c \wedge \exists y.\mathsf{prob}(y = x) = 1$ is valid from **RGV**. From this we can infer $\exists x.x = c \wedge P(x)$, where we have instantiated the universally quantified z with the rigid variable x. Subsequently, using the equality axioms, we can deduce $\exists x.P(c)$. The existential quantifier can then be dropped, as x does not occur in $P(c)$, leaving the desired conclusion $P(c)$. Here the variable x is being used as a temporary device to denote the same individual denoted by c *in the current world*. However, since variables are rigid x denotes this individual in all worlds, unlike c. Hence, x can be used to instantiate universally quantified variables. After we have performed the instantiation we can replace the variable with the original term by equality reasoning. Note, however, that this method does not work when the formula contains a propositional probability operator: we would not be able to perform the final replacement of the variable since the equality axioms do not allow one to substitute equals into the propositional probability operator. Thus although universal instantiation with non-rigid terms is allowed in formulas without the propositional probability operator, instantiation into the propositional probability operator is blocked.

4.4.3   Soundness and Completeness

It is not difficult to demonstrate that this proof theory is sound with respect to the combined probability structures. The axioms and all of the rules of inference are valid for exactly the same reasons that they were valid in the statistical and propositional probability structures; the interpretations of the probability operators are unchanged. We have also given arguments that demonstrate the validity of the changes we have made to accommodate non-rigid terms. The only two new axioms are **RGV** and **RGSP**, and an examination of their semantic interpretation should convince the reader that they are both valid.

As should be expected, a complete proof theory is not possible for the combined probability language. Any complete proof theory would also be complete for the statistical and propositional probability sublanguages, and it is known that there is no complete proof theory for these languages. However, just as was the case for the statistical and propositional languages, the proof theory is fairly complete for finite domains.

If we restrict the language by omitting the measuring functions and by disallowing any user defined numeric functions or predicates, and we extend the proof theory by including the axioms which define a real-closed field, i.e., axioms **RCF1** and **RCF2**$_n$ and which specify that the domain is bounded in size, i.e., axiom **FIN**$_N$ for some N^6, then the following theorem holds.

THEOREM 44 (HALPERN [43])
The extended proof theory in the restricted language is complete for combined probability structures where the domain $\mathcal{O}$ is bounded in size.

In addition to this result for finite domains, we also have empirical demonstrations of various types of reasoning that can be captured by the proof theory. In particular, all of the examples of reasoning with the propositional probability terms given in Chapter 2, as well as all of the examples of reasoning with the statistical probability terms given in Chapter 3, are captured by our proof theory: it includes all of the axioms and rules of inference that were used in these examples. Hence, we conclude that, although incomplete, the proof theory is very powerful, and that it captures a wide range of useful first-order, statistical probabilistic, and propositional probabilistic reasoning.

4.5 The Relation Between the Different Probabilities

The combined probability logic provides a useful unified framework for representing and reasoning with both statistical and propositional probabilities. In the language we can express assertions which contain either type of probability and we can reason about the valid consequences of these assertions. However, in the logic there is no intrinsic relationship between the two types of probabilities. That is, the distribution over the domain $\mu_{\mathcal{O}}$ places no restrictions on the distribution over the worlds μ_S.

There are some simple constraints between the statistical and propositional probabilities when we deal with universally quantified formulas. For example we have that all formulas of the following form are valid:

$$\mathsf{cert}\big([\alpha]_x = 1\big) \to \big[\mathsf{cert}(\alpha)\big]_x = 1.$$

This formula asserts that if in every world of non-zero probability every individual of non-zero probability is a satisfying instantiation of x in α,

---

[6] These axioms were given in Section 2.6.3.

then every individual of non-zero probability is a satisfying instantiation of x in α in every world of non-zero probability.

Once we move away from unit probabilities, however, the relationship between the two types of probabilities becomes weaker, even for universally quantified formulas. For example, the following formula is satisfiable:

$$\mathrm{cert}\big([\mathsf{P}(\mathbf{x})]_{\mathbf{x}} = .75\big) \wedge \big[\mathrm{cert}\big(\mathsf{P}(\mathbf{x})\big)\big]_{\mathbf{x}} < .75.$$

This formula says that it is possible that 75% of all individuals are P's (i.e., satisfy $\mathsf{P}(\mathbf{x})$) in every world of non-zero probability, but in the same structure less than 75% of the individuals are P's in every world of non-zero probability. Consider, for example, the structure which consists of four individual objects $\{o_1, o_2, o_3, o_4\}$ and four possible worlds $\{s_1, s_2, s_3, s_4\}$, and in which μ_S and μ_O are uniform distributions. If o_1 and o_2 are P's in every world, o_3 is a P in s_1 and s_2, and o_4 is a P in s_3 and s_4, then both of the above conjuncts are satisfied.

The most interesting kinds of relationships between propositional and statistical probabilities come from applications of direct inference, e.g., the inference that since most birds fly and Tweety is a bird, Tweety probably flies. These kinds of inferences arise from the assumption that the particular individual in question was randomly selected from some class of individuals, commonly referred to as the reference class. In the next chapter we will demonstrate how defeasible or default inferences can be generated from such assumptions. Here, however, we can note that the combined probability logic is by itself insufficient to capture this kind of inference from statistical to propositional probabilities. Statistical probabilities, like $[\mathtt{fly}(\mathbf{x})|\mathtt{bird}(\mathbf{x})]_{\mathbf{x}}$, place no constraints on propositional probabilities which involve particular constants, like $\mathrm{prob}\big(\mathtt{fly}(\mathtt{Tweety})\big)$, even if we know something about the value of the statistical probability in every world. For example, even if we are certain that $[\mathtt{fly}(\mathbf{x})|\mathtt{bird}(\mathbf{x})]_{\mathbf{x}} > .9$, i.e., we know that $\mathrm{cert}\big([\mathtt{fly}(\mathbf{x})|\mathtt{bird}(\mathbf{x})]_{\mathbf{x}} > .9\big)$, we cannot deduce anything about the value of $\mathrm{prob}\big(\mathtt{fly}(\mathtt{Tweety})\big)$.

4.6   An Expectation Operator

When we discuss direct inference in the next chapter we will need a slight extension to the combined probability language developed above. The combined logic contains non-rigid numeric terms. These terms can denote a different real number in every world. We also have a probability distribution over the worlds μ_S. Hence, it makes sense to talk about the expected value of non-rigid numeric terms, i.e., the weighted average of their value across the possible worlds, where μ_S determines the weight or influence of each individual world.

To refer to the expected value we can add an expectation operator to the language. In the sequel we will only apply the expectation operator to statistical probability terms, including the conditional statistical terms, and rigid numeric terms. These types of numeric terms have the important feature that there is a fixed upper and lower bound on the value that they can denote in any possible world. In the case of the statistical terms the upper bound is 1 and the lower bound is 0, while for the rigid terms the term's denotation serves as both upper and lower bound. Since the denotation of the term has fixed bounds, the expected value, which is taken over a possibly infinite number of worlds, will always exist. This is not necessarily the case for arbitrary numeric terms. For example, if we have an infinite number of worlds with non-zero probability $\langle s_1, \ldots, s_i, \ldots \rangle$, and if the denotation of the term t is $1/\mu_S(s_i)$ in every world s_i, then its expected value will be infinite. That is, its expected value will not be a real number. We avoid this problem by restricting the application of the expectation operator.

Syntactically, we add the following term formation rule to our language:

T2c) If t is a statistical probability term or if t is rigid f-term then $\mathsf{E}(t)$ is a new *f-term*. That is, the expectation operator acts syntactically like a monadic function; however, its semantic interpretation is quite different from ordinary functions. Note that all numeric constants formed from 1, 0, and -1 are rigid terms.

Semantically, these new terms are interpreted by the following rule.

T2c) Every f-term $\mathsf{E}(t)$ created by the E operator is given the interpretation,
$$\mathsf{E}(t)^{(M,s,v)} = \sum_{s' \in S} \mu_S(s') \times t^{(M,s',v)}.$$

The rule gives the promised interpretation of these terms: they denote the weighted average of their operand across the different possible worlds.

The following is an example of how the expectation operator could be used in the language.

EXAMPLE 18 (EXPECTED VALUES)
We can express assertions about the expected value of various statistical probability terms.

$$E\big([\mathtt{fly(x)}|\mathtt{bird(x)}]_\mathtt{x}\big) = E\big([\mathtt{fly(x)}|\mathtt{yellow(x)} \wedge \mathtt{bird(x)}]_\mathtt{x}\big).$$

This formula says the subclass of yellow birds has the same expected proportion of fliers as does its superclass, the set of all birds. By using the expectation operator we can make this assertion while still allowing the possibility that in some worlds being yellow does affect the chances of a bird being able to fly. In some worlds being yellow may have adverse effects on flying ability, while in other worlds it may have a positive effect. However, we are asserting that it has no net effect when weighed over all the possible worlds.

4.6.1   Properties of the Expectation Operator

Our use of the expectation operator will be fairly limited, so we will not attempt to develop a proof theory for the extended language. Instead, we will derive from the semantics certain results which identify some important properties of the operator. We could add these derived properties as additional axioms to the proof theory we have already developed. This would extend the proof theory, making it capable of reasoning with the expectation operator.

LEMMA 45 Expectations are rigid, as is obvious from their semantic definition. That is, for every expectation term $E(t)$ the following axiom is valid:

$$\exists r.\mathsf{prob}\big(r = E(t)\big) = 1.$$

Non-rigid numeric terms become rigid when insulated by the expectation operator.

In addition to rigidity there are a number of useful numeric properties of the expectation terms.

LEMMA 46 (PROPERTIES OF THE EXPECTATION TERMS)

1. If t is rigid, then $E(t) = t$.

2. $\text{cert}(t = t') \rightarrow E(t) = E(t')$.

3. $\text{cert}(t < t') \rightarrow E(t) < E(t')$.

4. $\text{cert}(t > t') \rightarrow E(t) > E(t')$.

5. $\text{cert}(t \leq t') \rightarrow E(t) \leq E(t')$.

6. $\text{cert}(t \geq t') \rightarrow E(t) \geq E(t')$.

7. $E(t) = 0 \equiv \text{cert}(t = 0)$.

8. $E(t) = 1 \equiv \text{cert}(t = 1)$.

9. $E(t + t') = E(t) + E(t')$.

10. If r is rigid, then $E(r \times t) = r \times E(t)$.

11. If r is rigid, then $E(t/r) = E(t)/r$.

Proof: The first item is obvious since t has the same denotation in every possible world.

For the other items, since the various relations between t and t' are certain, they hold in every world of non-zero probability. Furthermore, due to the restrictions on the application of the expectation operator all of the infinite sums generated from its definition have well-defined limits. Hence, the items in the lemma follow from elementary result about the limits of real-valued sums. The only possible source of subtlety lies in item 3 and 4. Two sequences, $\langle t_i \rangle$ and $\langle t'_i \rangle$, which have the property that $t_i < t'_i$ for all i may have equal limits: the difference $t_i - t'_i$ may tend to zero. Here, however, we are summing the items in the sequence; i.e., if $t_i = \mu_S(s_i) \times t^{(M,s_i,v)}$ for every world s_i (in some enumeration of the worlds which have non-zero probability), then $E(t) = \sum t_i$. Similarly, $E(t') = \sum t'_i$. The formula $\text{cert}(t < t')$ implies that $t_i < t'_i$ for every i; therefore, the difference between the sums increases as i increases. Hence, the expected values preserve the strict inequality.

Items 7 and 8 are subsumed by item 1 when t is rigid. Otherwise, t is a statistical probability term. Since 1 and 0 are upper and lower bounds on the value of these terms in all worlds, the expectations can only achieve these extremes if the value is extreme in every world of non-zero probability.

The last three items follow from the fact that expectations are linear operators. It should be noted, however, that it is not necessarily the case that $E(t \times t') = E(t) \times E(t')$ when both t and t' are non-rigid. For example, we could have two possible worlds (s_1, s_2). In s_1, t could have the value 1 and t' the value 0, while in s_2, t could have the value 0 and t' the value 1. We would then have $E(t) = E(t') = 1/2$, therefore $E(t) \times E(t') = 1/4$, but $E(t \times t') = 0$. ∎

5 Default Inferences from Statistical Knowledge

5.1 Direct Inference

We have presented a combined probability logic capable of dealing simultaneously with propositional and statistical probabilities. In this combined logic, however, there is no intrinsic relationship between the different probabilities; the two types of probabilities simply co-exist without significant interaction.

Although these are distinct types of probabilities, there is clearly a connection between them. As mentioned in Chapter 1, this connection is most apparent in actuarial situations, which often equate the two. When you apply for life insurance, for example, the insurance companies gather some relevant information about your health, job risk, etc., and consult their *statistical* information about deaths among a set of individuals similar to you in the relevant aspects. They then quote you a rate that is based on their belief that the probability of your death after any particular number of years is equal to the proportion of individuals in their reference set who die after that many years. They have inferred a propositional probability, the probability of a particular individual's death, from a statistical probability, the proportion of individuals who die, among a reference set.

In AI a interesting example of the connection between propositional and statistical probabilities occurs in expert systems which deal with uncertainty. In medical diagnosis systems, for example, information is gathered from an expert who has had experience with a population of patients. When a particular patient is diagnosed it is assumed that the expert's knowledge about the population is applicable to that particular patient. That is, it is assumed that the probability of a patient having a particular ailment, given that he displays a certain set of symptoms, is the same as the proportion of patients that have that ailment from among those patients who display the same symptoms.[1]

Another example comes from chance phenomena like tosses of a coin.

---

[1] Some systems claim to be using subjective (propositional) probabilities directly, e.g., Prospector [23], but these systems are really using an expert's subjective opinions about various statistical probabilities. Other systems which do not use probabilities still use similar assumptions: they gather information about a population or class of patients and during diagnosis apply this information to particular patients.

If you perform a particular toss of a coin, you are very likely to believe that the probability of its landing heads is 1/2. Clearly any *particular* toss will land either heads or tails, so in this situation probability is being used as a degree of belief, i.e., as a propositional probability. However, the assignment of the particular value of probability 1/2 to this proposition is based on statistical knowledge, knowledge about the proportion of coin tosses that result in heads.

It could be argued that in this particular case we may be using considerations of symmetry to arrive at our propositional probabilities, instead of statistical knowledge. The coin looks symmetric; hence, we assign equal probability to either face being up after a toss.[2] However, if we take a particular coin that to all appearances seems symmetric and toss it a large number of times finding that it lands heads 90% of the time, it is unlikely that we would continue to assign a probability of only 1/2 to the proposition that any particular toss of this coin will land heads. In other words, any considerations of symmetry will be superseded by empirical evidence. With this in mind it makes sense to regard considerations like symmetry as being mediated through the formation of statistical knowledge, rather than being applied directly to generate propositional probabilities. When they are applicable, we may well use considerations of symmetry to generate our statistical knowledge, so, for example, seeing that the coin is symmetric may lead us to believe that it will land heads 50% of the time. From our belief in this statistical assertion we may then conclude that the probability a particular toss will land heads is 1/2. However, our empirical experience is also a major input to our statistical knowledge. So if we toss the coin a number of times and find out that it lands heads in 90% of these cases, we may reject the previous statistical assertion which was based solely on symmetry, and accept instead the assertion that in general the coin will land heads 90% of the time. From this new statistical knowledge we may then conclude that the probability that a particular toss will land heads is 0.9.

In non-actuarial situations, however, the connection between these two types of probabilities is not as obvious. Nevertheless, it would be of great utility if a general connection could be made, applicable to a wider

---

[2] The idea of assigning probabilities from considerations of symmetry was the basis of LaPlace's infamous principle of indifference. It has subsequently been accepted that this principle cannot explain many common uses of probability in situations where there is no clear identification of what the equiprobable cases are (see Kyburg [66] for a useful discussion).

class of situations. The reason is that while statistical probabilities are directly related to features of the environment, propositional probabilities are not. Propositional probabilities act as degrees of belief assigned by the agent to various propositions. Objectively these propositions are either true or false. That is, in the agent's environment there is no probability attached to these propositions, just a truth value. Propositional probabilities of one or zero are relatively easy to understand, they correspond to the agent having full belief or full disbelief in a proposition. Such beliefs have the important property that they can be verified. That is, from various sources of information, e.g., sensory information or information from well verified scientific theories, the agent can become very confident that certain propositions are objectively true, confident enough to accept, i.e., assign full belief to, these propositions. However, there is no straightforward way of explaining non-extreme degrees of belief, unless we can connect them to *verifiable* statistical sources as is done in actuarial situations. Without a connection between empirically founded statistical probabilities and propositional probabilities, it becomes difficult to justify any assertion about the agent's propositional probabilities. How can we ever judge an agent's degrees of belief to be rational or justifiable if they do not have any empirical foundation?

The issue of empirical foundations for probabilities *used as degrees of belief* has been largely ignored in AI. Proponents of probabilities have always been quick to claim that probabilities are empirically founded, referring to statistical probabilities. Unfortunately, they often continue on to claim that propositional probabilities have the same advantage, without paying due attention to the serious problems involved in connecting propositional probabilities with empirical observations.

Work on a general connection between statistical and propositional probabilities has been carried out in philosophy, where the inference of a propositional probability from a statistical probability is often called *direct inference*. Perhaps the earliest principle of direct inference was stated by Reichenbach [113]. Reichenbach claimed that the probability of an individual having a property should be equal to the relative frequency of that property among the smallest class to which that individual belonged for which one had "reliable statistics." For example, say that we know that more than 75% of all birds are fliers and that all we know about Tweety is that she is a bird, then direct inference would sanction the conclusion that the probability Tweety can fly is greater than 0.75. If we also know that Tweety is yellow, then the smallest, or narrowest, class to which Tweety is known to belong would be the class of yellow birds. However, given that we have no reliable statistical information about the proportion of fliers among the class of yellow birds, Reichenbach's principle would still allow us to perform direct inference from the class of birds, as it remains the narrowest class for which we have reliable information. The class from which direct inference is performed is called the *reference class* [71].

Direct inference hinges on one's ability to choose an appropriate reference class, and unfortunately Reichenbach's notion of "adequate statistics" is far too imprecise to be of much help in this task. Sophisticated systems of direct inference have been developed by a number of writers, including Kyburg [67,71], Pollock [104,105], and Levi [80]. These systems present precise mechanisms for choosing the correct reference class. Once the reference class is chosen we infer the propositional probability from the statistical information we have about the reference class.

5.2   Performing Direct Inference

Using the logical formalisms we have developed, we can construct a mechanism of direct inference. This mechanism describes how an agent who has accepted some set of statistical assertions can generate degrees of belief that are founded on this statistical information. The mechanism differs from the philosophical approaches in a couple of important ways. First, it is constructed in the combined probability logic developed in Chapter 4. This logic supports a greater variety of qualitative probabilistic information and also possesses a more transparent semantics than previously used formalisms. Second, we examine the problem of choosing the correct reference class from the AI perspective of reasoning from lack of knowledge.

The mechanism we will develop is not only capable of generating empirically founded degrees of belief, but is also capable of capturing a wide range of default reasoning, which we characterize as reasoning to plausible conclusions from less than conclusive evidence. Default reasoning is one of the most important types of non-monotonic reasoning and has been the subject of much study in AI, e.g., see the articles in Ginsberg [39].

Our approach to direct inference uses the observation that Reichenbach's notion of "adequate statistics" can be viewed as being determined by what statistics are *not* known. Sanctioning the use of a wider reference class over a narrower one when there are no adequate statistics available for the narrower class is equivalent to concluding non-monotonically that the statistics over the narrower class do not differ from the statistics over the wider class. That is, a wider reference class is chosen over a narrower one if we have no knowledge that the statistics over the narrower class differ from the wider class. So in the above example we reject the narrower reference class yellow(x) ∧ bird(x) because we have no knowledge that the proportion of fliers in this class is different from the proportion of fliers in the wider class bird(x). This kind of inference from lack of knowledge has been extensively studied in AI, as a form of non-monotonic reasoning.[3]

In the direct inference mechanism we will develop, a form of consistency-based non-monotonic reasoning will be used. This form of non-monotonic reasoning is characterized by a willingness to accept an assumption if it is not contradicted by what we have already accepted. Consistency-based non-monotonic reasoning is the foundation of Reiter's default logic [114], and is also closely related to Moore's autoepistemic logic [91]. Our choice is partly a matter of convenience, and no doubt other non-monotonic reasoning formalisms could be applied.[4] In the framework we develop, however, consistency-based non-monotonic reasoning has the closest conceptual fit with the rest of the mechanism.

The resulting combination of direct inference along with non-monotonic reasoning to drive the choice of reference class has a number of advantages over the sole use of non-monotonic reasoning in performing default reasoning. After we present the details of our mechanism we will discuss these advantages and make some other comparisons.

---

[3] Here we distinguish between reasoning from lack of knowledge and default reasoning. We will argue later that although lack of knowledge plays an important role in default reasoning, such reasoning is also dependent on the presence of certain types of empirical knowledge. The argument that these two types of reasoning are distinct has been made before, e.g., Moore [91].

[4] Grosof [42] has done some work on the non-monotonic inference of conditional independence using circumscription. The inference of conditional independence is similar to what we require.

5.3   The Epistemological Framework

We have already discussed the manner in which the propositional probability logic gives a generalization of Hintikka-style belief logics. Asserting that a formula has probability one is equivalent to asserting full belief in that formula, and, more generally, one can assign gradations of belief by using intermediate probabilities. Furthermore, through the use of numeric predicates relating the probabilities we can assert various qualitative relations between the degrees of belief assigned to different propositions.

The combined probability logic developed in Chapter 4 generalizes this even further. Not only can it assign degrees of belief to first-order assertions, but it can also assign degrees of belief to statistical assertions. That is, the combined probability logic allows us to model the beliefs of an agent who can make assertions about his environment expressed in the statistical probability logic of Chapter 3, and it can model the agent having graded belief in those assertions.

Given a fixed underlying statistical probability language in which the agent can express assertions about his environment, we assume that the agent has accepted, i.e., assigned full belief to, some finite set of assertions expressed in this language. Using the combined probability language we will develop a mechanism whereby we can reason in the combined logic about the degree of belief the agent should assign to other assertions given his accepted base of beliefs.

The mechanism which determines the agent's degrees of belief, given the accepted base of beliefs, will be presented as a collection of formulas of the combined probability language. By reasoning with these formulas inside of the combined probability logic we will be able to deduce new formulas that give information about the agent's degrees of belief.

5.4   The Formalism

In the following we assume a fixed statistical probability language $\mathcal{L}^{\text{stat}}$; i.e., the set of predicate and function symbols of $\mathcal{L}^{\text{stat}}$ is unaltered throughout the course of reasoning. $\mathcal{L}^{\text{stat}}$ is the language in which the agent expresses assertions about his environment. We will call the assertions expressed in $\mathcal{L}^{\text{stat}}$ *objective* assertions, as they relate to the environment external to the agent. To represent the agent's degrees of belief in these assertions, we extend $\mathcal{L}^{\text{stat}}$ by adding the propositional probability operator **prob** and the expectation operator E. This gives us a combined probability language $\mathcal{L}^{\text{comb}}$, as developed in Chapter 4, that is capable of representing the assignment of degrees of belief to assertions written in $\mathcal{L}^{\text{stat}}$. $\mathcal{L}^{\text{stat}}$ is a sublanguage of $\mathcal{L}^{\text{comb}}$, and we will call the formulas of $\mathcal{L}^{\text{comb}}$ that are also in $\mathcal{L}^{\text{stat}}$ *objective* formulas.

Given a finite knowledge base expressed as a collection of objective formulas, i.e., formulas of $\mathcal{L}^{\text{stat}}$, let KB denote the conjunction of these formulas. KB is itself a formula of $\mathcal{L}^{\text{stat}}$, as it is the conjunction of a *finite* collection of formulas. KB corresponds to the set of objective assertions that the agent has accepted; hence, we could more accurately refer to KB as a belief base, the full beliefs of the agent. KB will usually include information about particular individuals, e.g., bird(Tweety), general logical relationships between properties, e.g., $\forall$x.bird(x) $\rightarrow$ animal(x), and *statistical information*, e.g., [fly(x)|bird(x)]$_\text{x}$ > 0.75.

DEFINITION 47 (RANDOMIZATION)
Let α be a formula of $\mathcal{L}^{\text{stat}}$. If $\langle c_1, \ldots, c_n \rangle$ are the n distinct object constants that appear in $\alpha \wedge$ KB and $\langle v_1, \ldots, v_n \rangle$ are n distinct object variables that do not occur in $\alpha \wedge$ KB, then let $\text{KB}^{\mathbf{V}}$ $(\alpha^{\mathbf{V}})$ denote the new formula which results from textually substituting c_i by v_i in KB (α), for all i.

With this notation we can present a preliminary mechanism of direct inference that specifies the agent's degree of belief in any objective formula, given that he has accepted KB and *nothing else*.[5] This preliminary mechanism does not quite accomplish our goal of being representable as a set of formulas of the combined probability logic, but it serves to clarify some underlying concepts.

DEFINITION 48 (PRELIMINARY DIRECT INFERENCE PRINCIPLE)
If α is a formula of $\mathcal{L}^{\text{stat}}$ and if KB is the complete set of objective formulas that the agent fully believes, then the agent's degree of belief in α, $\text{prob}(\alpha)$, should be determined by the equality

$$\text{prob}(\alpha) = [\alpha^{\mathbf{V}}|\text{KB}^{\mathbf{V}}]_{\vec{v}},$$

---

[5]KB is all that the agent knows (about objective propositions). Although we will not attempt to develop a formal model of this notion, its formal properties have been studied, e.g., Levesque [78], Halpern and Moses [45], Konolige [61].

where $\vec{v}$ is the vector of new object variables used in randomization. In addition, the agent must assume $[\mathrm{KB^V}]_{\vec{v}} > 0$.

Before we explain the principle in more detail we present an example of its use. Let

$$\mathrm{KB} = \ \mathrm{bird(Tweety)} \quad \wedge \quad [\mathrm{fly(x)|bird(x)}]_{\mathbf{x}} > 0.75,$$

i.e., Tweety is a bird and most birds fly. Say that we wish to determine the agent's degree of belief in fly(Tweety). Using the direct inference principle we obtain

$$\mathrm{prob}\big(\mathrm{fly(Tweety)}\big) = \big[\mathrm{fly(v)|bird(v)} \wedge [\mathrm{fly(x)|bird(x)}]_{\mathbf{x}} > 0.75\big]_{\mathbf{v}}.$$

Note that the statistical assertion $[\mathrm{fly(x)|bird(x)}]_{\mathbf{x}} > 0.75$ appears unchanged in the randomized KB: no constants appear in this formula. Hence, the random designator $\mathbf{v}$, used in the outermost statistical probability term, does not appear free in this inner formula, and since $[\mathrm{KB^V}]_{\vec{v}} > 0$, we have that the above statistical probability term is equal to the simpler term $[\mathrm{fly(v)|bird(v)}]_{\mathbf{v}}$, by Lemma 34. This term is an alphabetic variant of $[\mathrm{fly(x)|bird(x)}]_{\mathbf{x}}$, and from the information in KB we know it to be greater than 0.75. Hence, our principle of direct inference allows us to conclude that $\mathrm{prob}\big(\mathrm{fly(Tweety)}\big) > 0.75$. The end result is that the agent's degree of belief in fly(Tweety) is equal to the probability that a randomly selected bird will be able to fly.

Our mechanism of assigning degrees of belief replaces the constants in the formulas α and KB by random designators. Intuitively it says that the agent's degree of belief in α should be equal to the probability that a randomly selected tuple (of individuals) from the set of tuples which satisfy $\mathrm{KB^V}$, satisfies $\alpha^{\mathbf{V}}$. The assumption $[\mathrm{KB^V}]_{\vec{v}} > 0$, on the other hand, is equivalent to assuming that there is a non-zero probability that a tuple of objects could be encountered which together satisfy $\mathrm{KB^V}$ (Section 3.6). Such an assumption is not unreasonable given that the agent has accepted KB: KB already asserts that $\mathrm{KB^V}$ is satisfied by a tuple of objects, i.e., the tuple denoted by $\langle c_1, \dots, c_n \rangle$.

In the above example, α and KB contain exactly the same set of constants, the single constant Tweety, and the set of individuals that satisfy $\mathrm{KB^V}$ is exactly the set of birds. Hence, our principle of direct inference says that the probability that Tweety can fly is equal to the probability that a randomly selected bird can fly, which we know from KB to be greater than 0.75.

It may be and usually will be the case that KB contains other constants besides those that appear in α. For example, with α as above we could have

$$KB = \text{bird}(\text{Tweety}) \quad \wedge \quad \text{bird}(\text{Opus})$$
$$\wedge \quad [\text{fly}(x)|\text{bird}(x)]_x > 0.75,$$

where we also have some information about Opus. In this situation our principle of direct inference will yield the more complex equality

$$\text{prob}\big(\text{fly}(\text{Tweety})\big)$$
$$= \big[\text{fly}(v_1)\big|\text{bird}(v_1) \wedge \text{bird}(v_2) \wedge [\text{fly}(x)|\text{bird}(x)]_x > 0.75\big]_{\langle v_1, v_2 \rangle}.$$

Once again, however, we have by Lemma 34 that the right-hand side is equal to the simpler $[\text{fly}(v_1)|\text{bird}(v_1)]_{\langle v_1, v_2 \rangle}$, which by Lemma 36 is equal to $[\text{fly}(v_1)|\text{bird}(v_1)]_{v_1}$. Hence, we obtain that $\text{prob}\big(\text{fly}(\text{Tweety})\big)$ > 0.75: the same conclusion as before.

Lemma 34 demonstrates that although we condition on the entire knowledge base, this is equivalent to conditioning only on those formulas which are "related" to α. The other formulas of the knowledge base are irrelevant at this stage. The formula α is related to every formula $\beta \in$ KB (i.e., β is one of the conjuncts of KB) with which it shares a constant, and α is also related to every formula in KB which shares a constant with a formula related to α; i.e., "related" is a transitive notion. For example, if KB $= P(a, b) \wedge Q(b, c) \wedge R(d)$ and $\alpha = A(a)$, then α is related to $P(a, b)$ and $Q(b, c)$ but is not related to $R(d)$.

The formulas of KB that are not related to α may, however, still be relevant when deducing information about the statistical probability term that appears on the right-hand side of the direct inference equality. For example, $[\text{fly}(x)|\text{bird}(x)]_x > 0.75$ was irrelevant as a conditioning formula in the statistical term equivalenced to $\text{prob}\big(\text{fly}(\text{Tweety})\big)$, but it provided important information about the value of that term.

The reader may wonder why we do not simply randomize those constants that appear in α instead of randomizing all of the constants in KB. When we replace a constant in KB by a new random designator we are, in essence, making the assumption that KB contains all that we know about the individual denoted by the constant. In other words, we are assuming that for all we know the denoted individual was randomly encountered from among the set of individuals that share all of its known properties.[6] In applying the direct inference principle we want to make this assumption for all of the constants in α and KB, not only for the constants in α. This is best illustrated by an example.

EXAMPLE 19 Let KB $= R(a, b)$, and let α be the formula $Q(a)$. If we randomized only those constants appearing α we would obtain $\mathsf{prob}\big(Q(a)\big) = [Q(v)|R(v, b)]_v$. In other words, we would assign a degree of belief to $Q(a)$ equal to the probability that a randomly selected individual related to b via R has property Q. The problem here is that just as KB contains everything we know about a, it also contains everything we know about b.   Hence, if we are willing to assume that a was randomly selected we have no reason to be unwilling to assume that b was randomly selected: we should be willing to randomize b as well as a.   Note that when we randomize a constant we are not losing any information. That is, we always replace the constant with a random designator that *shares all of that constant's known properties*, since we make our substitution uniformly throughout KB.

If we randomize both a and b we will obtain

$$\mathsf{prob}\big(Q(a)\big) = [Q(v_1)|R(v_1, v_2)]_{\langle v_1, v_2 \rangle};$$

i.e., we would assign a degree of belief to $Q(a)$ equal to the probability that the first element x of a randomly selected *pair* of individuals $\langle x, y \rangle$ standing in the relation R has property Q. This is a different conclusion than the conclusion obtained when we randomize only a. But say that $[Q(v)|R(v, b)]_v$ was known to be different from $[Q(v_1)|R(v_1, v_2)]_{\langle v_1, v_2 \rangle}$. (It could be that those individuals related by R to b have a different chance of being Q's than average).   Would not the conclusion $\mathsf{prob}\big(Q(a)\big) = [Q(v)|R(v, b)]_v$ be more reasonable than the conclusion $\mathsf{prob}\big(Q(a)\big) = [Q(v_1)|R(v_1, v_2)]_{\langle v_1, v_2 \rangle}$? Yes it would be. But this is not a difficulty with our approach: in this case KB would contain more about b than it did before.

For example, let

$$KB = \begin{array}{l} [Q(x)|R(x, y)]_{\langle x, y \rangle} < 0.25 \quad \wedge \quad [Q(x)|R(x, b)]_x > 0.75 \\ \wedge \quad R(a, b). \end{array}$$

---

[6]Of course, it is quite possible that the set of individuals that share all of the denoted individual's known properties is a very small set. For example, KB may contain the information that Tweety is Mary's pet, and that Mary only has one pet. In this case the set of individuals that share all of Tweety's known properties is simply the singleton set consisting of the individual denoted by Tweety.

Applying the direct inference principle we obtain

$$\mathsf{prob}\big(\mathsf{Q}(\mathsf{a})\big) = \left[\mathsf{Q}(\mathsf{v}_1)\middle|\begin{array}{l} \mathsf{R}(\mathsf{v}_1,\mathsf{v}_2) \wedge ([\mathsf{Q}(\mathsf{x})|\mathsf{R}(\mathsf{x},\mathsf{y})]_{\langle \mathsf{x},\mathsf{y}\rangle} < 0.25) \\ \wedge ([\mathsf{Q}(\mathsf{x})|\mathsf{R}(\mathsf{x},\mathsf{v}_2)]_{\mathsf{x}} > 0.75) \end{array}\right]_{\langle \mathsf{v}_1,\mathsf{v}_2\rangle}.$$

Lemma 34 allows us to remove the conjunct $[\mathsf{Q}(\mathsf{x})|\mathsf{R}(\mathsf{x},\mathsf{y})]_{\langle \mathsf{x},\mathsf{y}\rangle} < 0.25$ from the conditioning formula, but we cannot remove the conjunct $[\mathsf{Q}(\mathsf{x})|\mathsf{R}(\mathsf{x},\mathsf{v}_2)]_{\mathsf{x}} > 0.75$ as it contains one of the random designators v_2. However, Lemma 39 allows us to demonstrate that the resulting statistical term,

$$\big[\mathsf{Q}(\mathsf{v}_1)\big|\mathsf{R}(\mathsf{v}_1,\mathsf{v}_2) \wedge ([\mathsf{Q}(\mathsf{x})|\mathsf{R}(\mathsf{x},\mathsf{v}_2)]_{\mathsf{x}} > 0.75)\big]_{\langle \mathsf{v}_1,\mathsf{v}_2\rangle}$$

has a value greater than 0.75. Thus our more specific information about b continues to have the proper effect on the induced degree of belief, even after it is replaced by a random designator. As long as we replace b with a random designator uniformly throughout KB we do not lose any of b's known properties, and b's known properties can include statistical properties.

Besides ensuring a consistent application of the randomization process, randomizing all of the constants in KB has the important property of ensuring that the assigned degrees of belief are in fact probabilities, a result that we will prove later.

5.4.1 Representing Direct Inference in the Combined Probability logic

As we mentioned above, we wish to represent the direct inference principle as a formula (schema) of the combined probability logic. Such a representation would allow us to reason about the consequences of the principle by reasoning formally within the combined logic. The preliminary direct inference principle presented above, however, does not achieve our desideratum.

The problem with the preliminary direct inference principle lies in the non-rigidity of the statistical probability terms. For example, consider the term $[\mathsf{P}(\mathsf{x})]_{\mathsf{x}}$. The set of satisfying instantiations of x in $\mathsf{P}(\mathsf{x})$ is exactly the denotation of the predicate symbol P. The denotation of P varies across possible worlds; therefore, the statistical term $[\mathsf{P}(\mathsf{x})]_{\mathsf{x}}$ denotes the probability of a varying set of individuals. That is, it is not a rigid term. On the other hand, the propositional probability terms are rigid. For example the term $\mathsf{prob}(\mathsf{P}(\mathsf{c}))$ denotes the probability of the set of possible worlds which satisfy $\mathsf{P}(\mathsf{c})$. In the combined probability structures the probability distribution over the worlds is fixed; hence, the value of $\mathsf{prob}(\mathsf{P}(\mathsf{c}))$ does not vary across possible worlds.

Therefore, the direct inference principle that we have given equates a rigid propositional probability with a non-rigid statistical probability. Hence, the truth value of this equality will depend on the current world. It may be true in some worlds and false in others.

We could make sense of this equality if we fix a distinguished world that we always use as the current world in our interpretation of the formulas. That is, the formulas of the combined probability language could always be interpreted with respect to a triple (M, s', v) where s' is the distinguished world of the structure M. In the equality given by the direct inference principle, $\mathsf{prob}(\alpha) = [\alpha^{\mathbf{v}}|\mathsf{KB}^{\mathbf{v}}]_{\vec{v}}$, the denotation of the statistical probability term $[\alpha^{\mathbf{v}}|\mathsf{KB}^{\mathbf{v}}]_{\vec{v}}$ would then be determined uniquely; its denotation will be its denotation in the distinguished world s'.[7] The problem with this approach is that it forces a move away from reasoning solely about the agent's beliefs. Now assertions must be made and conclusions drawn about what is true in the distinguished world. If the distinguished world is considered to be the real world, then we are making assertions about what is true in the real world instead of making epistemic assertions about the agent's beliefs.[8]

To this end we present another version of the direct inference principle. Here we let the propositional probabilities be equal to the expected value of the statistical probability terms. As we will demonstrate, if the agent is certain about various statistical probabilities, then these certainties will be reflected in the expected value. The advantage of the expected

---

[7] This is essentially the manner in which Moore [91] formalizes the interpretation of formulas of autoepistemic logic. In Moore's interpretation the fixed world is considered to be the "real" world, i.e., the agent's environment. In this manner Moore is able to interpret formulas which involve world dependent components, e.g., the formula $\mathsf{bird}(\mathsf{Tweety}) \wedge \neg B \neg \mathsf{fly}(\mathsf{Tweety}) \rightarrow \mathsf{fly}(\mathsf{Tweety})$. This formula expresses the default that if Tweety is a bird (in the real world) and the agent does not believe that Tweety cannot fly then Tweety can fly (in the real world). This type of interpretation leads to the rather questionable assumption that the agent has complete knowledge of the set of non-flying birds, or even more unreasonably, that the agent's beliefs can determine what is true in the *real* world.

[8] Of course, there are difficult and interesting questions pertaining to how an agent accumulates a base of accepted beliefs, i.e., its knowledge base and how he ensures the accuracy of those beliefs, but we will not address these questions here. Instead we are concerned with the issues that arise when representing and reasoning with a prespecified collection of beliefs.

values is that they are not dependent on the current world; i.e., they are rigid terms. Hence, the formulas produced by the direct inference principle are not dependent on the current world. The use of expected values also has important advantages when it comes to the problem of overly-specific reference classes, which we will discuss later.[9]

DEFINITION 49 (DIRECT INFERENCE PRINCIPLE)

If α is a formula of $\mathcal{L}^{\text{stat}}$ and if KB is the complete set of objective formulas that the agent fully believes, then the agent's degree of belief in α should be determined by the equality

$$\text{prob}(\alpha) = \mathsf{E}\big([\alpha^{\mathsf{V}}|\text{KB}^{\mathsf{V}}]_{\vec{v}}\big).$$

In addition, the agent must fully believe that $[\text{KB}^{\mathsf{V}}]_{\vec{v}} > 0$, i.e., $\text{cert}\big([\text{KB}^{\mathsf{V}}]_{\vec{v}} > 0\big)$.

The only change that has been made is that we use the expected value of the statistical terms instead of the plain statistical terms. The expected value terms are rigid; therefore this resolves the issues discussed above. The assumption $\text{cert}\big([\text{KB}^{\mathsf{V}}]_{\vec{v}} > 0\big)$ is simply a generalization of our previous assumption, and it has the same justification.

Before we demonstrate how the new principle works we will prove three theorems which demonstrate that our specification is coherent.

We have implicitly assumed, through our use of the prob operator, that the degrees of belief generated by the direct inference principle are in fact probabilities. The next theorem demonstrates that this is the case.

THEOREM 50 The degrees of belief assigned by the direct inference principle are probabilities.

---

[9] Another possible solution to our problem is to view the direct inference principle as being a meta-level connection between two languages, the pure statistical probability language $\mathcal{L}^{\text{stat}}$, and the combined probability language $\mathcal{L}^{\text{comb}}$. The knowledge base would then be expressed in $\mathcal{L}^{\text{stat}}$ and the meta-level connection would allow us to reason about the degrees of belief sanctioned by the knowledge base. One could perform all of the reasoning in the statistical language, using the direct inference principle to connect the statistical conclusions to conclusions about the degrees of belief. This is very similar to Levesque's functional view of knowledge bases [76], where one can reason about assertions expressed in an extended language containing knowledge modalities by querying a first-order knowledge base. Under this view the direct inference principle would be acting as an ASK interface to the statistical knowledge base. This approach, however, does not seem capable of dealing with the problem of overly-specific reference classes.

We would expect that if a perfectly rational agent gives full belief to KB then he should also give full belief to the logical consequences of KB. This is certainly a property of Hintikka-style models of belief. In particular, we would expect that if KB $\models \alpha$ then $\mathsf{prob}(\alpha)$ should be equal to 1. Furthermore, we would not expect to be able to validly infer $\mathsf{prob}(\alpha) = 1$ unless KB $\models \alpha$. The following theorem demonstrates that the direct inference principle has these important properties. Hence, the assigned degrees of belief are a *generalization of a deductively closed set of beliefs*.

THEOREM 51 $\mathsf{prob}(\alpha) = 1$ is a logical consequence of the direct inference principle if and only if KB $\models \alpha$.

The direct inference principle specifies a collection of equations (formulas) of $\mathcal{L}^{\text{comb}}$, one equation for every formula α of $\mathcal{L}^{\text{stat}}$. We have mentioned that we intend to reason with these formulas in the combined probability logic. The natural question is, is this set of formulas is consistent? As long as the agent starts off with a consistent set of fully accepted beliefs, the answer is yes. This is demonstrated by the last and most important coherency theorem. But first we must specify more precisely the theory generated by the direct inference principle.

DEFINITION 52 (THE THEORY T_0)
Let D_0 be a set of formulas of $\mathcal{L}^{\text{comb}}$ consisting of the formula $\mathsf{cert}\big([\text{KB}^{\mathbf{V}}]_{\vec{v}} > 0\big)$ along with all instances of the direct inference principle. That is, for all objective formulas α, i.e., $\alpha \in \mathcal{L}^{\text{stat}}$, D_0 will contain the formula $\mathsf{prob}(\alpha) = \mathsf{E}\big([\alpha^{\mathbf{V}}|\text{KB}^{\mathbf{V}}]_{\vec{v}}\big)$. Let T_0 denote the *closure of D_0 under logical consequence*.

T_0 is the theory that describes the agent's beliefs (both full beliefs and beliefs of intermediate degree) as determined by direct inference from KB. For example, by Theorem 51, T_0 will contain $\mathsf{prob}(\alpha) = 1$ for all α entailed by KB.

THEOREM 53 (T_0 IS SATISFIABLE)
If KB $\wedge [\text{KB}^{\mathbf{V}}]_{\vec{v}} > 0$ is satisfiable, then T_0 is satisfiable.

Of course, satisfiability implies consistency.

5.4.2   Proofs of the Coherency Theorems

Proof of Theorem 50   We show that the assigned degrees of belief obey the axioms of probability. That is, the degrees of belief are bounded above by 1 and below by 0, and the degree of a disjunction of two disjoint formulas is equal to the sum of the individual degrees.

First, $0 \leq \mathsf{prob}(\alpha) \leq 1$. From the properties of the statistical probability terms we have $0 \leq [\alpha^{\mathbf{V}}|\mathsf{KB}^{\mathbf{V}}]_{\vec{v}} \leq 1$ is valid and hence satisfied at every possible world in the combined probability structures. Therefore, we have that $\mathsf{cert}\big(0 \leq [\alpha^{\mathbf{V}}|\mathsf{KB}^{\mathbf{V}}]_{\vec{v}}\big) \wedge \mathsf{cert}\big([\alpha^{\mathbf{V}}|\mathsf{KB}^{\mathbf{V}}]_{\vec{v}} \leq 1\big)$. From the properties of the expectation operator (Lemma 46) we get that $0 \leq \mathsf{E}\big([\alpha^{\mathbf{V}}|\mathsf{KB}^{\mathbf{V}}]_{\vec{v}}\big) \leq 1$. Since this expectation term is equal to $\mathsf{prob}(\alpha)$, we have our result.

Second,

$$\mathsf{prob}(\alpha \wedge \beta) = 0 \rightarrow \mathsf{prob}(\alpha \vee \beta) = \mathsf{prob}(\alpha) + \mathsf{prob}(\beta).$$

The only complication here is that the set of constants in α and β may differ. Hence, the statistical probability terms whose expectations are equivalenced to $\mathsf{prob}(\alpha)$ and $\mathsf{prob}(\beta)$ may have different random designators. That is, we may have $\mathsf{prob}(\alpha) = \mathsf{E}\big([\alpha^{\mathbf{V}}|\mathsf{KB}^{\mathbf{V}}]_{\vec{v}}\big)$ and $\mathsf{prob}(\beta) = \mathsf{E}\big([\beta^{\mathbf{V}}|\mathsf{KB}^{\mathbf{V}}]_{\vec{v}'}\big)$ where $\vec{v} \neq \vec{v}'$. However, we can divide the constants in α, β, and KB into three disjoint sets: those constants unique to α, those unique to β, and the rest. The last set includes all of the constants in KB. During randomization let the constants unique to α be replaced by the variables $\vec{x}$, those unique to β be replaced by the variables $\vec{y}$, and the rest be replaced by the variables $\vec{z}$. As demonstrated in Lemma 36, one of the properties of the statistical probability terms is that $[\alpha]_{\vec{x}} = [\alpha]_{\langle \vec{x}, y \rangle}$ if y does not appear in α. Therefore, we have that $[\alpha^{\mathbf{V}} \wedge \mathsf{KB}^{\mathbf{V}}]_{\langle \vec{x}, \vec{z} \rangle} = [\alpha^{\mathbf{V}} \wedge \mathsf{KB}^{\mathbf{V}}]_{\langle \vec{x}, \vec{z}, \vec{y} \rangle}$, since no variable in $\vec{y}$ appears in $\mathsf{KB}^{\mathbf{V}}$ or $\alpha^{\mathbf{V}}$. We also have that $[\mathsf{KB}^{\mathbf{V}}]_{\langle \vec{x}, \vec{z} \rangle} = [\mathsf{KB}^{\mathbf{V}}]_{\langle \vec{x}, \vec{z}, \vec{y} \rangle}$. Thus we have that $[\alpha^{\mathbf{V}}|\mathsf{KB}^{\mathbf{V}}]_{\langle \vec{x}, \vec{z} \rangle} = [\alpha^{\mathbf{V}}|\mathsf{KB}^{\mathbf{V}}]_{\langle \vec{x}, \vec{z}, \vec{y} \rangle}$. Similarly we have that $[\beta^{\mathbf{V}}|\mathsf{KB}^{\mathbf{V}}]_{\langle \vec{z}, \vec{y} \rangle} = [\beta^{\mathbf{V}}|\mathsf{KB}^{\mathbf{V}}]_{\langle \vec{x}, \vec{z}, \vec{y} \rangle}$. Since these equalities hold at all possible worlds, they also hold for the expectations. From the direct inference principle we have that $\mathsf{prob}(\alpha \vee \beta) = \mathsf{E}\big([(\alpha \vee \beta)^{\mathbf{V}}|\mathsf{KB}^{\mathbf{V}}]_{\langle \vec{x}, \vec{z}, \vec{y} \rangle}\big)$, $\mathsf{prob}(\alpha) = \mathsf{E}\big([\alpha^{\mathbf{V}}|\mathsf{KB}^{\mathbf{V}}]_{\langle \vec{x}, \vec{z} \rangle}\big)$, and $\mathsf{prob}(\beta) = \mathsf{E}\big([\beta^{\mathbf{V}}|\mathsf{KB}^{\mathbf{V}}]_{\langle \vec{z}, \vec{y} \rangle}\big)$. Therefore, we have demonstrated that

$$\mathsf{prob}(\alpha \vee \beta) = \mathsf{prob}(\alpha) + \mathsf{prob}(\beta)$$

iff

$$E\big([(\alpha \vee \beta)^{\mathbf{V}}|\mathrm{KB}^{\mathbf{V}}]_{\langle \vec{x}, \vec{z}, \vec{y}\rangle}\big) = E\big([\alpha^{\mathbf{V}}|\mathrm{KB}^{\mathbf{V}}]_{\langle \vec{x}, \vec{z}, \vec{y}\rangle}\big) + E\big([\beta^{\mathbf{V}}|\mathrm{KB}^{\mathbf{V}}]_{\langle \vec{x}, \vec{z}, \vec{y}\rangle}\big).$$

But under the condition that

$$0 = \mathsf{prob}(\alpha \wedge \beta) = E\big([(\alpha \wedge \beta)^{\mathbf{V}}|\mathrm{KB}^{\mathbf{V}}]_{\langle \vec{x}, \vec{z}, \vec{y}\rangle}\big),$$

we have that $\mathsf{cert}\big([(\alpha \wedge \beta)^{\mathbf{V}}|\mathrm{KB}^{\mathbf{V}}]_{\langle \vec{x}, \vec{z}, \vec{y}\rangle} = 0\big)$, by the properties of the expectation operator. Therefore, we have that

$$\mathsf{cert}\Big([(\alpha \vee \beta)^{\mathbf{V}}|\mathrm{KB}^{\mathbf{V}}]_{\langle \vec{x}, \vec{z}, \vec{y}\rangle} = [\alpha^{\mathbf{V}}|\mathrm{KB}^{\mathbf{V}}]_{\langle \vec{x}, \vec{z}, \vec{y}\rangle} + [\beta^{\mathbf{V}}|\mathrm{KB}^{\mathbf{V}}]_{\langle \vec{x}, \vec{z}, \vec{y}\rangle}\Big),$$

by the properties of the statistical terms. From the properties of the expectation operator we obtain the above equality between the expected values of the statistical terms, as desired. ∎

Proof of Theorem 51 Say that $\mathrm{KB} \models \alpha$. This means $\mathrm{KB} \rightarrow \alpha$ is valid; it is satisfied by every world in every combined probability structure. Hence, if $\langle c_1, \ldots, c_n \rangle$ are the constants that appear in $\alpha \wedge \mathrm{KB}$, then no matter what their denotation is in a particular world, $\mathrm{KB} \rightarrow \alpha$ will be satisfied by that world. Therefore, $\forall \vec{v}.(\mathrm{KB} \rightarrow \alpha)^{\mathbf{V}}$ will also be satisfied by every world: it also will be valid. Thus from the properties of the statistical terms we obtain the validity of $[(\mathrm{KB} \rightarrow \alpha)^{\mathbf{V}}]_{\vec{v}} = 1$, and $[\alpha^{\mathbf{V}}|\mathrm{KB}^{\mathbf{V}}]_{\vec{v}} = 1$. Since this last is valid it is satisfied by every world, i.e., $\mathsf{cert}\big([\alpha^{\mathbf{V}}|\mathrm{KB}^{\mathbf{V}}]_{\vec{v}} = 1\big)$, and hence we have that $E\big([\alpha^{\mathbf{V}}|\mathrm{KB}^{\mathbf{V}}]_{\vec{v}}\big) = 1$. Thus we obtain $\mathsf{prob}(\alpha) = 1$ as a logical consequence of the direct inference principle.

In the opposite direction if $\mathrm{KB} \not\models \alpha$, then $\exists \vec{v}.\neg(\mathrm{KB} \rightarrow \alpha)^{\mathbf{V}}$ is satisfiable. Hence, $[\alpha^{\mathbf{V}}|\mathrm{KB}^{\mathbf{V}}]_{\vec{v}} < 1$ is satisfiable and so is $E\big([\alpha^{\mathbf{V}}|\mathrm{KB}^{\mathbf{V}}]_{\vec{v}}\big) < 1$. Therefore, $\mathsf{prob}(\alpha) = 1$ is not a logical consequence. ∎

Proof of Theorem 53 Let (M, s, v) be a triple that satisfies $\mathrm{KB} \wedge [\mathrm{KB}^{\mathbf{V}}]_{\vec{v}} > 0$. For simplicity we will ignore the possibility of this formula having any free variables, and therefore we can ignore the variable assignment function v. Let $M = \langle \mathcal{O}, S, \vartheta_c, \mu_S, \mu_{\mathcal{O}} \rangle$. It is not difficult to see that since $\mathrm{KB} \wedge [\mathrm{KB}^{\mathbf{V}}]_{\vec{v}} > 0$ is objective we can view (M, s) as being a statistical probability structure $M^{\mathrm{stat}} = \langle \mathcal{O}, \vartheta, \mu_{\mathcal{O}} \rangle$, where ϑ is simply the interpretation function at the satisfying world s, i.e., $\vartheta = \vartheta_c(s)$.

We will demonstrate how a combined probability structure M^{comb} can be constructed from M^{stat} such that M^{comb} satisfies T_0. We only need to demonstrate that M^{comb} satisfies all instances of the direct inference principle, along with $\mathsf{cert}([\mathsf{KB}^{\mathbf{v}}]_{\vec{v}} > 0)$; the logical consequences are guaranteed since M^{comb} is a model.

To simplify let us assume that $\langle c_1, \ldots, c_n \rangle$ are all the set of constants in $\mathcal{L}^{\mathrm{stat}}$, and furthermore that these are exactly the same constants that appear in KB. The extension to the more general case, where KB might contain only a subset of these constants or where KB might contain free variables, is straightforward. The extension to the case where $\mathcal{L}^{\mathrm{stat}}$ contains an infinite number of constants is more difficult, but can be dealt with by using the limit of the product probabilities over the domain, $\lim_{n \to \infty} \mu_{\mathcal{O}}^n$.[10]

Consider the set of n-ary vectors of individuals $\mathcal{O}^n$; this set is at most denumerable in cardinality. Therefore, we can index this set. Let I be an index of the elements of $\mathcal{O}^n$; i.e., $\vec{o}_i$ is the i-th vector in $\mathcal{O}^n$. We have that $M^{\mathrm{stat}} = \langle \mathcal{O}, \vartheta, \mu_{\mathcal{O}} \rangle$. From this we construct $M^{\mathrm{comb}} = \langle \mathcal{O}', S, \vartheta', \mu_S, \mu_{\mathcal{O}}' \rangle$. We let $\mathcal{O}' = \mathcal{O}$, and $\mu_{\mathcal{O}}' = \mu_{\mathcal{O}}$. For S we have a set of worlds $\{s_i\}$ indexed by I. That is, the cardinality of the set of worlds is equal to the cardinality of $\mathcal{O}^n$, and we index them both by the same set I. In the combined probability structure M^{comb}, ϑ' is a function from worlds to interpretations, while in the statistical structure M^{stat}, ϑ is simply an interpretation. We let ϑ' map every world s to a slightly altered version of this interpretation; i.e., for every world s, $\vartheta'(s)$ is a slightly altered version of ϑ. In particular, the denotation of every symbol except the constant symbols will be the same under $\vartheta'(s)$ as under ϑ, and for each world s_i we let $\vartheta'(s_i)$ map $\langle c_1, \ldots, c_n \rangle$ pointwise to the i-th vector in $\mathcal{O}^n$, $\vec{o}_i$.

For example, if $\mathcal{L}^{\mathrm{stat}}$ contains only the constants c_1 and c_2 and $\mathcal{O} = \{a, b\}$, then we will have that

1. $\mathcal{O}^2 = \{\langle a, a \rangle, \langle a, b \rangle, \langle b, a \rangle, \langle b, b \rangle\}$,

2. $S = \{s_1, s_2, s_3, s_4\}$,

3. $\langle c_1, c_2 \rangle^{\vartheta(s_1)} = \langle a, a \rangle$ $\langle c_1, c_2 \rangle^{\vartheta(s_2)} = \langle a, b \rangle$
   $\langle c_1, c_2 \rangle^{\vartheta(s_3)} = \langle b, a \rangle$ $\langle c_1, c_2 \rangle^{\vartheta(s_4)} = \langle b, b \rangle$

---

[10]This limit probability function is a well studied construct, e.g., Chung [14].

To define μ_S we first consider the set of vectors of $\mathcal{O}^n$ that satisfy $\mathrm{KB}^\mathbf{V}$ in M^{stat}; i.e., the set of vectors whose probability is denoted by $[\mathrm{KB}^\mathbf{V}]_{\vec{v}}$. Let this set of satisfying instantiations be denoted by SI. Note that this set is determined by M^{stat}, and that $SI \subseteq \mathcal{O}^n$. Next we let $\mu_S(s_i) = 0$ when $\vec{o}_i \notin SI$, and we let $\mu_S(s_i) = \mu_\mathcal{O}^n(\vec{o}_i)$ when $\vec{o}_i \in SI$. The last step is that we normalize μ_S by dividing by $\mu_\mathcal{O}^n(SI)$.

For example, if $\mathrm{KB} = P(c_1, c_2)$, $P^\vartheta = \{\langle a, b \rangle, \langle b, a \rangle\}$, and $\mu_\mathcal{O}(a) = \mu_\mathcal{O}(b) = 1/2$, then we will have that

1. $\mathrm{KB}^\mathbf{V} = P(v_1, v_2)$,

2. $SI = \{\langle a, b \rangle, \langle b, a \rangle\}$,

3. $\mu_\mathcal{O}^2(SI) = 1/2$,

4. $\mu_S(s_1) = 0$, $\mu_S(s_2) = 1/2$, $\mu_S(s_3) = 1/2$, and $\mu_S(s_4) = 0$.

It is now possible to check that $M^{\mathrm{comb}} \models T_0$. Briefly, we have that $[\alpha^\mathbf{V} | \mathrm{KB}^\mathbf{V}]_{\vec{v}}$ has the same denotation in every world of M^{comb}, and that this denotation is the same as the term's denotation in M^{stat}. Therefore, we have that $\mathsf{E}([\alpha^\mathbf{V} | \mathrm{KB}^\mathbf{V}]_{\vec{v}})$ will have this denotation in M^{comb}. All of this follows from the fact that $[\alpha^\mathbf{V} | \mathrm{KB}^\mathbf{V}]_{\vec{v}}$ contains no constants, and other than on the constants, the interpretation of all symbols is identical in every world. This statistical term denotes the relative measure of the set of n-ary vectors that satisfy $(\alpha \wedge \mathrm{KB})^\mathbf{V}$ from among the set of vectors SI. Consider the value of $\mathsf{prob}(\alpha)$ in M^{comb}. It is not difficult to see that any world s_i with non-zero probability will satisfy α if and only if $\vec{o}_i$ is in the set of satisfying instantiations of $(\alpha \wedge \mathrm{KB})^\mathbf{V}$. Furthermore, by our construction, the probability of the set of worlds that satisfy α will be equal to the relative measure of the set of n-ary vectors that satisfies $(\alpha \wedge \mathrm{KB})^\mathbf{V}$ from among the set of vectors SI. That is, we have that $M^{\mathrm{comb}} \models \mathsf{prob}(\alpha) = \mathsf{E}([\alpha^\mathbf{V} | \mathrm{KB}^\mathbf{V}]_{\vec{v}})$ as required. The fact that $M^{\mathrm{comb}} \models \mathsf{cert}([\mathrm{KB}^\mathbf{V}]_{\vec{v}} > 0)$ is easily seen to be true, as like the other statistical terms this term contains no constants. ∎

5.5 Examples

To demonstrate how the direct inference principle works we present a few examples.

EXAMPLE 20 (TWEETY FLIES.)
Let
$$KB = \text{bird}(\text{Tweety}) \wedge [\text{fly}(x)|\text{bird}(x)]_x > c,$$

where c is a *rigid* numeric constant that is strictly greater than 0.5. That is, the agent has accepted the assertions that Tweety is a bird and that the majority of birds fly. By using a non-specific constant like c instead of a more specific constant like 0.5 we can demonstrate that the inferences sanctioned by the knowledge base are not dependent on the exact denotation of c. That is, c could be any number greater than 0.5.

From this knowledge base we have by the direct inference principle that $\text{prob}(\text{fly}(\text{Tweety})) > c$, and furthermore, we can deduce this result by reasoning in the combined probability logic. In the proofs below we use the following abbreviations: (1) "expt. prop." indicating that we have used properties of the expectation operator as given in Lemma 46, (2) "dir. inf." indicating our initial application of the direct inference principle (we will usually remove all irrelevant conjuncts from the conditioning formula, as sanctioned by Lemma 34), and (3) "stat. prop." indicating the use of properties of the statistical probability terms as developed in Chapter 3. It should be noted that all valid properties of the statistical terms are certain, i.e., they have propositional probability one. This was demonstrated in Lemma 43.

$\text{prob}(\text{fly}(\text{Tweety}))$
$\quad = E\big([\text{fly}(v)|\text{bird}(v) \wedge [\text{fly}(x)|\text{bird}(x)]_x > c]_v\big)$ dir. inf.
$\text{cert}\big([\text{fly}(v)|\text{bird}(v) \wedge [\text{fly}(x)|\text{bird}(x)]_x > c]_v$
$\quad = [\text{fly}(v)|\text{bird}(v)]_v\big)$ stat. prop.
$E\big([\text{fly}(v)|\text{bird}(v) \wedge [\text{fly}(x)|\text{bird}(x)]_x > c]_v\big)$
$\quad = E\big([\text{fly}(v)|\text{bird}(v)]_v\big)$ expt. prop.
$\text{prob}(\text{fly}(\text{Tweety})) = E\big([\text{fly}(v)|\text{bird}(v)]_v\big)$
$\text{cert}\big([\text{fly}(v)|\text{bird}(v)]_v > c\big)$ Thm. 51
$E\big([\text{fly}(v)|\text{bird}(v)]_v\big) > E(c)$ expt. prop.

$$\mathsf{E}(c) = c \qquad\qquad\qquad\qquad c \text{ rigid}$$

$$\mathsf{prob}\big(\mathsf{fly}(\mathtt{Tweety})\big) > c$$

The steps involved in the proof are quite straightforward. First, one applies the direct inference principle to the formula of interest, in this case fly(Tweety). The properties of the statistical probability terms allow one to reject those parts of KB that are not related to the formula. One then proceeds to reason about the value of the statistical term that is the result of applying direct inference. As Theorem 51 demonstrates, any logical consequence of KB will be certain, i.e., have propositional probability one. The relationship between certainty and expected values means that the logical consequences of KB sanction conclusions about the expected values. Of course any conclusions about the expected values are conclusions about the assigned degrees of belief. In the above example we were able to deduce from KB that $[\mathtt{fly}(\mathtt{v})|\mathtt{bird}(\mathtt{v})]_{\mathtt{v}} > c$ (the variable name change is allowed by axiom **P5** of the statistical logic). This conclusion has probability one, i.e., it is certain, and hence this relationship also holds of the expected value and of the assigned degree of belief.

EXAMPLE 21 (OPUS DOES NOT FLY.)
Let

$$
\begin{aligned}
\mathsf{KB} = \;& \mathtt{bird}(\mathtt{Opus}) \quad\wedge\quad \mathtt{penguin}(\mathtt{Opus})\\
& \wedge \;\; [\mathtt{fly}(\mathtt{x})|\mathtt{bird}(\mathtt{x})]_{\mathtt{x}} > c \quad\wedge\quad [\mathtt{fly}(\mathtt{x})|\mathtt{penguin}(\mathtt{x})]_{\mathtt{x}} < 1 - c\\
& \wedge \;\; \forall \mathtt{x}.\mathtt{penguin}(\mathtt{x}) \to \mathtt{bird}(\mathtt{x}).
\end{aligned}
$$

With this knowledge we have that $\mathsf{prob}(\mathtt{fly}(\mathtt{Opus})) < 1 - c$ can be inferred from the direct inference principle.[11]

$$
\begin{aligned}
&\mathsf{prob}\big(\mathtt{fly}(\mathtt{Opus})\big)\\
&\qquad = \mathsf{E}\big([\mathtt{fly}(\mathtt{v})|\mathtt{bird}(\mathtt{v}) \wedge \mathtt{penguin}(\mathtt{v})]_{\mathtt{v}}\big) && \text{dir. inf.}\\
&\mathsf{cert}\big([\mathtt{fly}(\mathtt{v})|\mathtt{bird}(\mathtt{v}) \wedge \mathtt{penguin}(\mathtt{v})]_{\mathtt{v}}\\
&\qquad = [\mathtt{fly}(\mathtt{v})|\mathtt{penguin}(\mathtt{v})]_{\mathtt{v}}\big) && \text{stat. prop.}\\
&\mathsf{cert}\big([\mathtt{fly}(\mathtt{v})|\mathtt{penguin}(\mathtt{v})]_{\mathtt{v}} < 1 - c\big) && \text{stat. prop.}\\
&\mathsf{E}\big([\mathtt{fly}(\mathtt{v})|\mathtt{bird}(\mathtt{v}) \wedge \mathtt{penguin}(\mathtt{v})]_{\mathtt{v}}\big)
\end{aligned}
$$

---

[11] If KB were to contain the more reasonable assertion $\forall \mathtt{x}.\mathtt{penguin}(\mathtt{x}) \to \neg\mathtt{fly}(\mathtt{x})$, then $\mathsf{cert}(\neg\mathtt{fly}(\mathtt{Opus}))$ would be an immediate consequence of Theorem 51.

$$= \mathsf{E}\big([\mathtt{fly(v)}|\mathtt{penguin(v)}]_\mathbf{v}\big) < 1 - c \qquad \text{expt. prop.}$$
$$\mathtt{prob}\big(\mathtt{fly(Opus)}\big) < 1 - c$$

Because penguins are known to be a subset of the set of birds (i.e., $\forall \mathtt{x}.\mathtt{penguin(x)} \rightarrow \mathtt{bird(x)}$ is deducible from the knowledge base) we have by Lemma 37 that

$$[\mathtt{fly(v)}|\mathtt{bird(v)} \wedge \mathtt{penguin(v)}]_\mathbf{v} = [\mathtt{fly(v)}|\mathtt{penguin(v)}]_\mathbf{v}$$

is also deducible. Hence, this conclusion is certain and the equality also holds between the expected values.

In default logic this situation would correspond to knowing two defaults: one applicable to the class of birds and the other contradictory one applicable to the class of penguins, a subclass of the birds. Intuitively the default conclusion from the subclass should be preferred, and extra meta-logical machinery is often required to encode the subset preference criterion. An interesting feature of our system of direct inference is that this subset preference is an automatic consequence of the properties of the statistical terms.

EXAMPLE 22 (CLYDE LIKES TONY BUT NOT FRED.)
Let

$$
\begin{aligned}
\mathtt{KB} = \ & \mathtt{elephant(Clyde)} \quad \wedge \quad \mathtt{zookeeper(Tony)} \\
& \wedge \quad \mathtt{zookeeper(Fred)} \\
& \wedge \quad [\mathtt{likes(x,y)}|\mathtt{elephant(x)} \wedge \mathtt{zookeeper(y)}]_{\langle \mathtt{x,y} \rangle} > c \\
& \wedge \quad [\mathtt{likes(x,Fred)}|\mathtt{elephant(x)}]_\mathbf{x} < 1 - c.
\end{aligned}
$$

From this knowledge base we can construct the following derivation.

$\mathtt{prob}\big(\mathtt{likes(Clyde,Tony)}\big)$
$\qquad = \mathsf{E}\big([\mathtt{likes(u,v)}|\mathtt{elephant(u)} \wedge \mathtt{zookeeper(v)}]_{\langle \mathtt{u,v} \rangle}\big) \quad$ dir. inf.
$\mathtt{cert}\big([\mathtt{likes(u,v)}|\mathtt{elephant(u)} \wedge \mathtt{zookeeper(v)}]_{\langle \mathtt{u,v} \rangle} > c\big)$
$\mathsf{E}\big([\mathtt{likes(u,v)}|\mathtt{elephant(u)} \wedge \mathtt{zookeeper(v)}]_{\langle \mathtt{u,v} \rangle}\big) > c \qquad$ expt. prop.
$\mathtt{prob}\big(\mathtt{likes(Clyde,Tony)}\big) > c$

Therefore, the direct inference principle sanctions a high degree of belief in the proposition that $\mathtt{Clyde}$ likes $\mathtt{Tony}$.

The interesting case, however, is that $\mathtt{prob}\big(\mathtt{likes}(\mathtt{Clyde},\mathtt{Fred})\big) <$ $1 - c$. Let Φ abbreviate the formula

$$\mathtt{elephant(u)} \wedge \mathtt{zookeeper(v)} \wedge [\mathtt{likes(x,v)}|\mathtt{elephant(x)}]_\mathtt{x} < 1 - c$$

We then have:

$$\mathtt{prob}\big(\mathtt{likes(Clyde,Fred)}\big) = \mathsf{E}\big([\mathtt{likes(u,v)}|\Phi]_{\langle u,v\rangle}\big) \qquad \text{dir. inf.}$$
$$\mathtt{cert}\big([\mathtt{likes(u,v)}|\Phi]_{\langle u,v\rangle} < 1 - c\big) \qquad\qquad\qquad \text{stat. prop.}$$
$$\mathtt{prob}\big(\mathtt{likes(Clyde,Fred)}\big) < 1 - c$$

This proof hinges on the fact that

$$\big[\mathtt{likes(u,v)}\big|\Phi\big]_{\langle u,v\rangle} < 1 - c.$$

Again this follows from the properties of the statistical terms, in particular from Lemma 39. What happens here is that the statistical language is powerful enough to express not only an individual's first-order properties but also his statistical properties. In this case Fred is differentiated from Tony by the fact that he is generally unpopular with the elephants. This is a special statistical property that Fred possesses. When we condition on all that is known about Fred we also condition on this statistical property, and it influences the inferred degree of belief. That is a randomly selected elephant and a randomly selected zoo-keeper are probably in the likes relation, but a randomly selected elephant and a randomly selected *unpopular* zoo-keeper are probably not.

In default logic this would correspond to knowing a special default particular to the individual Fred and a more general default applicable to the class of zoo-keepers. Intuition mandates a preference for the more specific default. This preference is another feature of the system of direct inference; it follows directly from the properties of the statistical terms instead of requiring extra machinery.

It should be noted that there is a difference between what we have termed the subset preference and the specificity preference. The subset preference is a preference for information from a narrower class, while the specificity preference is a preference for information specific to the individuals in question. The specificity preference is not usually affected by other information, but the subset preference often is. For example, we might know that `Fred` was gentle and that elephants have a special liking for gentle zoo-keepers. This information could generate a subset preference. For example, if we know only that `Fred` is a zoo-keeper, then the information about `Fred`'s gentleness would be preferred. However, this information has no effect when we have specific information about `Fred`. If we know specifically that `Fred` is unpopular with the elephants, then other information about him does not matter. None of his other properties, like gentleness, will have an effect on his unpopularity; otherwise, his unpopularity would not be asserted in the knowledge base. One way of viewing this is that specific information about `Fred` is information from the narrowest possible class: the class consisting only of `Fred`.

5.6   Overly Specific Reference Classes

By conditioning on the entire knowledge base we are using the narrowest possible reference class. That is, we are taking into account all that is known about the individuals mentioned in α. This leads to Reichenbach's original problem of "adequate statistics." That is, the reference class generated by conditioning on all that is known may be so narrow that we have no useful statistical information about it.

For example let

$$KB = \; \texttt{bird(Tweety)} \; \land \; \texttt{yellow(Tweety)}$$
$$\land \; [\texttt{fly(x)}|\texttt{bird(x)}]_\texttt{x} > c.$$

That is, not only do we know that `Tweety` is a bird, but we also know that she is a yellow bird. Using the direct inference principle we obtain

$$\texttt{prob}\big(\texttt{fly(Tweety)}\big) = \mathsf{E}\big([\texttt{fly(v)}|\texttt{bird(v)} \land \texttt{yellow(v)}]_\texttt{v}\big).$$

Although we can derive some useful information about the expected value over the wider reference class $[\texttt{fly(v)}|\texttt{bird(v)}]_\texttt{v}$, we have no information about the narrower class of yellow birds. In particular, the proportion of fliers among the class of yellow birds is not constrained by the proportion of fliers among the class of birds.[12]

---

[12] The only constraints that are imposed on narrower classes by wider classes occur when the statistics in the wider class are extreme, i.e., 1 or 0. For example, $\mathsf{E}\big([\texttt{fly(x)}|\texttt{bird(x)}]_\texttt{x}\big) = 1 \rightarrow \mathsf{E}\big([\texttt{fly(x)}|\texttt{bird(x)} \land \texttt{yellow(x)}]_\texttt{x}\big) = 1$, and $\mathsf{E}\big([\texttt{fly(x)}|\texttt{bird(x)}]_\texttt{x}\big) = 0 \rightarrow \mathsf{E}\big([\texttt{fly(x)}|\texttt{bird(x)} \land \texttt{yellow(x)}]_\texttt{x}\big) = 0$.

Our solution to this problem is to assume non-monotonically that the proportion of fliers among the class of yellow birds is no different from the proportion of fliers among the class of birds. This inference would be legitimate whenever we have no knowledge to the contrary. That is, if KB does not entail that $[\mathtt{fly(v)|yellow(v)} \wedge \mathtt{bird(v)}]_\mathtt{v} \neq [\mathtt{fly(v)|bird(v)}]_\mathtt{v}$ and thus the agent does not have full belief in this inequality, then the agent can non-monotonically conclude that they are equal. There is an important difference, however, between this non-monotonic assumption and the assumption that we actually make.

Instead of non-monotonically assuming that

$$\mathsf{cert}\big([\mathtt{fly(v)|yellow(v)} \wedge \mathtt{bird(v)}]_\mathtt{v} = [\mathtt{fly(v)|bird(v)}]_\mathtt{v}\big),$$

we assume that

$$\mathsf{E}\big([\mathtt{fly(v)|yellow(v)} \wedge \mathtt{bird(v)}]_\mathtt{v}\big) = \mathsf{E}\big([\mathtt{fly(v)|bird(v)}]_\mathtt{v}\big).$$

Concluding the equality between the expected values is weaker than concluding that the statistical terms are certainly equal: the equality of the expected values is a consequence of the first equality. The reason for making the weaker assumption is illustrated by the problem of unit reference classes.

EXAMPLE 23 (UNIT REFERENCE CLASSES)
    Let

$$
\begin{aligned}
\mathtt{KB} = \ & \mathtt{bird(Tweety)} \quad \wedge \quad \mathtt{uniq(Tweety)} \\
& \wedge \quad 1 > [\mathtt{fly(x)|bird(x)}]_\mathtt{x} > c \\
& \wedge \quad \forall \mathtt{xy.uniq(x)} \wedge \mathtt{uniq(y)} \rightarrow \mathtt{x = y}.
\end{aligned}
$$

This knowledge base contains the assertions that Tweety is a bird, that most but not all birds fly, and that Tweety has the property uniq. Furthermore, it asserts that only one individual is a member of the denotation of uniq.

Inferring a degree of belief in fly(Tweety) from this knowledge base through direct inference produces the statistical term

$$[\mathtt{fly(v)|bird(v)} \wedge \mathtt{uniq(v)}]_\mathtt{v}.$$

An individual is a member of the set denoted by the conditioning formula if and only if that individual is a bird and that individual is in the denotation of the predicate uniq. Since uniq denotes a singleton set, the set denoted by the conditioning formula must also be a singleton set: the set consisting of the individual denoted by the constant Tweety. That is, the narrowest reference class that Tweety is known to belong to is a unit reference class.

Among the singleton set {Tweety} the proportion of fliers is either one or zero: either Tweety flies or does not fly. Hence, the statistical term generated by direct inference is equal to 1 or 0, and it is a logical consequence of KB that

$$[\texttt{fly(v)}|\texttt{bird(v)} \wedge \texttt{uniq(v)}]_\mathbf{v} \neq [\texttt{fly(v)}|\texttt{bird(v)}]_\mathbf{v}.$$

This inequality, being a logical consequence of KB, is certain, and therefore directly contradicts the strong non-monotonic assumption

$$\mathsf{cert}\big([\texttt{fly(v)}|\texttt{bird(v)} \wedge \texttt{uniq(v)}]_\mathbf{v} = [\texttt{fly(v)}|\texttt{bird(v)}]_\mathbf{v}\big).$$

It does not, however, contradict the weaker non-monotonic assumption

$$\mathsf{E}\big([\texttt{fly(v)}|\texttt{bird(v)} \wedge \texttt{uniq(v)}]_\mathbf{v}\big) = \mathsf{E}\big([\texttt{fly(v)}|\texttt{bird(v)}]_\mathbf{v}\big).$$

The term $[\texttt{fly(v)}|\texttt{bird(v)} \wedge \texttt{uniq(v)}]_\mathbf{v}$ may be 1 or 0 in every possible world, but its weighted average over all the worlds is not so constrained. In this case there is no contradiction in concluding that it is equal to $\mathsf{E}\big([\texttt{fly(v)}|\texttt{bird(v)}]_\mathbf{v}\big)$, which from the information in KB we know to be in the open interval $(c, 1)$.

The problem of unit reference classes is another important reason for using expected values in the direct inference principle.

5.7 Non-Monotonic Reasoning About Statistics

We now proceed to describe more formally the non-monotonic mechanisms which drive the choice of reference class when we are faced with an overly specific reference class.

The basic idea is that we will allow the non-monotonic inheritance of statistical information from superclasses; so our non-monotonic assumptions will have the following form:

$$\mathsf{cert}(\forall \vec{v}.\mathsf{KB}^\mathbf{V} \to \beta) \to \mathsf{E}\big([\alpha|\mathsf{KB}^\mathbf{V}]_{\vec{v}}\big) = \mathsf{E}\big([\alpha|\beta]_{\vec{v}}\big).$$

That is, if we are certain (i.e., if it is a logical consequence of KB) that $\lambda \vec{v}.\text{KB}^{\mathbf{V}}$ is a subset of $\lambda \vec{v}.\beta$, then we can conclude non-monotonically that the expected proportion of $\text{KB}^{\mathbf{V}}$'s that are α's is equal to the expected proportion of β's that are α's. Non-monotonic inferences of this form allow movement from the most specific reference class $\text{KB}^{\mathbf{V}}$, generated by conditioning on all that is known, to less specific reference classes, classes for which the agent might possess some useful information.

We do not, however, have to specify the non-monotonic assumptions in exactly this form. We can simplify our formulas by applying Lemma 34 to eliminate from $\text{KB}^{\mathbf{V}}$ those conjuncts that are not related to α. If we have that $\text{cert}\big([\alpha|\text{KB}^{\mathbf{V}}]_{\vec{v}} = [\alpha|\lambda]_{\vec{v}}\big)$, then the assumption $\mathsf{E}\big([\alpha|\lambda]_{\vec{v}}\big) = \mathsf{E}\big([\alpha|\beta]_{\vec{v}}\big)$ is equivalent to an assumption of the form specified.

One problem is that this schema specifies an infinite collection of non-monotonic assumptions or defaults. Traditional methods of default logic (Reiter [114]) do not have the flexibility we require to deal with such a large collection of defaults. In particular, we do not want to define an extension to be the result of drawing *all possible* default conclusions, as does Reiter. We want, instead, a system in which we can make some finite collection of non-monotonic assumptions, and furthermore we want to keep track of what assumptions are made.

Another problem is that the ability to make assumptions can destroy the natural subset preference of the statistical approach. For example, let

```
KB =  bird(Opus)  ∧  penguin(Opus)  ∧  black-white(Opus)
   ∧  [fly(x)|bird(x)]x > c ∧  ∀x.penguin(x) → bird(x)
   ∧  [fly(x)|penguin(x)]x < 1 − c.
```

That is, Opus is a black and white penguin, penguins are birds, most birds fly and most penguins don't fly.[13] From this we obtain by direct inference

$$\text{prob}\big(\texttt{fly(Opus)}\big) = \mathsf{E}\big([\texttt{fly(v)}|\texttt{bird(v)}\wedge\texttt{penguin(v)}\wedge\texttt{black-white(v)}]_{\mathbf{v}}\big).$$

We can deduce that this expectation is equal to $\mathsf{E}\big([\texttt{fly(v)}|\texttt{penguin(v)}\wedge$ $\texttt{black-white(v)}]_{\mathbf{v}}\big)$, but otherwise there is nothing in KB which can be

---

[13] If KB contains the assertion that penguins do not fly (i.e., categorically) or if it contains the assertion that penguins are black and white (again categorically), then there would be no need for any non-monotonic assumptions.

used to infer any useful information about the value of this expectation. Hence, we have to make some assumptions. We could assume non-monotonically that

1. $\mathsf{E}\big([\mathtt{fly(v)}|\mathtt{penguin(v)} \wedge \mathtt{black\text{-}white(v)}]_\mathbf{v}\big)$
   $= \mathsf{E}\big([\mathtt{fly(v)}|\mathtt{penguin(v)}]_\mathbf{v}\big)$, or

2. $\mathsf{E}\big([\mathtt{fly(v)}|\mathtt{penguin(v)} \wedge \mathtt{black\text{-}white(v)}]_\mathbf{v}\big)$
   $= \mathsf{E}\big([\mathtt{fly(v)}|\mathtt{bird(v)}]_\mathbf{v}\big).$[14]

In both cases we are inheriting expected statistical values from superclasses, and both assumptions allow us to infer some useful information about $\mathsf{prob}\big(\mathtt{fly(Opus)}\big)$. However, clearly there should be a preference for the first default, and this preference is reflected by the fact that $\mathtt{penguin(v)}$ is a subset of $\mathtt{bird(v)}$. That is, we prefer to inherit statistics from narrower reference classes. Every time we inherit statistics from a superclass we are throwing out some information. For example, in assuming that $\mathsf{E}\big([\alpha|\beta \wedge \delta]_{\vec{x}}\big) = \mathsf{E}\big([\alpha|\beta]_{\vec{x}}\big)$, we are assuming that the information given by δ is irrelevant. Clearly, we should prefer to keep as much information as possible, and this requires using the narrowest possible reference class.

The specificity preference, however, is not affected by the non-monotonic assumptions. We only make assumptions after we have applied the direct inference principle. At this stage there are no constants left in the resulting statistical terms, and as a result there are no more-specific or less-specific defaults to be accounted for. The robustness of the specificity preference will be demonstrated in our examples.

5.7.1   The Non-Monotonic Reasoning Framework

T_0 (Definition 52) is the base theory which results from the direct inference principle. It is to T_0 that we add the non-monotonic assumptions. These assumptions all have the same form and the set of legitimate assumptions is dependent on T_0.

DEFINITION 54 (NON-MONOTONIC ASSUMPTIONS)
If $\mathsf{cert}(\forall \vec{v}.\mathtt{KB}^\mathbf{V} \to \beta) \in T_0$, then

$$\mathsf{E}\big([\alpha|\mathtt{KB}^\mathbf{V}]_{\vec{v}}\big) = \mathsf{E}\big([\alpha|\beta]_{\vec{v}}\big)$$

---

[14]Note that, as we have discussed, the non-monotonic assumptions have been simplified by eliminating the formulas of KB that are not related to the conclusion $\mathtt{fly(Opus)}$.

is a legitimate non-monotonic assumption.

By Theorem 51, $\mathsf{cert}(\forall \vec{v}.\mathrm{KB}^\mathbf{V} \to \beta) \in T_0$ if and only if $\forall \vec{v}.\mathrm{KB}^\mathbf{V} \to \beta$ is a logical consequence of KB. This means that we can inherit expectations only from *known* supersets. This is reasonable as the agent should be willing to accept the conclusion that the expected proportion of α's among $\mathrm{KB}^\mathbf{V}$ is equal to the expected proportion among β only if he has already accepted β to be a superset of $\mathrm{KB}^\mathbf{V}$.

Reiter's default logic makes non-monotonic assumptions about particular individuals. For example, to conclude that Tweety the bird flies we must make an assumption particular to Tweety. To further conclude that Oscar the bird flies we must make an additional assumption, particular to Oscar. Since we may have an infinite number of individuals, default logic must be able to extend a base theory with a potentially infinite number of additional assumptions, and as a result defaults (non-monotonic assumptions) in default logic are often specified as schema where each instantiation of the schema is a legitimate assumption. In our case, however, each non-monotonic assumption can sanction conclusions about a potentially infinite number of individuals. For example, from the single assumption $\mathsf{E}\big([\mathtt{fly(v)}|\mathtt{magpie(v)}]_\mathbf{v}\big) = \mathsf{E}\big([\mathtt{fly(v)}|\mathtt{bird(v)}]_\mathbf{v}\big)$, we can draw conclusions about the agent's degree of belief in $\mathrm{prob}\big(\mathtt{fly(C)}\big)$ for every magpie C. This means that we can confine ourselves to dealing with a finite number of assumptions without losing much generality.

There are only a countable number of formulas of the combined probability language; hence, there are only a countable number of possible default assumptions. This means that the collection of all *finite* sets of default assumptions is also countable. Hence, we can fix an enumeration of these finite sets of defaults. We let D_i denote the i-th set of defaults under this enumeration, with $i \geq 1$. Each such finite set of defaults defines an extension to T_0.

DEFINITION 55 (NON-MONOTONIC THEORIES)
Let T_i be the closure under logical consequence of $T_0 \cup D_i$, where D_i is the i-th finite set of default assumptions. That is, $T_i = \{\alpha : T_0 \cup D_i \models \alpha\}$.

The theories T_i are much like Reiter's extensions except that we do not check for consistency before adding a default assumption. As a result some theories will be inconsistent. That is, some of the theories will contain every formula of the combined language. In addition to inconsistent theories some theories will be preferred over others due to our preference for inheriting statistical information from narrower reference classes. Both inconsistent and unpreferred theories are dealt with through a criterion that selects *viable* theories. This criterion is developed through the following definitions.

DEFINITION 56 (CONTRADICTED THEORIES)
A theory T_i *contradicts* a theory T_j if there exists a formula α such that $\alpha \in T_i$ and $\neg\alpha \in T_j$.

DEFINITION 57 (PREFERRED NON-MONOTONIC ASSUMPTIONS)
The non-monotonic assumption

$$\mathsf{E}\big([\alpha|\mathsf{KB}^{\mathsf{V}}]_{\vec{v}}\big) = \mathsf{E}\big([\alpha|\beta_1]_{\vec{v}}\big)$$

is *preferred* to the non-monotonic assumption

$$\mathsf{E}\big([\alpha|\mathsf{KB}^{\mathsf{V}}]_{\vec{v}}\big) = \mathsf{E}\big([\alpha|\beta_2]_{\vec{v}}\big).$$

if $\mathrm{cert}(\forall\vec{v}.\beta_1 \to \beta_2) \in T_0$. That is, we prefer to inherit expectations from narrower classes.

Note that the preference relation is reflexive. That is, a default assumption is always preferred to itself.

DEFINITION 58 (PREFERRED THEORIES)
The theory T_i is *preferred* to the theory T_j if for every default assumption $d \in D_i$, there exists a default assumption $d' \in D_j$ such that d is preferred to d'.

Note that in the above definition a preferred theory could contain more default assumptions: it is not strictly the number of assumptions made that counts, the "quality" of the assumptions is also important. If the "quality" is the same, then the number of default assumptions will make a difference. For example, if $D_1 \subset D_2$ we will always have that T_1 is preferred to T_2; for every $d \in D_1$ there will be $d' \in D_2$ such that d is preferred to d': simply let $d' = d$. This means that the theory with no default assumptions, T_0, is preferred to any other theory.

DEFINITION 59 (VIABLE THEORIES)
T_i is a *viable* if it is not contradicted by any preferred theory.

The intuitive idea is that the agent's beliefs may be described by any viable theory, but only by a viable theory. We will refer to the theory that describes the agent's beliefs as the agent's theory. If the agent's KB is very detailed then, direct inference might be sufficient to describe how the agent should assign his degrees of belief. That is, T_0 might contain sufficient information about $\mathrm{prob}(\alpha)$ for all α of interest. And indeed, even if KB is not that detailed T_0 may still contain useful information about the degree of belief assigned to some assertions. There will be many cases, however, where T_0 does not contain any useful information because the direct inference principle resulted in a reference class more specific than the statistical information in T_0.

The fact that many properties in the most specific reference class are irrelevant is the intuitive basis for allowing the inheritance of expected statistics, and the non-monotonic assumptions enable this kind of inheritance. The preference criterion captures the natural constraint that we should try to retain as much information as possible; i.e., we should use the narrowest reference class possible.

Different assumptions lead to different conclusions, and this is why some theories may contradict others. The preference ordering between the default assumptions induces a preference ordering between the different theories.

Under this preference ordering T_0 is preferred to all other theories: it contains no defaults, and thus it vacuously satisfies the preference criterion. However, T_0 does not contradict every other theory. Therefore, there are other viable theories besides T_0. Every theory, including the viable ones, will contain T_0, however. Furthermore, since the inconsistent theories contain every formula they will be contradicted by T_0, and thus no inconsistent theory will be viable. We cannot make a non-monotonic assumption that is inconsistent with T_0, nor can we make a contradictory set of assumptions: these do not produce viable theories. Therefore, inconsistent theories cannot serve as legitimate descriptions of the agent's beliefs.

There can, and usually will be, many different viable theories. Our formalism makes no attempt to determine the agent's theory uniquely. Various writers (e.g., Konolige and Myers [63], Doyle and Wellman [22]) have argued that a domain independent scheme that produces a unique theory in every situation is more than we can or should expect from a system of default reasoning. This position is supported by examples like the Nixon diamond (Example 24.1), where there seems to be no basis for choosing between the theory in which Nixon is a pacifist and the theory in which he is not. What a default reasoning system should provide is the ability generate the obvious, uncontroversial theories, and equally important, it should eliminate obviously incorrect theories. As will be demonstrated in our examples, the statistical approach is particularly adept at both of these tasks.

It should be noted than in general it is not possible to determine when a theory T_i is viable by reasoning inside the logic. The only theory we can be assured is viable is T_0, and even this depends on our ability to ensure that the agent's initial KB is consistent. Usually the viability of a theory T_i can only be demonstrated meta-logically, by reasoning outside of the logic. When reasoning inside the logic it is possible that a preferred theory contradicting T_i may be found after further reasoning; in general, there is no fixed amount of reasoning which will determine a theory's viability. This is a common situation in non-monotonic reasoning. For example, in general one can only determine the contents of an extension in default logic by reasoning meta-logically, outside of the logic.

We have already discussed this complexity problem in Chapter 1. We can note here, however, that reasoning inside of the logic can still provide a great deal of useful information. There are two obvious types of information that can be inferred in this manner. First, anything that can be deduced about T_0 will be true of the agent's theory, no matter which of the viable theories this is: every theory is an extension of T_0. As the examples will demonstrate, there are many situations in which T_0 will contain useful information. Second, we can demonstrate that a theory is *not* viable by deducing a contradiction from T_0. This serves the important function of eliminating many obviously incorrect theories.

Now we present some examples of how the combination of the direct inference principle and the non-monotonic mechanism operate together as a system of default reasoning.

5.8 More Examples

EXAMPLE 24 (INHERITANCE REASONING)
The mechanism can deal nicely with exception allowing inheritance reasoning.

1. Let

$$\text{KB} = \begin{array}{ll} [P(x)|Q(x)]_x > c & \wedge \quad [P(x)|R(x)]_x < 1 - c \\ \wedge \quad Q(n) \quad \wedge \quad R(n). \end{array}$$

KB is a schema for the classic Nixon diamond (Reiter and Criscuolo [117]). We have that

$$\text{prob}(P(n)) = E([P(v)|Q(v) \wedge R(v)]_v)$$

is in T_0, by direct inference. However, T_0 does not contain any useful information about this expectation term.

Let

$$
\begin{array}{lll}
D_1 & = & \{E([P(v)|Q(x) \wedge R(v)]) = E([P(v)|Q(v)]_x)\}, \\
D_2 & = & \{E([P(v)|Q(v) \wedge R(v)]) = E([P(v)|R(v)]_x)\}.
\end{array}
$$

It is easy to see that $\text{prob}(P(n)) < 1-c \in T_1$, and that $\text{prob}(P(n)) > c \in T_2$, and furthermore that neither theory is preferred over the other.

Letting $P(x)$ represent the set of pacifists, $R(x)$ the set of Republicans, $Q(x)$ the set of Quakers, and n Nixon, we have that there is a theory where the agent has a high degree of belief that Nixon is a pacifist and an alternate theory where the agent has low degree of belief in this assertion.

The formalism is not designed to serve as a final arbiter for the agent's beliefs. In this case the agent's accepted beliefs KB provides no reason to prefer T_1 over T_2. An important point, however, is that the formalism identifies what additional information could serve to decide between these two theories. That is, since $\text{prob}(P(n)) = E([P(v)|Q(v) \wedge R(v)]_v)$ is in T_0, we see that statistical information about $[P(v)|Q(v) \wedge R(v)]_v$ would allow the agent to decide between T_1 and T_2, or even to decide to reject both. In the case of Nixon, the agent could generate a preferred theory about Nixon's pacifism if he had statistical information about the proportion of pacifists among the class of Quaker-Republicans.

2. Let

$$\text{KB} = \begin{array}{ll} [B(x)|A(x)]_x > c & \wedge \quad [C(x)|B(x)]_x > c \\ \wedge \quad A(c), \end{array}$$

and

$$D_1 = \{E([C(v)|B(v) \wedge A(v)]_v) = E([C(v)|B(v)]_v)\}.$$

The theory T_1 contains the conclusion $\text{prob}(B(c)) > c$ and the conclusion $\text{prob}(C(c)) > c^2$. The first conclusion follows directly from the direct inference principle; it is contained in T_0. For the second conclusion we have the following derivation:

$\text{prob}(C(c)) = E([C(v)|A(v)]_v)$	dir. inf.
$\text{cert}([C(v)|A(v)]_v > [C(v) \wedge B(v)|A(v)]_v)$	stat. prop.
$\text{cert}([C(v) \wedge B(v)|A(v)]_v$	
$\quad = [C(v)|B(v) \wedge A(v)]_v \times [B(v)|A(v)]_v)$	stat. prop.
$\text{cert}([C(v) \wedge B(v)|A(v)]_v > [C(v)|B(v) \wedge A(v)]_v \times c)$	KB
$E([C(v)|A(v)]_v) > E([C(v)|B(v) \wedge A(v)]_v \times c)$	expt. prop.
$E([C(v)|A(v)]_v) > E([C(v)|B(v) \wedge A(v)]_v) \times c$	c rigid
$E([C(v)|A(v)]_v) > E([C(v)|B(v)]_v) \times c$	default
$E([C(v)|A(v)]_v) > c \times c$	KB

This example demonstrates that the formalism allows a weakened form of transitivity between default conclusions: since $c < 1$ we have that $c^2 < c$. This dilution in degree of belief seems to be intuitively correct. The conclusion that c is a B is a default inference, and if it is a B then the additional conclusion that it is a C is another default inference. It seems reasonable that our confidence in the final conclusion should diminish as we use more and more default inferences: each such inference has a chance of error.

Another feature of the formalism is that the assumption we make in order to sanction the transitivity effect is explicit. That is, the transitivity inference depends on the assumption that c's A-ness does not have any negative effect on its chance of being a C. The fact that we must be explicit about this assumption is not a difficulty with the formalism: it can be argued that in complex situations we will have to reason about the assumptions that are being made (Poole [109]), and thus we must be explicit about these assumptions.

3. More detailed information can block weak transitivity. Let

$$\text{KB} = [B(x)|A(x)]_x > c \quad \wedge \quad [C(x)|B(x)]_x > c$$
$$\wedge \quad [C(x)|A(x) \wedge B(x)]_x < [C(x)|B(x)]_x$$
$$\wedge \quad A(c) \quad \wedge \quad B(b).$$

With this KB we have that $\text{prob}(C(b)) > c \in T_0$, but we have no conclusions about $\text{prob}(C(c))$ in T_0. Furthermore, the theory T_1, formed from the default D_1 given in the previous example, is no longer viable: D_1 is contradicted by T_0.

If we let $A(x)$ represent the set of high-school dropouts, $B(x)$ the set of adults, and $C(x)$ the set of employed persons, then this KB contains the assertions that most high-school dropouts are adults, that most adults are employed, and that employment among the adult high-school dropouts is lower than among adults in general. From this KB an agent would have a high degree of belief in b, an adult, being employed, and would have a lower but otherwise unspecified degree of belief in c, a high-school dropout, being employed.

4. Let

$$\text{KB} = [B(x)|A(x)]_x > c \quad \wedge \quad \forall x.B(x) \rightarrow C(x)$$
$$\wedge \quad \forall x.C(x) \rightarrow D(x) \quad \wedge \quad A(c).$$

The theory T_0 contains the conclusions $\text{prob}(B(c)) > c$, $\text{prob}(C(c)) > c$, and $\text{prob}(D(c)) > c$. That is, categorical information gives strong transitivity without a need for non-monotonic assumptions (T_0 contains no assumptions). This case is to be distinguished from the previous one involving weak transitivity. Here the only *default* inference involved is the assumption that c is a B. Once this default inference is made it then follows deductively that c must also be a C and a D.

It is interesting to note that these results can be proved two different ways. First, we have that $\text{cert}(B(c) \rightarrow C(c)) \in T_0$, by Theorem 51. Therefore, by reasoning with the propositional probabilities we get that $\text{prob}(C(c)) > \text{prob}(B(c))$, and we have that $\text{prob}(B(c)) > c$ by direct inference. The alternative way that these results can be derived is by reasoning with the statistical probabilities. It is easy to see that $[C(x)|A(x)]_x > [B(x)|A(x)]_x$ is derivable from KB. Therefore, we have that $\text{cert}([C(x)|A(x)]_x > c) \in T_0$ and that $\text{prob}(C(c)) > c \in T_0$ by direct inference.

5. Let

$$KB = \begin{array}{l} [B(x)|A(x)]_x > c \quad \wedge \quad [C(x)|B(x)]_x > c \\ \wedge \quad [C(x)|A(x)]_x < 1 - c \\ \wedge \quad A(a) \quad \wedge \quad B(b) \\ \wedge \quad A(c) \quad \wedge \quad B(c). \end{array}$$

In this case T_0 contains the conclusions $\text{prob}(C(a)) < 1 - c$ and also $\text{prob}(C(b)) > c$. The problem comes from c because we know both $A(c)$ and $B(c)$.

Let

$$D_1 = \{ E([C(v)|A(v) \wedge B(v)]_v) = E([C(v)|A(v)]_v) \},$$
$$D_2 = \{ E([C(v)|A(v) \wedge B(v)]_v) = E([C(v)|B(v)]_v) \}.$$

It would seem that this situation is like that of the Nixon diamond and that we have two contradictory theories with neither one being preferred: T_1 with $\text{prob}(C(c)) < 1 - c$, and T_2 with $\text{prob}(C(c)) > c$. However, if we have a slightly stronger constraint on c, in particular if we assume that $c > (\sqrt{5} - 1)/2 \approx 0.62$ instead of the weaker $c > 0.5$, then it can be demonstrated that T_2 is in fact not viable: it will be contradicted by T_0. Thus we are left with T_1 and its conclusion that c is probably not a C. In other words, when we know that most A's are B's the formalism will entail a preference for information based on the reference class of A's, under the relatively innocuous demand that "most" entail greater than 62%.

To show this we demonstrate that if $c > (\sqrt{5} - 1)/2$ then $\text{prob}(C(c)) < c \in T_0$. Hence, T_0 will contradict T_2. We have by statistical reasoning from KB that

$$[C(v)|A(v) \wedge B(v)]_v = \frac{[C(v) \wedge B(v)|A(v)]_v}{[B(v)|A(v)]_v} < \frac{[C(v)|A(v)]_v}{[B(v)|A(v)]_v}$$
$$< \frac{1-c}{c} < c.$$

The last line holds when c is greater than the positive root of the equation $(1 - c)/c = c$. This root has value $(\sqrt{5} - 1)/2$. Since this is a deductive consequence of KB we have that $\text{cert}([C(v)|A(v) \wedge B(v)]_v < c) \in T_0$. By direct inference, $\text{prob}(C(c)) = E([C(v)|A(v) \wedge B(v)]_v)$, and thus we have $\text{prob}(C(c)) < c \in T_0$.

For example, if we let $A(x)$ represent the set of university students, $B(x)$ the set of adults, and $C(x)$ the set of employed persons, then we have that it is not viable to assign a high degree of belief to the assertion that an adult university student is employed, given that this is all that is known about the student. That is, we eliminate an unintuitive theory purely by statistical reasoning.

6. Let

$$
\begin{aligned}
KB = \ & \forall x. A(x) \to B(x) \quad \wedge \quad [C(x)|B(x)]_x > c \\
& \wedge \ [C(x)|A(x)]_x < 1 - c \\
& \wedge \quad A(a) \quad \wedge \quad B(a) \\
& \wedge \quad A(b) \quad \wedge \quad B(c) \\
& \wedge \quad A(d) \quad \wedge \quad B(d) \wedge \quad D(d).
\end{aligned}
$$

We have already demonstrated the essence of the reasoning involved in this example, but treat the example more completely here. In this case T_0 contains $prob\big(C(a)\big) < 1 - c$: from KB we can prove that $[C(x)|B(x) \wedge A(x)]_x = [C(x)|A(x)]_x$. Hence, when all A's are B's we get a preference for the narrower class as a consequence of the properties of the statistical terms. We also have in T_0 that $prob\big(C(b)\big) < 1 - c$ and $prob\big(C(c)\big) > c$.

With $A(x)$ representing the set of royal elephants, $B(x)$ representing the set of elephants, and $C(x)$ representing the property of being gray, this KB contains the assertions that most elephants are gray, royal elephants are elephants, and most royal elephants are not gray. The viable theories will assign high degrees of belief to the assertions that the elephant c is gray, the royal elephant b is not gray, and the royal elephant a who is also explicitly known to be an elephant is not gray.

For the individual d we have some irrelevant information (or at least information that is not known to be relevant). Let

$$
\begin{aligned}
D_1 \ &= \ \big\{ \, E\big([C(v)|A(v) \wedge B(v) \wedge D(v)]_v\big) = E\big([C(v)|A(v)]_v\big) \, \big\}, \\
D_2 \ &= \ \big\{ \, E\big([C(v)|A(v) \wedge B(v) \wedge D(v)]_v\big) = E\big([C(v)|B(v)]_v\big) \, \big\}.
\end{aligned}
$$

Since $cert\big(\forall x. A(x) \to B(x)\big) \in T_0$, we have that T_1 is preferred to T_2. Furthermore, since $prob\big(C(d)\big) < 1 - c < 0.5 \in T_1$ and $prob\big(C(d)\big) > c > 0.5 \in T_2$, we have that T_1 contradicts T_2. Hence, T_2 is contradicted by a preferred theory and it is not viable.

So if we let D(x) represent the property of being average in size, then it remains unviable for the agent to have a high degree of belief in the grayness of an average sized royal elephant d, given that this is all that is known about d.

7. The system can also deal with more extensive inheritance problems. For example it can deal with the extended Nixon diamond (due to Ginsberg). Let p-m be a predicate denoting the set of politically motivated individuals, repub a predicate denoting the set of republicans, and

$$
\begin{aligned}
KB = \quad & \text{quaker}(N) \quad \wedge \quad \text{repub}(N) \\
& \wedge \quad [\text{hawk}(x)|\text{repub}(x)]_x > c \quad \wedge \quad [\text{dove}(x)|\text{quaker}(x)]_x > c \\
& \wedge \quad \forall x.\text{hawk}(x) \rightarrow \neg\text{dove}(x) \\
& \wedge \quad \forall x.\text{hawk}(x) \rightarrow \text{p-m}(x) \quad \wedge \quad \forall x.\text{dove}(x) \rightarrow \text{p-m}(x).
\end{aligned}
$$

Let

$$
\begin{aligned}
D_1 \quad &= \quad \{ \mathsf{E}\big([\text{hawk}(x)|\text{quaker}(x) \wedge \text{repub}(x)]_x\big) \\
& \qquad = \mathsf{E}\big([\text{hawk}(x)|\text{repub}(x)]_x\big) \}, \\
D_2 \quad &= \quad \{ \mathsf{E}\big([\text{hawk}(x)|\text{quaker}(x) \wedge \text{repub}(x)]_x\big) \\
& \qquad = \mathsf{E}\big([\text{hawk}(x)|\text{quaker}(x)]_x\big) \}, \\
D_3 \quad &= \quad \{ \mathsf{E}\big([\text{p-m}(x)|\text{quaker}(x) \wedge \text{repub}(x)]_x\big) \\
& \qquad = \mathsf{E}\big([\text{p-m}(x)|\text{repub}(x)]_x\big) \}, \\
D_4 \quad &= \quad \{ \mathsf{E}\big([\text{p-m}(x)|\text{quaker}(x) \wedge \text{repub}(x)]_x\big) \\
& \qquad = \mathsf{E}\big([\text{p-m}(x)|\text{quaker}(x)]_x\big) \}.
\end{aligned}
$$

Then our conclusions will include the following:

a) $\text{cert}\big([\neg\text{hawk}(x)|\text{quaker}(x)]_x > c\big) \in T_0$. That is, the agent will be certain that most quakers are not hawks. We also have that $\text{cert}\big([\text{p-m}(x)|\text{repub}(x)]_x > c\big) \in T_0$. What is encoded as statistical information in our formalism would, in other systems of default reasoning, normally be represented as defaults. These intuitive conclusions indicate the benefit of being able to reason with the defaults.

b) $\text{prob}\big(\text{hawk}(N)\big) > c \in T_1$ and $\text{prob}\big(\text{hawk}(N)\big) < 1 - c \in T_2$, and neither is preferred over the other. We also have $\text{prob}\big(\text{dove}(N)\big) < 1 - c \in T_1$ and $\text{prob}\big(\text{dove}(N)\big) > c \in T_2$. That is, if the agent commits to either of D_1 or D_2 he will also be able to draw a conclusion about how committed he should be to Nixon being a dove.

c) $\text{prob}(\text{p-m}(\text{N})) > c$ is in both T_1 and T_2, but the agent cannot simultaneously assume D_1 and D_2 since their union leads to an inconsistent, nonviable theory. Furthermore, we have no mechanism for allowing the agent's theory to be an intersection of other theories. We do not, however, need to construct extra machinery to allow the agent to believe that Nixon is politically motivated without being committed to a belief about Nixon's hawkishness, as the next item demonstrates.

d) $\text{prob}(\text{p-m}(\text{N})) > c$ is in both T_3 and T_4, and they are not contradictory. Thus the agent can have a theory that concludes that Nixon is politically motivated without forcing any conclusion about his hawkishness. If we have no reason to choose between T_3 and T_4, we can form $D_5 = D_3 \cup D_4$. Nixon is probably politically motivated in T_5 as well. This combined theory will also contain the conclusion that $\text{E}([\text{p-m}(x)|\text{repub}(x)]_x) = \text{E}([\text{p-m}(x)|\text{quaker}(x)]_x)$, but it will *not contain* the conclusion

$$\text{cert}([\text{p-m}(x)|\text{repub}(x)]_x = [\text{p-m}(x)|\text{quaker}(x)]_x).$$

That is, T_5 does not force the agent into an extra belief about an *objective* assertion.

8. Let pdutch-speaker be a predicate denoting the set of Pennsylvania Dutch speakers (Horty and Thomason [52]), and let

$$
\begin{aligned}
\text{KB} = \ &\text{pdutch-speaker}(\text{Hermann}) \\
\wedge \ &[\text{pennsylvanian}(x)|\text{pdutch-speaker}(x)]_x > c \\
\wedge \ &[\text{american}(x)|\text{german-speaker}(x)]_x < 1 - c \\
\wedge \ &\forall x.\text{pennsylvanian}(x) \rightarrow \text{american}(x) \\
\wedge \ &\forall x.\text{pdutch-speaker}(x) \rightarrow \text{german-speaker}(x).
\end{aligned}
$$

That is, most speakers of Pennsylvania Dutch, a dialect of German, are born in Pennsylvania, a part of USA, but most German speakers are not Americans.

We have that $\text{prob}(\text{american}(\text{Hermann})) > c$ is in T_0. From KB we can derive that

$$
\begin{aligned}
&[\text{american}(x)|\text{pdutch-speaker}(x)]_x \\
&\quad > [\text{pennsylvanian}(x)|\text{pdutch-speaker}(x)]_x > c.
\end{aligned}
$$

Therefore, this relation is certain in T_0. Since by direct inference

$$\text{prob}(\texttt{american}(\texttt{Hermann}))$$
$$= \mathsf{E}([\texttt{american}(\texttt{v})|\texttt{pdutch-speaker}(\texttt{v})]_{\texttt{v}}),$$

we obtain our result from the properties of the expectation operator. This can be contrasted with the system presented by Horty and Thomason [52], which requires a rather complex syntactic mechanism to sanction these kinds of conclusions.

Note also that the fact that german-speaker(Hermann) is deducible from the knowledge base is irrelevant. This information is deducible from what we conditioned on, i.e., pdutch-speaker. If we had this formula as an explicit part of KB, we would still have by statistical reasoning that the reference class formed by intersecting the German and Pennsylvania Dutch speakers would be equal to the reference class that we used: the Pennsylvania Dutch speakers.

EXAMPLE 25 (RELATIONS)
When we move beyond unary predicates to relations, we have to deal with generalizations of property inheritance: the inheritance of relations based on other properties, and the precedence for sub-relations over super-relations. There is also a new type of precedence between possible inheritances: the preference for more specific defaults. We have already demonstrated the manner in which the properties of the statistical terms entail a natural specificity preference, and we can demonstrate that this specificity preference is relatively robust in the face of extra information.

1. Gullible citizens like elected crooks (Touretzky [129]). Let

$$
\begin{aligned}
\text{KB} =\ & [\texttt{likes}(\texttt{x},\texttt{y})|\texttt{citizen}(\texttt{x}) \wedge \texttt{crook}(\texttt{y})]_{\langle \texttt{x},\texttt{y}\rangle} < 1 - c \\
& \wedge\ \left[\texttt{likes}(\texttt{x},\texttt{y})\ \middle|\ \begin{array}{l}\texttt{citizen}(\texttt{x}) \wedge \texttt{gullible}(\texttt{x}) \\ \texttt{crook}(\texttt{y}) \wedge \texttt{elected}(\texttt{y})\end{array}\right]_{\langle \texttt{x},\texttt{y}\rangle} > c \\
& \wedge\ \texttt{citizen}(\texttt{Fred})\quad \wedge\quad \texttt{gullible}(\texttt{Fred}) \\
& \wedge\ \texttt{crook}(\texttt{Dick})\quad \wedge\quad \texttt{elected}(\texttt{Dick}).
\end{aligned}
$$

From this knowledge base we have $\text{prob}(\texttt{likes}(\texttt{Fred},\texttt{Dick})) > c \in T_0$. That is, the agent has a high degree of belief in the assertion that Fred the gullible citizen likes Dick the elected crook.

2. Let

$$
\begin{aligned}
\text{KB} = \ &\text{elephant(Clyde)} \quad \wedge \quad \text{zookeeper(Fred)} \\
&\wedge \quad [\text{likes}(x, y)|\text{elephant}(x) \wedge \text{zookeeper}(y)]_{\langle x, y \rangle} > c \\
&\wedge \quad [\text{likes}(x, \text{Fred})|\text{elephant}(x)]_{x} < 1 - c \\
&\wedge \quad \text{gentle(Fred)}.
\end{aligned}
$$

Here KB is the same as in our previous discussion of this example, except that the agent now knows that Fred is gentle. But even with this extra information about Fred we still have that $\text{prob}\big(\text{likes}(\text{Clyde}, \text{Fred})\big) < 1 - c \in T_0$. This result can be proved in exactly the same manner as when we did not know that Fred was gentle: we just have to use the more general Lemma 40 instead of Lemma 39.

The point here is that it does not matter what else is known about Fred, as long as we know that he is unpopular among the elephants. Any other information we may have about Fred does not alter his unpopularity; otherwise the assertion about his unpopularity would have been removed from KB. Given that all the agent knows about Clyde is that he is an elephant, Fred's unpopularity among the elephants will be the only pertinent fact in determining if Clyde likes Fred.

If, however, we have additional information about Clyde, then we will no longer be able to draw the same conclusion without an assumption that this extra information is irrelevant. For example, if we add the formula friendly(Clyde) to the above KB, then T_0 will no longer contain $\text{prob}\big(\text{likes}(\text{Clyde}, \text{Fred})\big) < 1 - c$. The difference here is that the information we have about Fred pertains to the class of elephants, not to the special class of elephants that Clyde belongs to, the friendly elephants. Although Fred is unpopular among the elephants, he may be popular among the subclass of friendly elephants. We have to assume that this special class of elephants is no different from the superclass of all elephants in order to apply our knowledge about Fred's unpopularity. That is, the agent's degree of belief remains the same only in a theory that makes the assumption that Clyde's friendliness is irrelevant.

We can construct such a theory by using an appropriate nonmonotonic assumption. However, it may also be the case that we have additional statistical information about friendly elephants.

For example, we may have explicit information about the proportion of zoo-keepers that are liked by the class of friendly elephants. In this case there may be an alternate viable theory in which, instead of assuming that Clyde's property of being friendly is irrelevant, the agent assumes that Fred's special unpopularity is irrelevant. It may even be the case that the agent retains T_0 as his theory and remains indeterminate about the probability of likes(Clyde,Fred).

EXAMPLE 26 (TEMPORAL REASONING)
Tenenberg and Weber [128,131] have recently developed an interesting approach to non-monotonic temporal reasoning using statistical information. They have used an approach based on direct inference, and have dealt with problems like the qualification problem. Here we recast their approach in our formalism.

The essential idea is that among the object or non-numeric terms of the language are a collection of temporal objects, in this case time points. That is, the domain of discourse contains a temporal domain. We assume that the temporal domain has a structure similar to the natural numbers; in particular, it is discrete and it is totally ordered by a successor function.

So along with possibly some other non-temporal object symbols (functions and predicates) the language in which we perform temporal reasoning will contain a set of time constants, a successor function s, and a collection of *fluents*. The fluents are monadic object predicates whose denotations are a collection of time points. For example, if we are reasoning about a particular car, a possible fluent might be turn-key. The open formula turn-key(x) will denote the set of moments when the car's key was turned, and a formula like turn-key(t) will denote that the car's key was turned at the particular temporal point denoted by the term t. For this example we will assume that there are no non-temporal objects, and that we only have monadic fluents.[15]

In this language we can encode statistical causal rules. These are rules

---

[15] We could easily have a more general domain with actual objects as well as temporal objects. In this case a sort predicate in the language, say temporal(x), would also be needed. This predicate would be true of a term if and only if the term denoted a temporal object. Similarly we could have parameterized fluents, e.g., turn-key(x, t), where the first argument denotes the particular car whose key was turned and the second argument denotes the time point the action occurred.

that relate fluents at a particular time t to fluents at t's successor $s(t)$. As argued by Tenenberg and Weber, it is quite reasonable to assume that an agent could accumulate such statistical information through experience gained when acting in his environment. A typical causal rule might be

$$[\mathtt{start(s(x))|turn\text{-}key(x)}]_x > 0.75.$$

This rule asserts that greater than 75% of the time turning the car's key results in starting the car. Unlike the formalism used by Tenenberg and Weber, our language also allows the expression of qualitative statistical rules. For example,

$$[\mathtt{start(s(x))|turn\text{-}key(x) \wedge cold(x)}]_x < [\mathtt{start(s(x))|turn\text{-}key(x)}]_x$$

asserts that the car starts less often when it is cold, but makes no commitment to the frequency of starts in either case.

Let $\mathtt{p\text{-}in\text{-}t}$ represent the fluent "potato in the tailpipe," $\mathtt{twin\text{-}exh}$ represent the fluent "twin exhaust," and let

$$
\begin{aligned}
\mathtt{KB} = {}& [\mathtt{start(s(x))|turn\text{-}key(x)}]_x > 0.75 \\
\wedge\ & [\mathtt{start(s(x))|turn\text{-}key(x) \wedge p\text{-}in\text{-}t(x)}]_x < 0.1 \\
\wedge\ & [\mathtt{start(s(x))|turn\text{-}key(x) \wedge p\text{-}in\text{-}t(x) \wedge twin\text{-}exh(x)}]_x > 0.5 \\
\wedge\ & [\mathtt{start(s(x))|turn\text{-}key(x) \wedge p\text{-}in\text{-}t(x) \wedge twin\text{-}exh(x)}]_x \\
& \quad < [\mathtt{start(s(x))|turn\text{-}key(x)}]_x \\
\wedge\ & \mathtt{turn\text{-}key(t_1)} \\
\wedge\ & \mathtt{turn\text{-}key(t_2)} \quad \wedge \quad \mathtt{p\text{-}in\text{-}t(t_2)} \\
\wedge\ & \mathtt{turn\text{-}key(t_3)} \quad \wedge \quad \mathtt{p\text{-}in\text{-}t(t_3)} \quad \wedge \quad \mathtt{twin\text{-}exh(t_3)}.
\end{aligned}
$$

Then we will have that T_0 contains the following conclusions:

1. $\mathrm{prob}\big(\mathtt{start(s(t_1))}\big) > 0.75$: it is likely that the car will be started in situation t_1.

2. $\mathrm{prob}\big(\mathtt{start(s(t_2))}\big) < 0.1$: due to the potato in the tailpipe, it is unlikely that the car will be started in situation t_2.

3. $\mathrm{prob}\big(\mathtt{start(s(t_1))}\big) > \mathrm{prob}\big(\mathtt{start(s(t_3))}\big) > 0.5$: since the car has a twin exhaust it is more likely than not that it will start in situation t_3; however, it is less likely to start than in situation t_1 when it did not have the potato in its tailpipe.

The statistical approach to non-monotonic temporal reasoning deals nicely with the qualification problem, i.e., the problem of predicting the effects of actions despite lack of knowledge about possible qualifications, like potatoes in the tailpipe, that might change the effects of those actions. The qualification problem forces causal prediction to be non-monotonic: conclusions may change in the light of additional information. As our example demonstrates, the agent's degree of belief in the car starting can change as more is known about the situation. The agent's degree of belief decreases if he also knows that there is a potato in the tailpipe, but it increases again if he knows that the car is equipped with a twin exhaust. This last is an exception to an exception, and is handled in a uniform manner by the formalism. Exceptions to exceptions have presented problems for other non-monotonic approaches to temporal reasoning (Ginsberg and Smith [40]).

Another feature of the statistical approach is that the statistical information about general situations includes the effect of more specific situations. For example, we have the following valid equality:

$$\begin{aligned}
[\text{start}(s(x))|\text{turn-key}(x)]_x \\
= [\text{start}(s(x))|\text{turn-key}(x) \wedge \text{p-in-t}(x)]_x \\
\times [\text{p-in-t}(x)|\text{turn-key}(x)]_x \\
+ [\text{start}(s(x))|\text{turn-key}(x) \wedge \neg\text{p-in-t}(x)]_x \\
\times [\neg\text{p-in-t}(x)|\text{turn-key}(x)]_x
\end{aligned}$$

That is, information about the possible effect of potatoes in tailpipes is embedded in the information about the more general situation, where we do not know if there is a potato in the tailpipe. If potatoes in tailpipes occurred more frequently, this would be reflected in the statistic $[\text{start}(s(x))|\text{turn-key}(x)]_x$: the car would start less frequently when the key was turned. In fact, statistics about general situations include information about *every* exception, even those the agent is not aware of.[16] And more importantly, all of these exceptions are *weighted* as to their relative impact. For example, the engine-missing exception might make it impossible to start the car, i.e., we might have

$$[\text{start}(s(x))|\text{turn-key}(x) \wedge \text{engine-missing}(x)]_x = 0,$$

but the chance of it occurring might be very small, i.e.,

$$[\neg\text{engine-missing}(x)|\text{turn-key}(x)]_x$$

---

[16] Elgot-Drapkin et al. [24] have pointed out that it may be *impossible* to write down all the qualifications needed to guarantee action success—the complexity of the domain might be beyond our ability to completely formalize.

may be much larger than

$$[\text{engine-missing}(x)|\text{turn-key}(x)]_x;$$

therefore, its net effect on the chance of the car starting may be negligible.

One final point that can be made about this approach to temporal reasoning is that the default conclusions made are not certain. That is, the agent is less than certain that the car will start, even in situation t_1 where we know nothing special about the turn-key event. In contrast, traditional non-monotonic approaches to this problem fail to distinguish default conclusions from purely deductive ones. This causes the problem that if the agent has no specific evidence to the contrary, he will conclude that the car will *always start*; so, e.g., he may conclude that there is no need for preventative maintenance. If we assume that the car-starting events are independent, we obtain

$$\text{prob}\big(\text{start}(t) \wedge \text{start}(t')\big) = \text{prob}\big(\text{start}(t)\big) \times \text{prob}\big(\text{start}(t')\big).$$

That is, the agent's degree of belief in the car starting at two different times t and t' will be lower than his degree of belief in the individual starts.

EXAMPLE 27 (REASONING WITH DEGREES OF BELIEF)
Previous examples have demonstrated that the ability to do probabilistic reasoning with the statistical information is very useful in eliminating unintuitive theories. This example illustrates that the ability to perform probabilistic reasoning with the degrees of beliefs induced by direct inference also plays an important role in the ultimate power of the system.
Let

$$
\begin{aligned}
\text{KB} = \ & \text{car}(\text{Car1}) \quad \wedge \quad \text{parked}(\text{Car1}, \text{Lot1}) \\
\wedge \ & [\text{towed}(x)|\text{car}(x) \wedge \text{parked}(x, \text{Lot1})]_x > c \\
\wedge \ & \text{owns}(\text{John}, \text{Car1}) \\
\wedge \ & \text{towed}(\text{Car1}) \rightarrow \text{angry}(\text{John}).
\end{aligned}
$$

That is, John has parked his car in a lot where it is likely to be towed, and if it is towed he will be angry. Say we wish to determine how angry he will be, i.e., $\text{prob}\big(\text{angry}(\text{John})\big)$. We have in T_0 that $\text{prob}\big(\text{angry}(\text{John})\big) =$

$\mathsf{E}([\mathrm{angry}(\mathsf{v})|\mathsf{KB}^\mathsf{V}]_{\vec{v}})$. Written out explicitly $\mathsf{E}([\mathrm{angry}(\mathsf{v})|\mathsf{KB}^\mathsf{V}]_{\vec{v}})$ is

$$\mathsf{E}\left(\left[\mathrm{angry}(\mathsf{v_1})\;\middle|\;\begin{array}{l}\mathrm{car}(\mathsf{v_2}) \wedge \mathrm{parked}(\mathsf{v_2},\mathsf{v_3})\\ \wedge\, [\mathrm{towed}(\mathsf{x})|\mathrm{car}(\mathsf{x}) \wedge \mathrm{parked}(\mathsf{x},\mathsf{v_3})]_\mathsf{x} > c\\ \wedge\, \mathrm{owns}(\mathsf{v_1},\mathsf{v_2}) \wedge (\mathrm{towed}(\mathsf{v_2}) \to \mathrm{angry}(\mathsf{v_1}))\end{array}\right]_{\vec{v}}\right).$$

The problem here is that in this KB the formulas are all tightly coupled; every formula of KB is related to the constant John. Hence, this complex statistical term does not reduce to anything simpler. It is clear that T_0 does not contain any useful information about this expectation term. Furthermore, it is not obvious what default assumptions can be used to generalize the reference class. There is no obvious superclass for which T_0 contains explicit information.

However, the formalism allows a less direct approach to the problem. Since $\mathrm{towed}(\mathrm{Car1}) \to \mathrm{angry}(\mathrm{John})$ is in KB, we have $\mathrm{cert}(\mathrm{towed}(\mathrm{Car1}) \to \mathrm{angry}(\mathrm{John})) \in T_0$. Simple probabilistic reasoning with the degree of belief probabilities yields the conclusion that $\mathrm{prob}(\mathrm{angry}(\mathrm{John})) > \mathrm{prob}(\mathrm{towed}(\mathrm{Car1})) \in T_0$. Hence, this relation between the two degrees of belief is in every other theory as well. This means that we can generate useful conclusions about $\mathrm{prob}(\mathrm{angry}(\mathrm{John}))$ in those theories that have something to say about $\mathrm{prob}(\mathrm{towed}(\mathrm{Car1}))$.

In particular, in the theory where we have the default assumption that $\mathsf{E}([\mathrm{towed}(\mathsf{v_2})|\mathsf{KB}^\mathsf{V}]_{\vec{v}})$ is equal to

$$\mathsf{E}\left(\left[\mathrm{towed}(\mathsf{v_2})\;\middle|\;\begin{array}{l}\mathrm{car}(\mathsf{v_2}) \wedge \mathrm{parked}(\mathsf{v_2},\mathsf{v_3})\\ \wedge\, [\mathrm{towed}(\mathsf{x})|\mathrm{car}(\mathsf{x}) \wedge \mathrm{parked}(\mathsf{x},\mathsf{v_3})]_\mathsf{x} > c\end{array}\right]_{\vec{v}}\right),$$

we have the conclusion that $\mathrm{prob}(\mathrm{towed}(\mathrm{Car1})) > c$: this follows immediately from Lemma 39. Hence, this theory also contains the conclusion that $\mathrm{prob}(\mathrm{angry}(\mathrm{John})) > c$.

EXAMPLE 28 (KYBURG'S PREFERENCE RULES)

Perhaps the most far reaching theory of direct inference has been developed by Kyburg [67]. In [71] and elsewhere, Kyburg argues that the problem of choosing the correct reference class cannot be solved by a simple preference for narrower reference classes. He argues that there are certain cases where a preference should exist between two reference classes even though there is no subset-superset relation between them.

1. One preference criterion that is not subsumed by the subset preference is Kyburg's strength rule. For example, the agent's knowledge

base may be

$$\begin{aligned}
\texttt{KB} = \quad & [\texttt{fly(x)}|\texttt{bird(x)}]_{\mathbf{x}} \in (0.8, 0.9) \\
\wedge \quad & [\texttt{fly(x)}|\texttt{parrot(x)}]_{\mathbf{x}} \in (0.5, 0.95) \\
\wedge \quad & \forall \texttt{x.parrot(x)} \rightarrow \texttt{bird(x)} \\
\wedge \quad & \texttt{parrot(Polly)}.
\end{aligned}$$

Such a knowledge base may occur quite naturally if the agent obtains his statistical knowledge from his day to day experiences. For example, the agent may have encountered a large number of birds. If the agent uses classical statistical techniques in obtaining his base of accepted statistical beliefs, then this large sample may legitimate the acceptance of an assertion that the actual percentage of flying birds is within tight bounds of the percentage encountered in the agent's sample.[17] On the other hand, the agent may have encountered very few parrots, and may have no other sources of information about them. This would legitimate the acceptance of only loose bounds on the proportion of parrots that are fliers.

In this case we have more exact statistical information about the superclass bird than about the subclass parrot. Kyburg argues that in such situations since the stronger statistical information about the superclass does not conflict with the weaker information about the subclass, we should use the more informative superclass as our reference class. That is, we should conclude that $\mathsf{prob}\big(\texttt{fly(Polly)}\big) \in (0.8, 0.9)$, rather than $\mathsf{prob}\big(\texttt{fly(Polly)}\big) \in (0.5, 0.95)$. In our formalism we have that the latter conclusion, rather than the former, is in T_0.

However, we can still draw Kyburg's conclusion, simply by being explicit about the assumption involved. Let

$$D_1 \quad = \quad \big\{ \mathsf{E}\big([\texttt{fly(x)}|\texttt{bird(x)}]_{\mathbf{x}}\big) = \mathsf{E}\big([\texttt{fly(x)}|\texttt{parrot(x)}]_{\mathbf{x}}\big) \big\}.$$

Then we have that $\mathsf{prob}\big(\texttt{fly(Polly)}\big) \in (0.8, 0.9)$ is in T_1. Since $[\texttt{fly(x)}|\texttt{bird(x)}]_{\mathbf{x}} = [\texttt{fly(x)}|\texttt{parrot(x)}]_{\mathbf{x}}$ is consistent with KB, T_1 is not contradicted by T_0; rather it simply makes the extra assumption that the proportion of fliers among parrots is the same

---

[17]Classical statistical testing is built around the set theoretical fact that most samples of a population will display a relative frequency close to the population's actual relative frequency, and that as the sample size increases so does the chance of agreement.

as the proportion of fliers among birds (more precisely that the expected proportions are the same).

This example shows that Kyburg's strength rule is consistent with our formalism. All that we require is to make explicit the assumption that Kyburg is making implicitly.

2. Another case pointed out by Kyburg is what he calls a preference for the product reference class. Say that we have a room containing three cages, two of which contain a healthy sparrow and three penguins, while the third contains 40 healthy sparrows and two penguins. If we first select a cage at random and then select a bird from that cage, again at random, then most of the time the bird selected by this process will not be a flier. At the same time, however, most of the birds in the room are fliers. Furthermore, there is no subset of the set of birds in the room for which we know (1) the selected bird is a member and (2) the majority of birds in that subset are non-fliers. Thus it would seem that we cannot find a preferred theory which will contradict the theory that assumes that the bird was randomly selected from among all of the birds in the room; i.e., it would seem that we cannot remove the theory which says that the bird selected is likely to be a flier. Again, however, by making some of Kyburg's implicit assumptions explicit we can deal with this situation.[18]

Our probability structures only have one distribution over the domain, and under this distribution the relative measure of flying birds from among the set of birds can have only one value. But in this example the agent also has knowledge about the process by which the bird is selected, and therefore this knowledge should be included in the agent's knowledge base.

With this aim, we admit a collection of trials into the domain of objects. These trials are of two types. One type of trial occurs when a bird is selected at random from among all of the birds in the room (i.e., every bird has an equal chance of being selected). We will use the predicate symbol from-room to denote trials of this type. The second type of trial occurs when we first select a cage at random and then we select a bird from that cage, again at

---

[18]The example is much like the situation we discussed in Section 3.6. The mechanism which we use to deal with it, i.e., admitting an explicit notion of trial into the domain, was also discussed in that section.

random. We will use from-cage as a predicate denoting trials of this type.

Let result be a function symbol denoting the function that maps trials to their outcomes. For example, if t is a trial, of either type, then result(t) will denote the bird that was selected by t. Now let

$$
\begin{aligned}
\text{KB} = \ & [\texttt{fly(result(x))}|\texttt{from-room(x)}]_x = 42/50 \\
\wedge \ & [\neg\texttt{fly(result(x))}|\texttt{from-cage(x)}]_x = 1/2 + 1/63 \\
\wedge \ & \texttt{from-cage(t}_1\texttt{)} \quad \wedge \quad \texttt{from-room(t}_2\texttt{)}.
\end{aligned}
$$

KB contains the numeric information that we have. We have made the example simpler by including in KB the calculated probability of a trial of type from-cage resulting in a non-flier. It should be noted that we could have encoded in KB the information that was actually given in the example. That is, trials of type from-cage can be exhaustively decomposed into three mutually disjoint subtypes corresponding to the three different cages that could be selected at the first stage. For each of these subtypes the example gives explicit information about the probability of a flier being selected. From this more primitive encoding we could have *deduced* the conclusion $[\neg\texttt{fly(result(x))}|\texttt{from-cage(x)}]_x = 1/2 + 1/63$.

It is not difficult to see that we have the desired conclusions in T_0. That is, $\texttt{prob}\big(\texttt{fly(result(t}_2\texttt{))}\big) = 42/50 \in T_o$, and

$$
\texttt{prob}\big(\texttt{fly(result(t}_1\texttt{))}\big) = 1 - (1/2 + 1/63) \in T_o.
$$

There are a couple of other preference rules cited by Kyburg. One is a preference for super-samples over sub-samples when inferring a statistical assertion from information about particular cases, in direct contrast to the preference for subsets. This kind of situation does not, however, occur in our formalism. The formalism we have developed (so far) is not as far reaching as Kyburg's. In particular, we have not addressed the problem of inferring statistical information from information about particular cases; we have only addressed the opposite problem of inferring information about particular cases from statistical information. (But see Example 29 for a description of how statistical information might be inferred in our formalism).

EXAMPLE 29 (BELIEF IN STATISTICAL ASSERTIONS)
Let r be a numeric constant whose denotation is the actual proportion of fliers among the set of birds. Let sample-100 be a predicate whose denotation is the set of all possible samples one hundred birds; i.e., if sample-100(c), then c will denote a particular sample of a hundred birds. Let *freq* be a measuring function that maps particular samples to the proportion of fliers among that sample; i.e., *freq*(c) will be a numeric term denoting the number of flying birds among the 100 birds in the sample c.

Say that the agent has knowledge of the manner in which the samples sample-100 are gathered, so that from classical statistical theory he can determine the proportion of samples that have a relative frequency of fliers close to the real frequency r. For example, the birds may have been sampled with replacement, so that the proportions are determined by the binomial distribution.

Using these symbols let

$$\text{KB} = \quad [\texttt{fly(x)}|\texttt{bird(x)}]_x = r$$
$$\wedge \quad [(\textit{freq}(x) - r) \in [-0.1, 0.1]|\texttt{sample-100(x)}]_x > 0.95$$
$$\wedge \quad \texttt{sample-100(c)} \quad \wedge \quad \textit{freq}(c) = 0.85.$$

That is, more than 95% of the samples have a frequency of fliers that is within ±0.1 of the true frequency, and c is a particular sample.

In the theory which regards the particular value of *freq*(c) to be irrelevant, the agent will have a high degree of belief (> 0.95) that the frequency of fliers in c is close to the real relative frequency. Therefore, in this theory we will also have $\texttt{prob}([\texttt{fly(x)}|\texttt{bird(x)}]_x \in [0.75, 0.95]) > 0.95$.

This example demonstrates that the agent can generate degrees of belief from sampling information, and it points to an interesting area for future research; the learning of statistical information from samples. Many details remain to be worked out, e.g., determining the manner in which the samples have been accumulated and reasoning to conclusions about the distribution of the frequencies displayed by the samples. Another feature that might be required is a rule of acceptance. All that is produced by the system is a high degree of belief in the statistical assertion; we would need a rule of acceptance of obtain a KB in which the agent was certain of the statistical information. A reasonable rule of acceptance is a difficult problem, as such rules often lead to instances of the lottery paradox (see Section 5.10.2).

5.9   Conditional Degrees of Belief

There are certain situations where the agent may wish to engage in *hypothetical* reasoning. That is, the agent may wish to assume some extra premise and then evaluate how this premise would affect his degree of belief. This kind of reasoning is a powerful tool in probabilistic reasoning. If one can identify a set of mutually exclusive and exhaustive hypotheses, one can reason about the degree of belief in a premise α sanctioned by each hypothesis. The alternative degrees of belief in α can then be combined by weighing them with respect to the probability of each hypothesis. This kind of reasoning is at the heart of Bayesian methods.

Although we could perform this kind of reasoning with a meta-level control that temporarily added the new information to the knowledge base, it is possible to do this kind of reasoning without such a meta-level. In particular, we can perform hypothetical reasoning in the same logical formalism by using conditional probabilities, just as is done in Bayesian methods. To do this we just need a small extension to the formalism we have already developed.

A conditional probability like $\mathsf{prob}(\alpha|\beta)$ denotes the relative measure of the set of worlds that satisfy α from among those worlds that satisfy β. Hence, it is reasonable to interpret it as being the agent's degree of belief in α given that he has accepted the hypothesis β. For it to be a true model of the kind of hypothetical reasoning described above we would want the following equality to be true:

$$\mathsf{prob}(\alpha|\beta) = \mathsf{E}\big([\alpha^{\mathbf{V}}|(\beta \wedge \mathtt{KB})^{\mathbf{V}}]_{\vec{v}}\big).$$

That is, we want the conditional probability of α given β to be equal to the agent's degree of belief in α if the agent had added β to his knowledge base. Our current formalism comes close to satisfying this equality, but does not quite succeed.

Under the current direct inference principle we have that $\mathsf{prob}(\alpha|\beta) =$

$\mathsf{prob}(\alpha \wedge \beta)/\mathsf{prob}(\beta)$, and this in turn is equal to

$$\frac{\mathsf{E}\big([(\alpha \wedge \beta)^{\mathbf{V}}|\mathrm{KB}^{\mathbf{V}}]_{\vec{v}}\big)}{\mathsf{E}\big([\beta^{\mathbf{V}}|\mathrm{KB}^{\mathbf{V}}]_{\vec{v}'}\big)}.$$

It is a consequence of probability theory that

$$\frac{[(\alpha \wedge \beta)^{\mathbf{V}}|\mathrm{KB}^{\mathbf{V}}]_{\vec{v}}}{[\beta^{\mathbf{V}}|\mathrm{KB}^{\mathbf{V}}]_{\vec{v}'}} = [\alpha^{\mathbf{V}}|(\beta \wedge \mathrm{KB})^{\mathbf{V}}]_{\vec{v}},{}^{19}$$

which has the form we want, but unfortunately this equality does not hold for the expected values. In particular, it is not necessarily true that $\mathsf{E}(t)/\mathsf{E}(t') = \mathsf{E}(t/t')$; if it were we would have the equality that we require.

So in order to capture the kind of hypothetical reasoning that we want we need to extend our formalism by making an additional continuity assumption for the pair of objective formulas α and β

DEFINITION 60 (CONTINUITY ASSUMPTION)
Given two objective formulas α and β, the continuity assumption for this pair of formulas is that

$$\frac{\mathsf{E}\big([(\alpha \wedge \beta)^{\mathbf{V}}|\mathrm{KB}^{\mathbf{V}}]_{\vec{v}}\big)}{\mathsf{E}\big([\beta^{\mathbf{V}}|\mathrm{KB}^{\mathbf{V}}]_{\vec{v}'}\big)} = \mathsf{E}\left(\frac{[(\alpha \wedge \beta)^{\mathbf{V}}|\mathrm{KB}^{\mathbf{V}}]_{\vec{v}}}{[\beta^{\mathbf{V}}|\mathrm{KB}^{\mathbf{V}}]_{\vec{v}'}}\right).$$

We have that $\mathsf{E}\big([(\alpha \wedge \beta)^{\mathbf{V}}|\mathrm{KB}^{\mathbf{V}}]_{\vec{v}}/[\beta^{\mathbf{V}}|\mathrm{KB}^{\mathbf{V}}]_{\vec{v}'}\big) = \mathsf{E}\big([\alpha^{\mathbf{V}}|(\beta \wedge \mathrm{KB})^{\mathbf{V}}]_{\vec{v}}\big)$ is valid, as these two terms are certainly equal. Therefore, the behavior that we want from the conditional degrees of belief is a consequence of the continuity assumption and the direct inference principle.

The continuity assumption is an assumption that the ratio of the statistical terms $[(\alpha \wedge \beta)^{\mathbf{V}}|\mathrm{KB}^{\mathbf{V}}]_{\vec{v}}/[\beta^{\mathbf{V}}|\mathrm{KB}^{\mathbf{V}}]_{\vec{v}'}$ is fairly constant across the different possible worlds. In fact, the continuity assumption will be true whenever this ratio is rigid. We also have the following theorem which demonstrates that the continuity assumption is fairly innocuous:

THEOREM 61 If KB is satisfiable then so is the union of T_0 and all instances of the continuity assumption.

---

[19] Note that this equality is true even though the vector of random designators may not be the same for both terms; i.e., it may be that $\vec{v} \neq \vec{v}'$. The important point is that all of the free variables in $\mathrm{KB}^{\mathbf{V}}$ are in both $\vec{v}$ and $\vec{v}'$; therefore, the complexities introduced by the different vectors of random designators can be handled with the techniques used in Theorem 50.

Proof: First, we note that any instance of the continuity assumption for a particular β will be satisfied if $[\beta^{\mathbf{V}}|\text{KB}^{\mathbf{V}}]_{\vec{v}}$ has the same denotation in every possible world. In this case the term will be rigid, and we can take rigid terms in and out of the expectation operator; i.e., we have $\mathsf{E}(t)/\mathsf{E}(t') = \mathsf{E}(t/t')$ if t' is rigid.

In Theorem 53 we demonstrated that if KB is satisfiable then so is T_0, and we did this by constructing a satisfying model of T_0, M^{comb}. In M^{comb} only the denotation of the constants varies from world to world. Since $[\beta^{\mathbf{V}}|\text{KB}^{\mathbf{V}}]_{\vec{v}}$ has no constants, it will be a rigid term in that model. Therefore, in addition to satisfying T_0, M^{comb} will also satisfy all instances of the continuity assumption. ∎

As a demonstration of how the continuity assumption can be used we present the following example due to Pollock [105].

EXAMPLE 30 X is a genetic abnormality linked to heart disease, and the statistical probability of a person having both syndrome X and heart disease is 0.005. However, the statistical probability of a person of Slavic descent having the syndrome is 0.1, and the probability of a male with the syndrome having heart disease is 0.3. Boris is a male of Slavic descent.

Let us assume that the domain of discourse consists only of people. This allows us to avoid conditioning on a "person" predicate.

Let

```
KB =  male(Boris)   ∧   slavic(Boris)
      ∧  [heart(z) ∧ X(z)]_z = 0.005   ∧   [X(z)|slavic(z)]_z = 0.1
      ∧  [heart(z)|X(z) ∧ male(z)]_z = 0.3.
```

Say that we wish to determine the agent's degree of belief that Boris has both heart disease and syndrome X.

We have that

$$\text{prob}\big(\text{X(Boris)} \wedge \text{heart(Boris)}\big)$$
$$= \mathsf{E}\big([\text{X(v)} \wedge \text{heart(v)}|\text{male(v)} \wedge \text{slavic(v)}]_{\mathbf{v}}\big).$$

Let D_1 be the assumption

$$\big\{\mathsf{E}\big([\text{X(v)} \wedge \text{heart(v)}|\text{male(v)} \wedge \text{slavic(v)}]_{\mathbf{v}}\big) = \mathsf{E}\big([\text{X(v)} \wedge \text{heart(v)}]_{\mathbf{v}}\big)\big\}.$$

The right-hand side of this assumption involves an unconditional probability, but it is not significantly different from the default assumptions that we have specified before. That is, we have that

$$E\big([X(v) \wedge \text{heart}(v)]_v\big) = E\big([X(v) \wedge \text{heart}(v)|\text{true}]_v\big);$$

unconditional statistical terms can be considered to be conditioned on a tautology. This is equivalent to conditioning on the widest possible reference class: the entire domain. In this case we have agreed that the domain consists only of people.

We have that $\text{prob}\big(X(\text{Boris}) \wedge \text{heart}(\text{Boris})\big) = 0.005 \in T_1$. However, there is a better theory than T_1 which contradicts it, making it non-viable.

By reasoning with the probabilistic degrees of belief we have

$$\begin{aligned}\text{prob}\big(&X(\text{Boris}) \wedge \text{heart}(\text{Boris})\big) \\ &= \text{prob}\big(\text{heart}(\text{Boris})|X(\text{Boris})\big) \times \text{prob}\big(X(\text{Boris})\big).\end{aligned}$$

Furthermore, if we include the continuity assumption in T_0, then we will have

$$\begin{aligned}\text{prob}\big(&\text{heart}(\text{Boris})|X(\text{Boris})\big) \\ &= E\big([\text{heart}(v)|X(v) \wedge \text{male}(v) \wedge \text{slavic}(v)]_v\big).\end{aligned}$$

We also have in T_0

$$\text{prob}\big(X(\text{Boris})\big) = E\big([X(v)|\text{male}(v) \wedge \text{slavic}(v)]_v\big) \in T_o.$$

Let

$$\begin{aligned}D_2 = \quad &\{E\big([\text{heart}(v)|X(v) \wedge \text{male}(v) \wedge \text{slavic}(v)]_v\big) \\ &\quad = E\big([\text{heart}(v)|X(v) \wedge \text{male}(v)]_v\big), \\ &E\big([X(v)|\text{male}(v) \wedge \text{slavic}(v)]_v\big) = E\big([X(v)|\text{slavic}(v)]_v\big)\}.\end{aligned}$$

Then $\text{prob}\big(\text{heart}(\text{Boris})|X(\text{Boris})\big) = 0.3 \in T_2$, and $\text{prob}\big(X(\text{Boris})\big) = 0.1 \in T_2$. Therefore, $\text{prob}\big(\text{heart}(\text{Boris}) \wedge X(\text{Boris})\big) = 0.03 \in T_2$.

T_2 contradicts T_1, and it is also preferred to T_1. We have that $\forall v.X(v) \wedge \text{male}(v) \rightarrow \text{true}$, and similarly for $\text{slavic}(v)$. Therefore, both defaults in D_2 are preferred to a default in D_1, and T_1 is not a viable theory.

5.10   Discussion and Comparison

Research on non-monotonic reasoning has been an active area in AI over the past ten years (see Reiter [115] for a useful survey). The formalism presented here offers a statistical perspective on non-monotonicity in *common sense reasoning*. Applications to common sense reasoning are to be distinguished from other applications of non-monotonic reasoning. In particular, non-monotonic reasoning formalisms have been applied to the study of closed-world assumptions in databases and negation as failure in logic programming (e.g., Clark [15], Lifschitz [82], Reiter [116], Przymusinski [112]). The closed-world assumption and negation as failure are computational mechanisms that have found use in practical systems. The closed-world assumption is often used in databases, and negation as failure has been used as the basis of procedural non-monotonicity in AI. Using non-monotonic reasoning formalisms to analyze these mechanism provides useful information, and helps us understand their ad-hoc use in various systems. However, although this is a useful application of non-monotonic reasoning, the exact relationship between closed-world databases and negation as failure on the one hand and common sense reasoning on the other is not clear. Certainly, they are not to be identified with each other. The statistical approach to non-monotonic reasoning does not provide any additional insights into these mechanisms, but, as the examples have demonstrated, it does provide a powerful system of non-monotonic reasoning for common sense applications.

The formalism offers two major contributions to the study of non-monotonicity in common sense reasoning. First, it demonstrates the importance of recognizing formally the difference between default conclusions, which are conclusions that the agent considers to be plausible but not certain, and defaults, which are the rules of thumb that the agent has accepted. By making this differentiation it is possible represent and interpret the defaults in a standard manner. The defaults are assertions about the agent's environment like every other component of the agent's knowledge: they are simply weaker assertions that admit exceptions. Another advantage of this differentiation is that default conclusions are formally distinguished from logically valid conclusions: they are weak conclusions which the agent has less confidence in. Second, it demonstrates the advantage of viewing defaults from a statistical perspective.

In the next two sections we describe more fully the contributions of the statistical approach to default reasoning and offer comparisons with other approaches.

When there is a conflicting collection of relevant information, i.e., alternate default conclusions or multiple extensions, the statistical approach provides a powerful mechanism for resolving the conflicts. However, it does not provide a mechanism for excluding irrelevant information. The problem of relevance and irrelevance is an important issue in default reasoning, and it occurs either implicitly or explicitly in every non-monotonic formalism. In the last section we will discuss the issue of relevance and irrelevance in more detail.

5.10.1 The Statistical Interpretation of Defaults

Although our system uses non-monotonic assumptions that are based on the traditional approach of preserving consistency, for the most part defaults in our system are represented as assertions about the agent's environment. In particular, they are represented as qualitative statistical assertions. Although the interpretation of defaults as statistical assertions may be controversial, it has many benefits, some of which we enumerate below.

1. This representation of the defaults makes them just like any other component of the agent's knowledge: they are assertions about the agent's environment. This means that we can represent the defaults in a traditional manner as formulas of a suitable logical language. In this way, the defaults are given a declarative representation, and a well specified interpretative semantics.

2. Statistical assertions are transparently related to features of the agent's environment. Hence, an agent can learn various defaults (qualitative statistical assertions) though his experience with his environment, and he can test the validity of various defaults by examining features of his environment.

3. We can reason with the defaults by reasoning about statistics. So, for example, from the default "Typically canaries are yellow," and the terminological assertion "All yellow objects are not green" we can deduce the default "Typically canaries are not green." That

is,

$$\vdash \begin{pmatrix} [\texttt{yellow}(\texttt{x})|\texttt{canary}(\texttt{x})]_\texttt{x} > c \\ \forall \texttt{x}.\texttt{yellow}(\texttt{x}) \rightarrow \neg\texttt{green}(\texttt{x}) \end{pmatrix} \rightarrow [\neg\texttt{green}(\texttt{x})|\texttt{canary}(\texttt{x})]_\texttt{x} > c.$$

Example 14 (Chapter 3) demonstrates the extensive range of reasoning made possible by interpreting the defaults statistically. It is also important to note that the conclusions generated from such reasoning matches general intuitions about how defaults should behave. This is evidence that the statistical interpretation of defaults is reasonable.

4. Once we accept the intuitively reasonable assumption that default conclusions should be based on everything that is known, the commonly used subset and specificity preferences follow directly from the semantic properties of the statistics.

5. Reasoning with the statistics provides a natural mechanism for eliminating certain unintuitive theories (extensions). In Example 24.5 we demonstrated that it was statistically impossible for the majority of adult university students to be employed given that most university students are adult and that most are unemployed. That is, we are able to eliminate an unintuitive possibility by reasoning with the defaults.

6. By treating the defaults as simply a different type of assertion we have been able to develop a logical representation that can deal with relations and other more complex forms of default assertions in a uniform manner. Furthermore, there is no conflict between default assertions that involve statistical terms, categorical assertions that involve the universal quantifier, and assertions about particular individuals. All are given an semantic treatment that respects their fundamental differences. As a result, the formalism can reason about the interaction between these types of assertions, and can deal with situations where different types of knowledge are present, as demonstrated in Example 24.8. Furthermore, by treating each type of assertion in a semantically different and coherent manner we do not require that the knowledge base be split between evidence and background context (cf. the approach of Geffner and Pearl [36]).

7. The formalism offers a unified approach to both qualitative common sense reasoning and more quantitative and exact evidential reasoning. We do not have two distinct modes of reasoning, "common sense" and "scientific"; instead there is a single framework that adapts to the quality of information that the agent possesses. If the agent has precise numeric information the formalism can reason quantitatively, otherwise it can reason qualitatively about the underlying, but unknown, quantities.

Our interpretation of defaults as qualitative statistical assertions is a major difference between our approach and that taken by other nonmonotonic reasoning formalisms. Below we contrast this interpretation of defaults with that given by some of the alternate formalisms that have been developed.

Default and Autoepistemic Logics

Default logic and autoepistemic logic have much in common, as is perhaps best demonstrated by the existence of certain formal translations between the two (Konolige [62], Marek and Truszczynski [86]). Although defaults in default logic exist outside of the language, as extra rules of inference, they are interpreted in a manner similar to their use in autoepistemic logic; namely, they are treated as policies or rules that an agent may follow which allow him to extend his beliefs beyond what is allowed by logical consequence, subject to the condition of maintaining consistency. In default logic there is no explicit mention of the agent whose beliefs are being extended. However, there is clearly an implicit reference to an agent. For example, a program that uses defaults to extend its knowledge base can be viewed as being an agent who believes the contents of the knowledge base and who uses the defaults as policies for expanding its set of beliefs. Autoepistemic logic makes the agent explicit, and encodes defaults as formulas which involve an explicit belief operator. For example, in autoepistemic logic the default "Birds typically fly" is commonly encoded as the formula $\forall x.\text{bird}(x) \land \neg B \neg \text{fly}(x) \to \text{fly}(x)$. This says that the agent's lack of belief in a bird being unable to fly is sufficient reason to conclude that it can fly.

The use of a belief operator gives autoepistemic logic an advantage over default logic: it can provide an explicit representation and interpretation for the defaults by representing them as formulas of the language. The meaning or interpretation of the defaults is then determined by the formal semantic interpretation of the formulas used to represent them. Therefore, it would seem that autoepistemic logic is capable of reasoning with the defaults. However, this is true only to a limited extent. For example, from the default "Typically canaries are yellow," and the terminological assertion "All yellow objects are not green" we cannot deduce the default "Typically canaries are not green." Rather we can only deduce the formula

$$\forall x.\text{canary}(x) \wedge \neg B\neg \text{yellow}(x) \rightarrow \neg \text{green}(x).$$

As pointed out by Reiter [115], it is not clear whether this last formula can legitimately be interpreted as meaning "Typically canaries are not green;" certainly, there is a difference between this formula and the formula that would normally be used to represent the default: $\forall x.\text{canary}(x) \wedge \neg B\text{green}(x) \rightarrow \neg \text{green}(x)$. The normal representation relates the properties of being green and being a canary, while the inferred formula contains an extraneous reference to the property of being yellow. Furthermore, autoepistemic logic is quite incapable of performing the sophisticated kinds of reasoning with defaults possible in the statistical approach. For example, we cannot eliminate unintuitive extensions by reasoning with the defaults in autoepistemic logic.

Autoepistemic and default logics' limited ability to reason with defaults stems from the fact that they interpret defaults purely as rules acting on the agent's beliefs. Under this view the logical connections between the defaults depend only on the logical connections between the agent's beliefs, and these are not necessarily very strong.

These logics fail to capture the empirical component of defaults. For example, there are certain properties of the agent's *environment* that makes the policy $\forall x.\text{bird}(x) \wedge \neg B\neg \text{fly}(x) \rightarrow \text{fly}(x)$ a reasonable policy for the agent to follow, and that makes the policy $\forall x.\text{bird}(x) \wedge \neg B\text{fly}(x) \rightarrow \neg \text{fly}(x)$ an unreasonable policy. There is no attempt in default or autoepistemic logics to capture these empirical features. The statistical approach, on the other hand, makes a direct attempt to model the empirical content of the defaults. On this view the reason that the first policy is preferable to the second is the statistical fact that most birds fly. Therefore, the agent will be more often right than wrong if he uses the first policy and more often wrong than right if he uses the second. This empirical interpretation forces strong logical connections between the defaults, and thus permits an extensive amount of reasoning.

Conventions

There is, however, an alternate view of defaults under which there is no reason to suppose that defaults have an empirical component. This is the view that defaults express conventions, and that non-monotonic reasoning models a notion of reasoning with conventions (e.g. Reiter [115], McCarthy [87]). Under this view $\forall x.\text{bird}(x) \wedge \neg B\text{fly}(x) \rightarrow \text{fly}(x)$ is a reasonable policy because it expresses a communication convention. It does not depend on the objective truth of "Most birds fly" for its justification; rather, once the convention is agreed upon it is not subsequently influenced by any empirical features of the agent's environment. If another agent tells you that Tweety is a bird and nothing else, then, under the assumption that the other agent is following conventions, that agent is really telling you that Tweety is a bird *and* that she flies. Hence, you can legitimately infer that Tweety flies just from the information that she is a bird.

It is true that convention plays a role in the non-monotonicity of common sense reasoning. For example, conventions play an important role when solving puzzles like the missionaries-and-cannibals problem. However, common sense reasoning must *also* depend on empirical information.

The reason is that communication conventions are not of any assistance when the agent has to deal with his environment, as compared to dealing with other agents. The world does not follow our conventions; rather we have to accumulate empirical information to understand how the world behaves. For example, if we discover that Tweety is a bird, we cannot expect that if Tweety lacked the ability to fly the world would have displayed this information to us. This means that the viewpoint of non-monotonic reasoning as reasoning about conventions tells us very little about how an agent should make default inferences when reasoning about his environment.

This problem occurs even when the agent is interacting with other agents. Say that the communicating agent does not know anything about Tweety's flying ability. When he tells another agent that Tweety is a bird he will be obligated, under convention, to also inform the other agent that he does not know if Tweety can fly. Now the agent who re-

ceived the information about Tweety is in a situation where convention
cannot legitimize the default inference "Tweety flies." Only empirical
information can justify this inference. The ultimate source of information for all agents is their external environment, and typically it does
not disclose everything. This suggests that much of the information obtained from other agents will be incomplete, and will not be suitable for
sanctioning default conclusions by convention. What legitimizes many
default inferences must be knowledge of general empirical features of the
environment. So, for example, what legitimizes or justifies the inference
that Tweety flies is, on the statistical view, general empirical knowledge
about the proportion of birds that fly. This property of the world makes
it more often true than false that an arbitrary bird will be able to fly.

It is instructive to examine the formalism developed here in light of
our discussion of conventions versus general empirical knowledge. The
formalism uses both kinds of knowledge in its default reasoning: empirical defaults encoded as statistical assertions, and "conventional" defaults encoded as assumptions that the agent can make to extend his
base theory. The latter type of defaults are based on, or can potentially be justified by, the conventions which the agent uses to determine
the meaning of his language. Therefore, these defaults, although they
are different from the typical default in autoepistemic logic, can still be
viewed as being defaults based on convention.

To see why this is so we can examine the form of these defaults. They
are all formulas similar to $\mathsf{E}\big([\mathsf{P}(\mathbf{x})|\mathsf{Q}(\mathbf{x})]_{\mathbf{x}}\big) = \mathsf{E}\big([\mathsf{P}(\mathbf{x})|\mathsf{R}(\mathbf{x})]_{\mathbf{x}}\big)$, where Q is
a subset of R. From the semantics of the language this asserts that the
expected proportion of P's in the subset Q is equal to the expected proportion in the superset R. It is a set-theoretic fact that the proportion of
P's in most subsets of R will be close to the proportion of P's in R, with
the agreement becoming better as R increases in size. Although things
are not so simple in our semantic models (e.g., the denotation of R may
vary and we may be dealing with non-uniform distributions), this fact
gives some justification for our default. That is, the default is based
on, and can potentially be justified by, the semantic interpretation of
the language. If the agent was to choose to interpret his language by
a different set of conventions these defaults may no longer be applicable. On the other hand, the empirical defaults represent features of the
agent's environment. Their form would change if the agent changed his
language, but their content and applicability would not.

Of course, although the reader might accept our argument that both conventions and empirical information have an important role in non-monotonic reasoning, he may still question our interpretation of the empirical information as statistical information. One argument in favor of the statistical interpretation is the transparent relationship between statistical assertions and intuitive features of the environment. However, the strongest argument that can be offered lies in the examples we have presented. These examples have demonstrated that the conclusions arrived at by reasoning with defaults under the statistical interpretation match our intuitions. The formalism produces the intuitively correct theories that other formalisms aim to achieve.

Circumscription

In the circumscriptive approach to default reasoning, defaults are encoded using abnormality predicates, ab. The default "Birds typically fly" would be represented by the formula $\forall x.\text{bird}(x) \wedge \neg\text{ab}(x) \rightarrow \text{fly}(x)$, which says that normal birds fly. Here the set of birds is divided into two subsets: those that are abnormal and those that are normal. All the normal birds are fliers. The statistical encoding accomplishes something similar. Instead of introducing an abnormality predicate it simply divides the set of birds into the two subsets fliers and non-fliers. The statistical assertion $[\text{fly}(x)|\text{bird}(x)]_x > c$ then specifies that most birds are in the former subset.

The intuition in the circumscriptive approach is that abnormal birds are rare, and therefore we can circumscribe the ab predicate forcing it to have a minimum extension. However, the circumscription process which minimizes the extension of the ab predicate is outside of the logic, and generally cannot be represented or reasoned with inside of the language.[20] That is, the minimality which is part of the meaning of the ab predicates is only captured meta-logically. The statistical approach, on the other hand, uses an explicit representation of the fact that the set of non-flying birds is small, and it can reason with this fact in the logic. This gives it an advantage when dealing with complex interactions between "abnormalities." In certain cases, as demonstrated in the examples, one can resolve these interactions by reasoning with the statistics.

---

[20] In some rare cases the minimization (a second-order formula) can be represented in the language, as an equivalent first-order formula (Lifschitz [83,81]).

The major difficulty with the circumscriptive approach to default reasoning, however, is an unresolved problem, originally pointed out by Perlis [103]. Say that KB consists of the formulas

$$KB = \quad \forall x.bird(x) \wedge \neg ab(x) \rightarrow fly(x)$$
$$\wedge \quad \exists x.bird(x) \wedge \neg fly(x)$$
$$\wedge \quad bird(Tweety).$$

From this knowledge circumscription is incapable of producing the default inference fly(Tweety). This results from the fact that $\exists x.ab(x)$ is a logical consequence of KB, and in some minimal models (i.e., minimal with respect to the extension of ab) Tweety is that abnormal bird. Therefore, Tweety is not a flier in all the minimal models; i.e., fly(Tweety) is not entailed by the class of minimal models. This result runs counter to intuition, as the entire enterprise of default reasoning is to make conclusions under full awareness that exceptions exist. Knowledge of exceptions does not present a problem for the statistical approach. In fact, from the statistical information $[fly(x)|bird(x)]_x < 1$ we can deduce $\exists x.bird(x) \wedge \neg fly(x)$.

Other Probabilistic Approaches

Geffner and Pearl [35,36,102] have developed an alternative probabilistic approach to non-monotonic reasoning based on ϵ-probabilities. In this approach defaults are encoded as statements of almost extreme probability. For example, the default "Birds typically fly" would be encoded as $prob(fly(x)|bird(x)) \geq 1 - \epsilon$; i.e., the probability that x flies given that x is a bird is greater than $1 - \epsilon$ for any $\epsilon > 0$.

The system of inference built around this encoding of defaults is, like our statistical formalism, divided into two parts which Pearl calls the "conservative core" and the "adventurous shell." The conservative core is a variant of Adams's conditional logic [2], and involves reasoning with ϵ-probabilities. The adventurous shell is similar to our own system of non-monotonic reasoning with the statistical terms. It invokes assumptions of irrelevance to sanction default conclusions in the face of extra information. For example, knowing that a bird is yellow prohibits the conservative core from making the inference that it flies. The adventurous shell allows the assumption that being yellow does not affect the probability of a bird flying; i.e., it permits the assumption that $prob(fly|bird) = prob(fly|bird \wedge yellow)$. This is very similar to the default assumption used in our system:

$$E\big([\texttt{fly}(\texttt{x})|\texttt{bird}(\texttt{x})]_\texttt{x}\big) = E\big([\texttt{fly}(\texttt{x})|\texttt{bird}(\texttt{x}) \wedge \texttt{yellow}(\texttt{x})]_\texttt{x}\big).$$

The main difference in this approach lies in its use of ϵ-probabilities instead of ordinary probabilities.

Pearl makes a convincing argument that empirical support is required in non-monotonic reasoning. However, when he advocates the use of ϵ-probabilities it is no longer clear that his system has the empirical support he argues is so important. That is, although the empirical content of ordinary non-extreme statistical assertions is clear, the empirical content of a statement like $\texttt{prob}(\texttt{fly}(\texttt{x})|\texttt{bird}(\texttt{x})) \geq 1 - \epsilon$ is not. Certainly, the proportion of flying birds is not arbitrarily close to one: the set of non-flying birds has a finite size. The difference between real world frequencies and ϵ-probabilities leads to conflicts between the two.

Geffner and Pearl [36] have identified five rules of inference that are sound and complete for ϵ-probabilities. Three of these rules remain valid when we interpret defaults as statements of statistical majority. The other two, however, are not valid for ordinary probabilities.

1. One of the valid rules for ϵ-probabilities is the rule of cumulativity: from $\alpha \vdash_\Delta \beta$ and $\alpha \vdash_\Delta \lambda$ infer $\alpha \wedge \beta \vdash_\Delta \lambda$, where $\vdash_\Delta$ indicates entailment under ϵ-probabilities. This inference is valid under the semantics of ϵ-probabilities, but not under real frequencies. For example, we can have a collection of 100 objects in a box $(\alpha = \texttt{in-box}(\texttt{x}))$ of which 51 are balls $(\beta = \texttt{ball}(\texttt{x}))$ and 51 are black $(\lambda = \texttt{black}(\texttt{x}))$, and at the same time we could have only 2 black balls in the box, giving $[\texttt{black}(\texttt{x})|\texttt{ball}(\texttt{x}) \wedge \texttt{in-box}(\texttt{x})]_\texttt{x} = 2/51$.

   In this situation the properties of being black and being a ball are highly negatively correlated. We could make the cumulativity inference in the statistical approach if we make the assumption $E\big([\lambda|\alpha \wedge \beta]_\texttt{v}\big) = E\big([\lambda|\alpha]_\texttt{v}\big)$. That is, if we make the assumption that being a ball has no influence on the chance of being black, then we will be able to make the cumulative inference that a ball in the box is likely to be black.[21]

---

[21] Note that if all we know about an individual t is that it is in the box, T_0 would contain both $\texttt{prob}(\texttt{black}(\texttt{t})) > 0.5$ and $\texttt{prob}(\texttt{ball}(\texttt{t})) > 0.5$, but it would not contain $\texttt{prob}(\texttt{black}(\texttt{t}) \wedge \texttt{ball}(\texttt{t})) > 0.5$. We will discuss this point in more detail later.

2. The other valid rule for ϵ-probabilities is the rule of contraction:
from $\alpha \vdash_\Delta \beta$ and $\alpha \wedge \beta \vdash_\Delta \lambda$ infer $\alpha \vdash_\Delta \lambda$. Again this rule can
be violated by real frequencies. With a different collection of 100
objects in the box we could have that 75 of the objects are balls,
and that 49 of these balls are black ($\approx 65\%$), but at the same time
have only 49 black objects in the box (i.e., only the black balls).

Once again we can capture the contraction rule in the statistical
approach by making the assumption involved explicit, i.e., with
the non-monotonic assumption $\mathsf{E}([\lambda|\alpha]_\mathbf{x}) = \mathsf{E}([\lambda|\alpha \wedge \beta]_\mathbf{x})$ which is
the assumption that being a ball has no influence on the chance of
being black.[22]

Pearl claims that ϵ-probabilities are an abstraction or simplification of
reality, and therefore we should expect there to be situations in which the
abstraction is not applicable. He further claims that [102, p. 513] "Each
abstraction constitutes an expedient simplification of reality, tailored to
serve a specialized set of tasks. Each simplification is supported *by a*
different symbol processing machinery..." (emphasis added).

It is true that there are many situations where these two special rules
valid only for ϵ-probabilities seem to be reasonable, and Pearl's claim
that ϵ-probabilities form a useful abstraction may be correct. However,
these examples demonstrate that there are perfectly understandable situations in which ϵ-probabilities are inapplicable. These situations are
not beyond our common sense intuitions: someone can understand them
even if they know very little about probability theory. Hence, it is not
clear if there exists any easily identifiable boundaries separating the
tasks for which ϵ-probabilities are applicable from those where they are
not. Furthermore, it should be noted that with ϵ-probabilities the extra
assumptions are inextricably bound into the formalism. Hence, as Pearl
points out, different situations may force us to switch our entire mode
of reasoning: we are faced with the situation where we have completely
different logics determining our reasoning in different situations.

This is to be contrasted with the statistical approach. As we have
demonstrated, the extra inferences sanctioned by ϵ-probabilities can be
captured by making extra assumptions of conditional independence. By
making extra assumptions we retain the same underlying logic, the logic

---

[22] Note that without any assumptions $\mathsf{E}\big([\texttt{black(x)}|\texttt{in-box(x)}]_\mathbf{x}\big) > c^2$ can be de-
rived, but if c is not large enough this conclusion may not be sufficient.

determined by the semantics of the statistical assertions. When we are faced with a situation that violates our assumptions we can retract our assumptions, we do not have to retract *our entire logic*.[23] In fact, the approach of ϵ-probabilities already requires a mechanism for making and retracting such assumptions: the adventurous shell must make and retract assumptions of conditional independence to deal with irrelevant information.

Perhaps there are real advantages to the abstraction offered by ϵ-probabilities, advantages that outweigh the complexities of shifting logics. Even in this case, however, the statistical approach offers the important contribution of increasing our understanding of the assumptions being made by this abstraction.

Conditional Logics

Delgrande [18,19] has applied conditional logics to default reasoning (see also recent work by Boutilier [8]). Conditional logics are logics that have been developed in philosophy to account for the properties of conditional statements in natural language. It is well known that conditionals in natural language cannot be represented accurately by standard material implication. For example, we can assert the two conditionals "If a match were struck, it would light" and "If a wet match were struck, it would not light." It seems reasonable to assume that both of these statements are true, but if we attempt to use material implication to represent these conditionals we would obtain a contradictory pair of formulas $M \rightarrow L$ and $(M \wedge W) \rightarrow \neg L$.

Conditional logics attempt to solve this problem by adding a new connective, a conditional connective '$\Rightarrow$'. In most conditional logics the two formulas $M \Rightarrow L$ and $(M \wedge W) \Rightarrow \neg L$ are not contradictory. To supply a semantic interpretation for this new connective, conditional logics rely on possible world semantics, making the truth value of formulas like $M \Rightarrow L$ dependent on the possible worlds that are accessible from the current world.

Delgrande's approach to default reasoning interprets the accessibility

---

[23]This is more in accord with the manner in which abstractions are used in other sciences. For example, in physics the abstraction of a frictionless plane is an assumption that can be retracted without retracting the underlying logic of mechanics. There may be such a shift in "logics", e.g., when we move from Newtonian mechanics to reasoning about relativistic effects, but clearly one does not want to perform such major shifts unless absolutely necessary.

relation in these possible world semantics as a relationship of uniformity. Under this interpretation the world w_2 is accessible from w_1, $w_1 R w_2$, if w_2 is at least as uniform or at least as unexceptional as w_1. Using this interpretation he proceeds to develop a conditional logic suitable for default reasoning. In this approach defaults are represented using the conditional connective, with the default "Birds typically fly" being represented by the formula $\forall x.\mathtt{bird}(x) \Rightarrow \mathtt{fly}(x)$. These formulas are intended to represent the assertion that every bird normally flies. However, given $\mathtt{bird(Tweety)}$ the default conclusion $\mathtt{fly(Tweety)}$ cannot be inferred: inference in the logic is not sufficient to generate default conclusions. To obtain the expected types of default inferences we must invoke two extra assumptions.

One assumption is that the world being modeled is one of the least exceptional worlds, and the other is that information not known to be relevant to the default inference is assumed to be irrelevant. The assumption that the world is unexceptional is required since the conditional connective used to represent the defaults refers to conditions that hold in the least exceptional worlds; it does not make any assertions about the other worlds. The assumption of relevance, on the other hand, is required because the conditional connective is not robust under strengthening of the antecedent. That is, $A \Rightarrow B$ does not entail that $(A \wedge C) \Rightarrow B$, and indeed, as we saw with the wet match example, it should not. For example, this means that $\forall x.\mathtt{bird}(x) \Rightarrow \mathtt{fly}(x)$ does not imply $\forall x.(\mathtt{bird}(x) \wedge \mathtt{yellow}(x)) \Rightarrow \mathtt{fly}(x)$. Hence, an extra assumption is needed to conclude that being yellow does not affect a bird's flying ability.

The approach of conditional logics is in some ways the closest of the alternative approaches to the statistical formalism presented here. In particular, the two assumptions made in the conditional logic approach have analogues in the statistical approach. The obvious case is the assumption of irrelevance. Like the conditional connective, probabilistic conditioning is not robust under strengthening, e.g., $[\mathtt{fly}(x)|\mathtt{bird}(x) \wedge \mathtt{yellow}]_x$ is not constrained by $[\mathtt{fly}(x)|\mathtt{bird}(x)]_x$. This is why we need a mechanism for performing nonmonotonic reasoning with the statistical terms. The assumption of normality also has an analogue in our system, as our principle of direct inference. Direct inference involves the randomization of the particular individuals under consideration. When we randomize the individuals we are assuming that they are unexceptional instances of the class of individuals that share all the same properties.

Conditional logic also comes closest to the statistical approach in its ability to reason with the defaults. For example, if all yellow objects are necessarily not green, then conditional logic can deduce the default 'Typically canaries are not green" from the default "Typically canaries are yellow." That is,

$$\forall x.\text{canary}(x) \Rightarrow \text{yellow}(x)$$
$$\rightarrow \forall x.\text{canary}(x) \Rightarrow \neg \text{green}(x)$$

is valid in Delgrande's logic. However, it cannot capture more intricate forms of reasoning, e.g., the reasoning involved in eliminating unintuitive theories as in Example 24.5. Another advantage of the statistical approach lies in its ability to integrate qualitative and quantitative reasoning, offering a smooth transition from rough default reasoning to more exact evidential reasoning.

The most important advantage, however, of the statistical approach over conditional logics lies in the transparency of the semantic notions. There is a clear and obvious relationship between statistical assertions and properties of the world that we can detect and validate, measure and learn; the same cannot be said of the rather abstract "uniformity" relationship over possible worlds.

It is possible, however, that like ϵ-probabilities conditional logics can serve as useful abstractions in certain situations. In this case the statistical approach can serve the important function of increasing our understanding of this abstraction. In particular, it may be able to provide a better intuitive understanding of the notion of "uniformity" by relating this notion to well understood statistical notions.

Prototypes

There is one other issue that must be addressed in any discussion of the semantics of defaults: prototypes. We have written our default about birds as "Birds typically fly," and as Reiter and Criscuolo [117] have pointed out, there are usually two connotations of the word "typical." One interpretation, that we have use extensively here, is the statistical interpretation of majority; "Birds typically fly" is to be interpreted as "Most birds fly." The other interpretation is that this is an assertion about the prototypical bird; "Birds typically fly" is to be interpreted as "The prototypical bird flies." The notion of a prototype is one of the intuitions behind Minsky's concept of frames [90]. When an individual instantiates a frame he inherits all of the prototypical properties of the class of individuals identified by that frame.

It has often been claimed that the notion of 'most' has no relationship to the notion of prototype. The typical argument (e.g., Konolige and Myers [63]) points out that generally the majority of the members of a class do not have *all* of the properties of the prototypical individual, and then concludes that the two notions cannot be related. For example, if we say that the prototypical banker is a Republican, is more than 50 years old, wear glasses, is married, etc., there may be a very small number of bankers with all of these properties. The confusion in this argument lies in its failure to distinguish between the probability of a property and the probability of a conjunction of properties. It is perfectly consistent to assert that for each of prototypical property most bankers have that property and at the same time assert that only a very small number, or none at all, have all of these properties. In the formalism developed here the agent could have a high degree of belief in an individual possessing each one of these properties, while at the same time having a low degree of belief in the individual possessing their conjunction. In fact, this seems to be the reasonable thing to do. In what sense is it reasonable or rational to conclude by default that an *arbitrary* individual has the conjunction of all the properties possessed by a prototypical individual? This amounts to assuming that the individual is a prototypical individual, and prototypes may be very rare, or worse non-existent.[24]

The non-trivial question about prototypes and majority is whether or not the *primitive* properties of a prototypical instance of a class are shared by the majority of members of the class. This is a difficult question to answer, since the notion of a prototype is imprecisely specified. However, when we are performing default inferences we are making inferences about particular individuals, individuals who are known to be members of various classes. There is no reason to suppose that these individuals are prototypes (whatever that may be). When making default inferences about a particular individual, information about prototypes

---

[24]If the agent knows that no prototypical individuals exist, then this willingness to impart the conjunction of the prototypical properties to an arbitrary individual leads to inconsistency. This is a form of the lottery paradox, which will be discussed later.

is only useful if it reflects what is usually the case among the classes to which the individual belongs. That is, regardless of whether or not the primitive properties of a prototype are shared by the majority, it is the general properties of the entire class of individuals not the properties of the prototypical individual that are important in default reasoning.

Other Statistical Notions Besides Majority

Although we have concentrated almost exclusively on default notions represented as assertions of statistical majority, it should be noted that the formalism we have developed is much more general: it can deal with other kinds of qualitative statistical information which sanction other kinds of default inferences.

For example, as Ginsberg has pointed out some nonmonotonic formalisms allow contraposition [37]. So, for example, in the circumscriptive approach to default reasoning one can infer the default "Non-flying objects are typically not birds," from the default "Birds typically fly." However, indiscriminate applications of contraposition often leads to incorrect inferences (Konolige and Myers [63]). Contraposition is not sanctioned by statistical majority. For example, a reasonable default, that also makes sense when interpreted as a statement of statistical majority, is "Living things are typically not fliers," but from this default we do not want to conclude the contrapositive "Fliers are typically not living things," as there are many more living fliers, e.g., insects, than there are non-living fliers, e.g., planes.

However, the inference that a non-flier is not a bird seems reasonable, and in fact this inference can be captured and, more importantly, explained by the statistical interpretation. The statistical information that is used to make this inference is not, however, statistical majority.

EXAMPLE 31 (OTHER TYPES OF STATISTICS)
Say that the agent has the reasonable beliefs that birds are more likely to be fliers than non-birds, and that birds are only a minority of the objects that exist. We can represent this information in the following knowledge base:

$$\text{KB} = [\text{fly}(x)|\text{bird}(x)]_x > [\text{fly}(x)|\neg\text{bird}(x)]_x$$
$$\wedge \quad [\neg\text{bird}(x)]_x > [\text{bird}(x)]_x$$
$$\wedge \quad \neg\text{fly}(\text{Object}).$$

From KB the direct inference mechanism produces the inference that

$\text{prob}(\text{bird}(\text{Object})) < 0.5 \in T_0$; i.e., it is unlikely that a non-flier like Object is a bird.

From $[\text{fly}(\text{x})|\text{bird}(\text{x})]_\text{x} > [\text{fly}(\text{x})|\neg\text{bird}(\text{x})]_\text{x}$ we can deduce that

$$1 - [\neg\text{fly}(\text{x})|\text{bird}(\text{x})]_\text{x} > 1 - [\neg\text{fly}(\text{x})|\neg\text{bird}(\text{x})]_\text{x},$$

since $1 - [\neg\alpha|\beta]_{\vec{z}} = [\alpha|\beta]_{\vec{z}}$. Therefore, have that

$$[\neg\text{fly}(\text{x})|\text{bird}(\text{x})]_\text{x} < [\neg\text{fly}(\text{x})|\neg\text{bird}(\text{x})]_\text{x}$$

is deducible from KB. This means that the likelihood ratio of $\neg\text{fly}$ given bird is less than one; i.e., $[\neg\text{fly}(\text{x})|\text{bird}(\text{x})]_\text{x}/[\neg\text{fly}(\text{x})|\neg\text{bird}(\text{x})]_\text{x} < 1$.

We also have that $[\text{bird}(\text{x})]_\text{x}/[\neg\text{bird}(\text{x})]_\text{x} < 1$; i.e., the a priori odds of an object being a bird is less than one. It is a statistical fact that

$$\frac{[\text{bird}(\text{x})|\neg\text{fly}(\text{x})]_\text{x}}{[\neg\text{bird}(\text{x})|\neg\text{fly}(\text{x})]_\text{x}} = \frac{[\neg\text{fly}(\text{x})|\text{bird}(\text{x})]_\text{x}}{[\neg\text{fly}(\text{x})|\neg\text{bird}(\text{x})]_\text{x}} \times \frac{[\text{bird}(\text{x})]_\text{x}}{[\neg\text{bird}(\text{x})]_\text{x}}.$$

This is simply Bayes's rule expressed in terms of odds and likelihood ratios (see, e.g., Pearl [101, p. 35]). Since the two fractions of the right-hand side are both less than one, we have that the left-hand side is less than one. That is, from KB we can deduce that $[\text{bird}(\text{x})|\neg\text{fly}(\text{x})]_\text{x} < 0.5$. Applying direct inference to the formula bird(Object) gives the stated result.

This example demonstrates that the formalism is capable of reasoning with other types of statistical information besides majority, e.g., qualitative information about likelihood ratios, and that other types of statistical information may serve as useful representations for some forms of default information.[25] The example also gives another demonstration of the usefulness of the statistical interpretation. Under this interpretation there is a clear explanation of why the contrapositive inference is legitimate. The inference in this example depended on two facts, (1) birds are more likely to be fliers than non-birds, and (2) birds are in the minority. With the default "Living things are typically not fliers" although we have that living things are in the minority (among all of the

---

[25] Another interesting type of qualitative probabilistic information that has been investigated is the notion of changes in probability (Neufeld [96], Wellman [132]). That is, relations of the form $[\text{P}(\text{x})|\text{Q}(\text{x})]_\text{x} > [\text{P}(\text{x})]_\text{x}$; i.e., learning Q changes the probability of P. It is not difficult to see that our logic is also capable of reasoning with this type of statistical information.

objects in the world), we do not have that living things are more likely to be non-fliers than non-living things. Hence, the semantics provides a criterion for detecting when the inference is not applicable.

5.10.2 Default versus Deductive Conclusions

Another contribution of our approach is its formal distinction between deductive and default conclusions. In our system of default reasoning the logical consequences of KB are the only assertions that will be fully believed by the agent, i.e., assigned probability one; all default conclusions will be assigned probability less than one. One of the advantages of this distinction is that the probabilistically graded default conclusions avoid the lottery paradox.

Various writers (e.g., Etherington [26]) have noted that default conclusions should be distinguished from deductive conclusions. This follows from the need to revise one's beliefs when faced with new information. Clearly, if there is a choice between retracting a deductive conclusion or a default conclusion, one should retract the default conclusion; it is less certain. However, none of the other approaches to default reasoning discussed here are capable of making this distinction.[26] To be sure, one can keep a record of the source of the conclusions, marking those that depended on default reasoning. But such an approach is a meta-level control on reasoning; it is not part of the logical specification of reasoning. This problem becomes particularly acute when the agent must reason in situations that have different costs of error, the typical case for intelligent agents. Under such circumstances, approaches with ungraded default conclusions provide very little guidance for the agent. For example, Langlotz and Shortliffe have argued that traditional non-monotonic methods are not suitable for critical application like medical diagnosis [74]. The statistical approach, on the other hand, provides probabilistically graded conclusions and these lead naturally to decision theory, a well studied mechanism for dealing with the cost of error.[27]

---

[26] The Theorist system (Poole et al. [110]) does make a distinction between conclusions that follow from facts versus conclusions that follow from facts plus assumptions. However, this distinction is more in the spirit of a meta-level control: whenever an assumption is used the conclusion is tagged by the reasoner.

[27] Of course, there are open problems to be solved before decision theory can be applied in conjunction with our formalism. For example, our formalism generally produces qualitative probabilities; it is not clear how decision theory can be applied with such probabilities, but see Loui [84] for some work on decision theory with indeterminate probabilities.

The Lottery Paradox

An important property of the probabilistic conclusions generated by our formalism is that they avoid the lottery paradox (Kyburg [65]). Consider a fair lottery with one winner and 1,000,000 tickets. The chance of any particular ticket winning is very small (1/1,000,000). Furthermore, we can make this probability as small as we wish, by increasing the number of tickets in the lottery. Surely by any definition of default, a reasonable default would be that any particular ticket will not win.[28] Hence, by default reasoning we conclude that ticket #1 will not win; similarly we conclude that ticket #2 will not win, and so on for all of the tickets. Now we have concluded by default that every ticket will not win. If default conclusions are accorded the same status as deductive conclusions, in particular if we sanction the conjunction of two default conclusions, thus sanctioning the conjunction of any finite number of default conclusions, we will be faced with a logical contradiction. The conjunction of all of these default conclusions, one for every ticket, contradicts the fact that there must a winning ticket.

Poole [109] has pointed out that the lottery paradox can occur in real applications of non-monotonic reasoning; it is far from being an artificial phenomena. Our previous discussion on the rarity of prototypes is very similar to the example that Poole uses. He points out that every particular class of birds is exceptional in some aspect. Therefore, if we conclude by default that a particular bird is unexceptional in each aspect and conjoin these conclusions, we will be faced with a contradiction, as every bird is a member of some particular class of birds.

As Kyburg [69] has pointed out the culprit in the lottery paradox is not the acceptance of the default conclusions, rather is it the acceptance of the conjunction of the default conclusions. In the formalisms we have described, default conclusions have the same status as deductive conclusions, and since deductive conclusions are closed under conjunction so are the default conclusions. Hence, these formalisms are paralyzed by the lottery paradox.

Before we discuss the specific problems these approaches have in dealing with the lottery, let us be more explicit about the instance of the paradox we will consider. Assume that by default birds have properties

---

[28] Note that by making the lottery large enough we can make the default conclusion more reliable than any of the agent's beliefs, i.e., more reliable than the premises from which deductive conclusions are drawn.

P_1 through P_n, but that no bird has all of these properties, and let T be an individual for whom all we know is bird(T).

Default and autoepistemic logics generate multiple extensions or theories. In each one of these theories the bird T will be abnormal with respect to some property P_i; i.e., in each theory T will fail to have property P_i for some i. Hence, these approaches provide no guidance to the agent. If each extension is a viable description of the agent's beliefs (e.g., Reiter [115]), then an extension will exist that contains the negation of every default conclusion. But there is no reason for the agent to decide that T fails to have P_i for any particular i. This makes these extensions questionable descriptions of the agent's beliefs, as each one contains an arbitrary choice. If the intersection of the different extensions describes the agent's beliefs (e.g., Przymusinski [111]), then this intersection will contain no default conclusions. That is, the strongest statement the intersection will contain is the formula $\neg P_1(T) \vee \cdots \vee \neg P_n(T)$, but this formula was already a consequence of the initial description. In either case the formalism fails to match our intuition that the default conclusion should be made in spite of the paradox. Note that we cannot base our conclusions on what is true in the majority of extensions, as then we would be using statistical considerations without any explicit representation of the underlying statistical information.

Conditional logics suffer from similar difficulties. Dependent on what meta-logical assumptions are made these logics can either produce multiple extensions each failing to conclude P_i from some i, or a single extension containing no default conclusions.

The circumscriptive approach of minimizing abnormalities is the only one of the traditional approaches that offers a possible solution to the lottery paradox, but this solution has some unsatisfactory features. In the circumscriptive approach the defaults are encoded using abnormality predicates, e.g., the i-th default is represented as $\forall x.\text{bird}(x) \wedge \neg \text{ab}_i(x) \rightarrow P_i(x)$. If one minimizes all of the abnormality predicates in parallel (Lifschitz [83]), then for every i the class of minimal models will contain a model that satisfies $\neg P_i(T)$. Therefore, none of the default conclusions will be true in every minimal model: the class of minimal models will not entail any default conclusions. Prioritized circumscription offers a possible solution. One can add an extra default property P_{n+1}, where the interpretation of this property is "not-prototypical;" i.e., by default birds are not prototypical—they normally fail to have at least one of the properties of a prototypical bird. If this property has lowest priority during circumscription, the minimal models will satisfy $P_i(T)$ for $1 \le i \le n$, and will also satisfy $\neg P_{n+1}(T)$; i.e., the bird will be prototypical with all of the properties of a prototypical bird. If we know that T is exceptional in some other aspect, i.e., fails to have property P_i for some $i \ne n + 1$, then circumscription would conclude that T is not prototypical, i.e., $P_{n+1}(T)$. However, there are problems with this solution and with the circumscriptive approach to default reasoning in general. The major problem is that now the default "Birds typically have property P_{n+1}" no longer acts like a default. That is, when all we know is that T is a bird we can no longer conclude that he has property P_{n+1} by default. Furthermore, in general circumscription is still incapable of making any default inferences when we assert that exceptions exist: if we add $\exists x.\mathtt{bird}(x) \wedge \neg P_i(x)$ we can no longer conclude $P_i(T)$. This situation exists with the classical lottery: we know that a winning ticket exists.

The approach of ϵ-probabilities has the most difficult in dealing with the lottery. In this formalism the lottery is inconsistent. The set of conditional probabilities $\mathtt{prob}[P_i|\mathtt{bird}] < 1 - \epsilon$ $(i = 1,\dots,n)$ is inconsistent with $\mathtt{prob}[\neg(P_1 \wedge \cdots \wedge P_n)|\mathtt{bird}] = 1$ for small values of ϵ. Pearl claims that the failure to represent the lottery paradox is not problematic for nonmonotonic reasoning. But, as we have argued above, this leads to the position where one posits an entirely separate logic for common sense reasoning, instead of the more attractive position that common sense reasoning involves making extra assumptions in a constant underlying logic.

In the statistical formalism the lottery is easily and naturally dealt with. The agent will have a high degree of belief in $P_i(T)$ for all i, but will also be certain that T does not have *all* of these properties simultaneously: the agent simply loses confidence when asked to make more commitments. That is, we have that

$$\mathtt{prob}\big(P_1(T)\big) < \mathtt{prob}\big(P_1(T) \wedge P_2(T)\big) < \cdots < \mathtt{prob}\big(P_1(T) \wedge \cdots \wedge P_n(T)\big) = 0.$$

5.11 Relevance and Irrelevance

The notion of relevance and irrelevance plays an important role in non-monotonic reasoning, and it appears, either implicitly or explicitly, in every non-monotonic reasoning formalism.

In the system we have developed here we have approached the issue of relevance from the dual perspective of irrelevance. In particular, when we condition on all that the agent knows we are assuming that everything is relevant. The problem then becomes one of making assumptions of irrelevance to retreat from this extreme position. This retreat is necessary because the default conclusions are sensitive to extra information, and reasonable conclusions are no longer sanctioned in the face of irrelevant information. Obviously irrelevant information can be detected by Lemma 34, but otherwise the formalism is unable to identify irrelevant information.

The formalism can, however, represent and reason with fine grained notions of irrelevance. For example, the agent's knowledge base could include the assertion $[\texttt{fly(x)}|\texttt{bird(x)}]_x = [\texttt{fly(x)}|\texttt{bird(x)} \wedge \texttt{yellow(x)}]_x$. With this assertion of conditional independence in the agent's knowledge the system would be able reason that the property of being yellow does not affect a bird's flying ability. Unfortunately, this type of representation seems to be too fine grained; there are simply too many independencies of this type—some sort of closed-world assumption is needed for independencies. Our system of non-monotonic reasoning with the statistics can be viewed as being an particular implementation of such a closed-world assumption.

This sensitivity to irrelevant information is also shared by the approaches of conditional logic and ϵ-probabilities. However, neither of these approaches can represent notions of irrelevance, even at a fine grain.

One way of viewing this sensitivity to extra information is to consider it to be a cautious approach. Since there is no knowledge that the extra information is not relevant these systems act cautiously and assume that it is. Default and autoepistemic logics, on the other hand, are bold approaches. They continue to sanction the default conclusion unless the extra information directly contradicts this conclusion; that is, the negation of the default conclusion must be a logical consequence of this extra information. If the negation of the default conclusion is simply a default consequence of the extra information, then a competing extension is generated but the original default conclusion is not blocked.

For example, say we have the defaults "Birds typically fly" and "Penguins typically do not fly," and the categorical assertions "All penguins are birds" and "No ostrich flies." Then from "Tweety is a bird and an ostrich" these approaches would not generate the default conclusion "Tweety flies" as this is logically contradicted by the fact that she is an ostrich. However, nothing weaker than a logical contradiction will suffice, so from "Tweety is a penguin" two extensions would be generated, one in which Tweety flies and one in which she does not.

Circumscription seems to be somewhere between these cautious and bold approaches. Extra information can affect the default conclusion not only by logically contradicting it, but also by affecting the extension of the abnormality predicates. So, for example, knowing that a non-flying bird exists affects the extension of the abnormality predicate for non-flying birds, and thus affects default conclusions about the flying ability of particular birds.

5.11.1   The Need for a Theory of Relevance

When we are asked how probable a certain proposition is we often have a very good idea about what information is relevant to this assessment and what is not. For example, in most situations a doctor will quite confidently assert that the color of his patient's shoes is irrelevant to his diagnosis. Hence, it is not unreasonable to assume that agents have knowledge of relevance and irrelevance. An important area for future research is the development of a formalism for representing and reasoning about relevance at some reasonable level of abstraction. As we pointed out above, the logical formalisms developed here can deal with conditional independencies (an important type of irrelevance), but only at a very fine grain.[29]

Where a theory of relevance would be of particular benefit is in the arbitration between the possible non-monotonic theories T_i. We have provided a very simple subset preference criterion, and although the criterion is quite powerful, there are certain cases that it cannot deal

---

[29]Some work on a theory of relevance has been done; e.g., Subramanian and Genesereth have developed a theory of logical irrelevance [127], and Pearl et al. have worked on probabilistic theories of irrelevance [101].

with. Two such cases are disjunctive reference classes and redundant statistical information.

5.11.2 Disjunctive Reference Classes

EXAMPLE 32 Let

$$KB = \text{bird(Tweety)} \quad \wedge \quad \text{uniq(Tweety)}$$
$$\wedge \quad \forall xy.\text{uniq}(x) \wedge \text{uniq}(y) \rightarrow x = y.$$

If we wish to determine the agent's degree of belief in fly(Tweety) we obtain

$$\text{prob}\big(\text{fly(Tweety)}\big) = \mathsf{E}\big([\text{fly}(v)|\text{bird}(v) \wedge \text{uniq}(v)]_v\big).$$

The non-monotonic assumption

$$D_1 = \big\{\mathsf{E}\big([\text{fly}(v)|\text{bird}(v) \wedge \text{uniq}(v)]_v\big) = \mathsf{E}\big([\text{fly}(v)|\text{bird}(v)]_v\big)\big\},$$

leads to the theory T_1 containing the intuitively reasonable conclusion that Tweety is as likely to fly as the average bird. However, by forming a disjunctive reference class we can obtain a misleading theory that is preferred to T_1.

Since Tweety is the sole member of uniq's denotation and we know bird(Tweety), we have that the reference class specified by direct inference, $\text{bird}(v) \wedge \text{uniq}(v)$, is equal to the class $\text{uniq}(v)$. Hence, the disjunctive reference class $\text{uniq}(v) \vee \big(\neg\text{fly}(v) \wedge \text{bird}(v)\big)$ is a superclass of the class specified by direct inference. Furthermore, this class is a subset of $\text{bird}(v)$, i.e., $\forall v.\big(\text{uniq}(v) \vee (\neg\text{fly}(v) \wedge \text{bird}(v))\big) \rightarrow \text{bird}(v)$. Therefore, letting

$$D_2 = \big\{\mathsf{E}\big([\text{fly}(v)|\text{bird}(v) \wedge \text{uniq}(v)]_v\big)$$
$$= \mathsf{E}\big([\text{fly}(v)|\text{uniq}(v) \vee (\neg\text{fly}(v) \wedge \text{bird}(v))]_v\big)\big\},$$

we obtain a *preferred* theory T_2. Under most distributions the probability of the set of non-flying birds, $[\neg\text{fly}(v) \wedge \text{bird}(v)]_v$, will be much larger than the probability of the singleton set uniq, $[\text{uniq}(v)]_v$, as the former set has many more members than the latter. If this is the case, the relative frequency of non-flying birds in $\text{uniq}(v)$ will be overwhelmed by the relative frequency of non-flying birds in the larger set $\neg\text{fly}(v) \wedge \text{bird}(v)$. Hence, $[\neg\text{fly}(v)|\text{uniq}(v) \vee (\neg\text{fly}(v) \wedge \text{bird}(v))]_v$ will be close to 1, and we will have that $\text{prob}\big(\text{fly(Tweety)}\big)$ is close to zero in T_2.

This example demonstrates the problem that disjunctive reference classes can cause. If we know, for example, that Tweety is a member of the set bird(v), then we also know that she is a member of any set formed from the union of bird(v) and any other irrelevant set; e.g., she is a member of bird(v) ∨ elephant(v). Normally, we will have information about the narrower class that will be preferred over the disjunctive class; e.g., we will usually have information about bird(v). However, this is not always the case, especially when we have uniq predicates as in our example.[30]

Clearly we should prohibit the inheritance of statistical information from disjunctive reference classes like bird(v) ∨ elephant(v) when all we know is bird(v): the information elephant(v) is irrelevant to forming beliefs about birds. The difficulties with disjunctive reference classes have long been noted in work on direct inference. Kyburg and Pollock both explicitly prohibit the use of disjunctive reference classes in their systems, and they accomplish this by syntactic criteria. We could deal with this problem in the same manner: by syntactic criteria which determine the class of legitimate non-monotonic assumptions (Definition 54). The problem with this approach is that we may have disjunctive information in KB. For example, if we know moody(Tweety) → ¬fly(Tweety), it does not seem reasonable to exclude this information. A better approach might be to use pragmatic considerations when searching for possible non-monotonic assumptions, e.g., never generalizing to a disjunctive class unless the disjunct is *explicitly* part of KB.

In either case, however, these "solutions" are rather ad-hoc. What is really needed is a more sophisticated theory of relevance which will recognize misleading disjunctive reference classes as being irrelevant in the formation of degrees of belief.

5.11.3 Redundant Statistical Information

Pollock has pointed out another case where a richer theory of relevance is required [105].

---

[30] Note that we must have a special predicate symbol specifying that the individual is unique. For example, the formula Tweety = Tweety does not affect the base reference class KB$^{\lor}$: it becomes the tautology v = v when the direct inference principle is applied.

EXAMPLE 33 Let

$$KB = [\text{cancer}(x)|\text{canadian}(x)]_x = 0.1$$
$$\wedge \quad [\text{cancer}(x)|\text{canadian}(x) \wedge \text{red-hair}(x)]_x$$
$$= [\text{cancer}(x)|\text{canadian}(x)]_x$$
$$\wedge \quad [\text{cancer}(x)|\text{canadian}(x) \wedge \text{smoker}(x)]_x = 0.3$$
$$\wedge \quad \text{red-hair}(\text{John}) \quad \wedge \quad \text{canadian}(\text{John})$$
$$\wedge \quad \text{smoker}(\text{John}).$$

In this KB the agent has some information about the incidence of cancer among Canadians and among smoking Canadians. He also knows that having red hair is irrelevant to the chance of cancer, but instead of representing this information as an explicit statement of irrelevance he has represented it as and assertion of equality between the proportions in the two cases. From this KB we have that

$$\text{prob}\big(\text{cancer}(\text{John})\big)$$
$$= E\big([\text{cancer}(v)|\text{canadian}(v) \wedge \text{smoker}(v) \wedge \text{red-hair}(v)]_v\big)$$

Let

$$D_1 = \big\{ E\big([\text{cancer}(v)|\text{canadian}(v) \wedge \text{smoker}(v) \wedge \text{red-hair}(v)]_v\big)$$
$$= E\big([\text{cancer}(v)|\text{canadian}(v) \wedge \text{smoker}(v)]_v\big) \big\},$$
$$D_2 = \big\{ E\big([\text{cancer}(v)|\text{canadian}(v) \wedge \text{smoker}(v) \wedge \text{red-hair}(v)]_v\big)$$
$$= E\big([\text{cancer}(v)|\text{canadian}(v) \wedge \text{red-hair}(v)]_v\big) \big\}.$$

We have that $\text{prob}\big(\text{cancer}(\text{John})\big) = 0.3 \in T_1$ and $\text{prob}\big(\text{cancer}(\text{John})\big) = 0.1 \in T_2$, with no preference between the two theories. Clearly, there should be a preference for T_1.

Pollock uses examples such as this to motivate what he calls *domination defeaters*: a preference criterion which checks for numerically equal statistics. However, this check seems quite ad hoc. Numeric equality does not *represent* irrelevance, and indeed Pollock has difficulties in ensuring that the equality is not accidental instead of being a result of irrelevance.

What is really needed to deal with this kind of situation is an explicit representation of irrelevance. For example, we could use the formula schema

$$[\text{cancer}(x)|\beta(x) \wedge \text{red-hair}]_x = [\text{cancer}(x)|\beta(x)]_x,$$

where each formula β specifies an instantiation of the schema. With this schema it is not difficult to demonstrate that the base theory T_0 will contain the intuitively correct answer $\mathsf{prob}\big(\mathsf{cancer}(\mathsf{John})\big) = 0.3$. Whether or not this is the best representation, however, is something that must be determined by further research.

These two examples demonstrate that a mechanism for representing and reasoning with relevance and irrelevance would be very useful in further extending the range of our system. We still would not expect that considerations of relevance would determine a unique theory for the agent in all cases, but it would help to resolve a wider range of cases.

Bibliography

[1] M. Abadi and J. Y. Halpern. Decidability and expressiveness of first-order logics of probability. Technical Report RJ. 7220 (67987) 12/18/89, IBM Research, Almaden Research Center, 650 Harry Road, San Jose, California, 95120–6099, 1988.

[2] E. W. Adams. *The Logic of Conditionals: an Application of Probability to Deductive Logic.* D. Reidel, Dordrecht, Netherlands, 1975.

[3] R. Aleliunas. A new normative theory of probability logic. In *Proceedings of the Canadian Artificial Intelligence Conference*, pages 67–74. Morgan Kaufmann, San Mateo, California, 1988.

[4] L. Åqvist, J. Hoepelman, and C. Rohrer. Adverbs of frequency. In C. Rohrer, editor, *Time, Tense and Quantifiers: Proceedings of the Stuttgart Conference on the Logic of Tense and Quantification.* M. Niemeyer, Tubingen, 1980.

[5] F. Bacchus. *Representing and Reasoning With Probabilistic Knowledge.* PhD thesis, The University of Alberta, 1988. Available as University of Waterloo Research Report CS-88-31, Department of Computer Science, Waterloo, Ontario, Canada, N2L 3G1. pp. 1-135.

[6] F. Bacchus, H. E. Kyburg, Jr., and M. Thalos. Against conditionalization. *Synthese*, in press, 1990.

[7] J. Bell and M. Machover. *A Course in Mathematical Logic.* Elsevier, Amsterdam, 1977.

[8] C. Boutilier. Default reasoning with the conditional logic E. Master's thesis, University of Toronto, Department of Computer Science, University of Toronto, Jan. 1988.

[9] R. J. Brachman, H. J. Levesque, and R. Reiter, editors. *Proceedings of the First International Conference on Principles of Knowledge Representation and Reasoning.* Morgan Kaufmann, San Mateo, California, 1989.

[10] A. Bundy. Incidence calculus: A mechanism for probabilistic reasoning. *Journal of Automated Reasoning*, 1:263–283, 1985.

[11] R. Carnap. *Logical Foundations of Probability.* University of Chicago Press, 1962.

[12] P. Cheeseman. A method of computing generalized Bayesian probability values. In *Proc. International Joint Conference on Artifical Intelligence (IJCAI)*, pages 198–202, 1983.

[13] P. Cheeseman. An inquiry into computer understanding. *Computational Intelligence*, 4(1), Feb. 1988.

[14] K. L. Chung. *A Course in Probability Theory*. Academic Press, New York, 1974.

[15] K. L. Clark. Negation as failure. In Ginsberg [39], pages 311–325.

[16] B. De Finetti. *Probability, Induction and Statistics*. John Wiley and Sons, New York, 1972.

[17] J. de Kleer. An assumption-based TMS. In Ginsberg [39], pages 280–297.

[18] J. P. Delgrande. A first-order conditional logic for prototypical properties. *Artificial Intelligence*, 33:105–130, 1987.

[19] J. P. Delgrande. An approach to default reasoning based on a first-order conditional logic: Revised report. *Artificial Intelligence*, 36:63–90, 1988.

[20] D. R. Dowty, R. E. Wall, and S. Peters. *Introduction to Montague Semantics*. D. Reidel, Dordrecht, Netherlands, 1987.

[21] J. Doyle. A truth maintenance system. In Ginsberg [39], pages 259–279.

[22] J. Doyle and M. P. Wellman. Impediments to universal preference-based default theories. In Brachman et al. [9], pages 94–102.

[23] R. O. Duda, P. E. Hart, and N. J. Nilsson. Subjective Bayesian methods for rule-based inference systems. In B. L. Webber and N. J. Nilsson, editors, *Readings in Artificial Intelligence*, pages 192–199. Morgan Kaufmann, San Mateo, California, 1981.

[24] J. Elgot-Drapkin, M. Miller, and D. Perlis. The two frame problems. In F. M. Brown, editor, *The Frame Problem in Artificial Intelligence*, pages 23–28. Morgan Kaufmann, San Mateo, California, 1987.

[25] J. Elgot-Drapkin and D. Perlis. Reasoning situated in time I: Basic concepts. Technical Report UMIACS–TR–88–29, Institute of Advanced Computer Studies, University of Maryland, College Park, MD 20742, 1988.

[26] D. W. Etherington. *Reasoning with Incomplete Information*. Morgan Kaufmann, San Mateo, California, 1988.

[27] D. W. Etherington, A. Borgida, R. J. Brachman, and H. Kautz. Vivid knowledge and tractable reasoning (preliminary report). In *Proc. International Joint Conference on Artifical Intelligence (IJCAI)*, pages 1146–1152, 1989.

[28] O. Etzioni. Tractable decision-analytic control. In Brachman et al. [9], pages 114–125.

[29] R. Fagin and J. Y. Halpern. Belief, awareness and limited reasoning. *Artificial Intelligence*, 34:39–76, 1988.

[30] R. Fagin and J. Y. Halpern. Uncertainty, belief, and probability. In *Proc. International Joint Conference on Artifical Intelligence (IJCAI)*, pages 1161–1167, 1989.

[31] R. Fagin, J. Y. Halpern, and N. Megiddo. A logic for reasoning about probabilities. Technical Report RJ 6190 4/88, IBM Research, Almaden Research Center, 650 Harry Road, San Jose, California, 95120–6099, 1988.

[32] H. Field. Logic, meaning, and conceptual role. *Journal of Philosophy*, 77:374–409, 1977.

[33] H. Gaifman. Concerning measures in first-order calculi. *Israel Journal of Mathematics*, 2:1–18, 1964.

[34] P. Gärdenfors. *Knowledge in Flux*. MIT-Press, Cambridge, Massachusetts, 1988.

[35] H. Geffner. On the logic of defaults. In *Proc. AAAI National Conference*, pages 449–454, 1988.

[36] H. Geffner and J. Pearl. A framework for reasoning with defaults. Technical Report 870058 (R-94), Cognitive Systems Laboratory, U.C.L.A., Los Angeles, CA. 90024–1596, U.S.A., 1988.

[37] M. L. Ginsberg. Introduction. In *Readings in Nonmonotonic Reasoning* [39], pages 1–23.

[38] M. L. Ginsberg. Multi-valued logics. In *Readings in Nonmonotonic Reasoning* [39], pages 251–255.

[39] M. L. Ginsberg, editor. *Readings in Nonmonotonic Reasoning*. Morgan Kaufmann, San Mateo, California, 1987.

[40] M. L. Ginsberg and D. E. Smith. Reasoning about action II: The qualification problem. Technical report, Knowledge Systems Laboratory, Stanford University, 1987.

[41] A. Goldberg, P. Purdom, and C. Brown. Average time analyses of simplified Davis-Putnam procedures. *Information Processing Letters*, 15(2):72–75, 1982.

[42] B. N. Grosof. Non-monotonicity in probabilistic reasoning. In L. N. Kanal and J. F. Lemmer, editors, *Uncertainty in Artificial Intelligence Vol I*, pages 91–98. North-Holland, Amsterdam, 1986.

[43] J. Y. Halpern. An analysis of first-order logics of probability. In *Proc. International Joint Conference on Artifical Intelligence (IJCAI)*, pages 1375–1381, 1989. (Revised version) *Artificial Intelligence* (in press).

[44] J. Y. Halpern. The relationship between knowledge, belief, and certainty: Preliminary report. In *Proceedings of the Fifth Workshop on Uncertainty in Artificial Intelligence*, pages 143–151, 1989.

[45] J. Y. Halpern and Y. Moses. Towards a theory of knowledge and ignorance: Preliminary report. In *The Non-Monotonic Reasoning Workshop*, pages 125–143. AAAI Press, 1984.

[46] J. Y. Halpern and Y. Moses. A guide to the modal logics of knowledge and belief. In *Proc. International Joint Conference on Artifical Intelligence (IJCAI)*, pages 480–490, 1985.

[47] P. J. Hayes. In defense of logic. In *Proc. International Joint Conference on Artifical Intelligence (IJCAI)*, pages 559–564, 1977.

[48] P. J. Hayes. The second naive physics manifesto. In J. R. Hobbs and R. C. Moore, editors, *Formal Theories of The Commonsense World*, pages 71–107. Ablex Publishing, 1985.

[49] C. Hewitt. Meta-critique of McDermott and the logicist approach. *Computational Intelligence*, 3(3), 1987.

[50] J. Hintikka. *Knowledge and Belief.* Cornell University Press, Ithaca, 1962.

[51] J. E. Hopcroft. Computer science: The emergence of a discipline. *Communications of the ACM*, 30(3):198, 1987.

[52] J. F. Horty and R. H. Thomason. Mixing strict and defeasible inference. In *Proc. AAAI National Conference*, pages 427–432, 1988.

[53] E. J. Horvitz. Reasoning under varying and uncertain resource constraints. In *Proc. AAAI National Conference*, pages 111–116, 1988.

[54] G. E. Hughes and M. J. Cresswell. *A Companion to Modal Logic.* Methuen, London, 1984.

[55] D. J. Israel. What's wrong with non-monotonic logic. In *Proc. AAAI National Conference*, pages 99–101, 1980.

[56] R. W. Johnson. Independence and Bayesian updating methods. *Artificial Intelligence*, 29:217–222, 1986.

[57] D. Kalish and R. Montague. *Logic; Techniques of Formal Reasoning.* Harcourt, Brace and World, New York, 1964.

[58] H. Kautz and B. Selman. Hard problems for simple default logics. In Brachman et al. [9], pages 189–197.

[59] H. J. Keisler. Probability quantifiers. In J. Barwise and S. Feferman, editors, *Model Theoretic Logics*, chapter XIV. Springer-Verlag, New York, 1985.

[60] A. Kolmogorov. *Foundations of the Theory of Probability.* Chelsea Publishing Company, New York, 1950.

[61] K. Konolige. Circumscriptive ignorance. In *Proc. AAAI National Conference*, pages 202–204, 1982.

[62] K. Konolige. On the relation between default and autoepistemic logic. In Ginsberg [39], pages 195–226.

[63] K. Konolige and K. Myers. Representing defaults with epistemic concepts. *Computational Intelligence*, 5(1):32–44, 1989.

[64] B. O. Koopman. The axioms and algebra of intuitive probability. *Annals of Mathematics*, 41(2):269–292, Apr. 1940.

[65] H. E. Kyburg, Jr. *Probability and the Logic of Rational Belief.* Wesleyan University Press, Middletown, Connecticut, 1961.

[66] H. E. Kyburg, Jr. *Probability and Inductive Logic.* Macmillan, London, 1970.

[67] H. E. Kyburg, Jr. *The Logical Foundations of Statistical Inference.* D. Reidel, Dordrecht, Netherlands, 1974.

[68] H. E. Kyburg, Jr. Bets and beliefs. In *Epistemology and Inference* [70].

[69] H. E. Kyburg, Jr. Conjunctivitis. In *Epistemology and Inference* [70].

[70] H. E. Kyburg, Jr. *Epistemology and Inference.* University of Minnesota Press, 1983.

[71] H. E. Kyburg, Jr. The reference class. *Philosophy of Science*, 50(3):374–397, Sept. 1983.

[72] H. E. Kyburg, Jr. Subjective probabilities: Criticisms, reflections and problems. In *Epistemology and Inference* [70].

[73] H. E. Kyburg, Jr. Bayesian and Non-Bayesian evidential updating. *Artificial Intelligence*, 31:271–293, 1987.

[74] C. Langlotz and E. H. Shortliffe. Logical and decision-theoretic methods for planning under uncertainty. *AI Magazine*, 10(1):39–48, 1989.

[75] H. LeBlanc. Alternatives to standard first-order semantics. In D. Gabbay and F. Guenthner, editors, *Handbook of Philosophical Logic. Vol II*, pages 225–258. D. Reidel, Dordrecht, Netherlands, 1983.

[76] H. J. Levesque. Foundations of a functional approach to knowledge representation. *Artificial Intelligence*, 23:155–212, 1984.

[77] H. J. Levesque. A logic of implicit and explicit belief. In *Proc. AAAI National Conference*, pages 198–202, 1984.

[78] H. J. Levesque. All I Know: A study in autoepistemic logic. Technical Report KRR–TR 89–3, University of Toronto, Toronto, Ont., Canada M5S 1A4, 1989.

[79] H. J. Levesque. Logic and the complexity of reasoning. Technical Report KRR–TR 89–2, University of Toronto, Toronto, Ont., Canada M5S 1A4, 1989.

[80] I. Levi. *The Enterprise of Knowledge*. MIT-Press, Cambridge, Massachusetts, Cambridge, Massachusetts, 1980.

[81] V. Lifschitz. Computing circumscription. In Ginsberg [39], pages 167–173.

[82] V. Lifschitz. On the declarative semantics of logic programs with negation. In J. Minker, editor, *Foundations of Deductive Databases and Logic Programming*. Morgan Kaufmann, San Mateo, California, 1987.

[83] V. Lifschitz. Pointwise circumscription. In Ginsberg [39], pages 179–193.

[84] R. P. Loui. Decisions with indeterminate probabilities. *Theory and Decision*, 21, 1986.

[85] R. P. Loui. Defeat among arguments. *Computational Intelligence*, 3, 1987.

[86] W. Marek and M. Truszczynski. Relating autoepistemic and default logics. In Brachman et al. [9], pages 276–288.

[87] J. McCarthy. Applications of circumscription to formalizing common-sense knowledge. *Artificial Intelligence*, 28:86–116, 1986.

[88] J. McCarthy and P. J. Hayes. Some philosophical problems from the standpoint of artificial intelligence. In Ginsberg [39], pages 26–45.

[89] S. Miller and L. Schubert. Using specialists to accelerate general reasoning. In *Proc. AAAI National Conference*, pages 161–165, 1988.

[90] M. Minsky. A framework for representing knowledge. In R. J. Brachman and H. J. Levesque, editors, *Readings in Knowledge Representation*, pages 245–262. Morgan Kaufmann, San Mateo, California, 1985.

[91] R. C. Moore. Semantical considerations on nonmonotonic logic. In Ginsberg [39], pages 127–136.

[92] C. G. Morgan. Simple probabilistic semantics for propositional K, T, B, S4 and S5. *Journal of Philosophic Logic*, 11:443–458, 1982.

[93] C. G. Morgan. There is a probabilistic semantics for every extension of classical sentence logic. *Journal of Philosophic Logic*, 11:431–442, 1982.

[94] C. G. Morgan. Weak conditional comparative probability as a formal semantic theory. *Zeit. fur Math. Log.*, 30:199–212, 1984.

[95] Y. Moses. Resource-bounded knowledge. In *Proceedings of the second conference on Theoretical Aspects of Reasoning about Knowledge*, pages 261–275, 1988.

[96] E. Neufeld. Defaults and probabilities; extensions and coherence. In Brachman et al. [9], pages 312–323.

[97] A. Newell. The knowledge level. *Artificial Intelligence*, 18:87–127, 1982.

[98] N. J. Nilsson. Probabilistic logic. *Artificial Intelligence*, 28:71–87, 1986.

[99] D. Nute. Conditional logic. In D. Gabbay and F. Guenthner, editors, *Handbook of Philosophical Logic. Vol II*, pages 387–440. D. Reidel, Dordrecht, Netherlands, 1983.

[100] J. Pearl. Fusion, propagation, and structuring in belief networks. *Artificial Intelligence*, 29:241–288, 1986.

[101] J. Pearl. *Probabilistic Reasoning in Intelligent Systems*. Morgan Kaufmann, San Mateo, California, 1988.

[102] J. Pearl. Probabilistic semantics for nonmonotonic reasoning: A survey. In Brachman et al. [9], pages 505–516.

[103] D. Perlis. On the consistency of commonsense reasoning. *Computational Intelligence*, 2:180–190, 1986.

[104] J. L. Pollock. A theory of direct inference. *Theory and Decision*, 15:29–96, 1983.

[105] J. L. Pollock. Foundations for direct inference. *Theory and Decision*, 17:221–256, 1984.

[106] J. L. Pollock. *The Foundations of Philosophical Semantics*. Princeton University Press, 1984.

[107] J. L. Pollock. Defeasible reasoning. *Cognitive Science*, 12, 1987.

[108] J. L. Pollock. OSCAR: A general theory of reasoning. (unpublished manuscript), 1988.

[109] D. Poole. What the lottery paradox tells us about default reasoning. In Brachman et al. [9], pages 333–340.

[110] D. Poole, R. Goebel, and R. Aleliunas. Theorist: a logical reasoning system for defaults and diagnosis. In N. J. Cercone and G. McCalla, editors, *The Knowledge Frontier: Essays in the Representation of Knowledge*, pages 331–352. Springer-Verlag, New York, 1987.

[111] T. C. Przymusinski. Query-answering in circumscriptive and closed-world theories. In *Proc. AAAI National Conference*, pages 186–190, 1986.

[112] T. C. Przymusinski. Three-valued formalizations of nonmonotonic reasoning. In Brachman et al. [9], pages 341–348.

[113] H. Reichenbach. *Theory of Probability*. University of California Press, Berkeley, 1949.

[114] R. Reiter. A logic for default reasoning. *Artificial Intelligence*, 13, 1980.

[115] R. Reiter. Nonmonotonic reasoning. In J. F. Traub, N. J. Nilsson, and B. J. Grozf, editors, *Annual Review of Computing Science*. Annual Reviews Inc., 1987.

[116] R. Reiter. On closed world data bases. In Ginsberg [39], pages 300–310.

[117] R. Reiter and G. Criscuolo. On interacting defaults. In *Proc. International Joint Conference on Artifical Intelligence (IJCAI)*, pages 270–276, 1981.

[118] M. J. Schervish, T. Seidenfeld, and J. B. Kadane. The extent of non-conglomerability of finitely additive probabilities. *Zeitschrift für Wahrscheinlichkeitstheorie und verwandte Gebiete*, 66:205–226, 1984.

[119] L. K. Schubert, M. A. Papalaskaris, and J. Taugher. Accelerating deductive inference: Special methods for taxonomies, colours, and times. In N. J. Cercone and G. McCalla, editors, *The Knowledge Frontier: Essays in the Representation of Knowledge*, pages 187–220. Springer-Verlag, New York, 1987.

[120] D. Scott and P. Krauss. Assigning probabilities to logical formulas. In J. Hintikka and P. Suppes, editors, *Aspects of Inductive Logic*. North-Holland, Amsterdam, 1966.

[121] T. Seidenfeld. Why I am not an Objective Bayesian. *Theory and Decision*, 11:413–440, 1979.

[122] B. Selman. Analogues. Technical Report CSRI–47, Department of Computer Science, University of Toronto, Toronto, Ont., Canada M5S 1A4, 1987.

[123] B. Selman and H. Kautz. The complexity of model-preference default theories. In *Proceedings of the Canadian Artificial Intelligence Conference*, pages 102–109. Morgan Kaufmann, San Mateo, California, 1988.

[124] G. A. Shafer. *A Mathematical Theory of Evidence*. Princeton University Press, 1979.

[125] J. R. Shoenfield. *Mathematical Logic*. Addison-Wesley, London, 1967.

[126] M. E. Stickel. Theory resolution: Building in nonequational theories. In *Proc. AAAI National Conference*, pages 391–397, 1983.

[127] D. Subramanian and M. R. Genesereth. The relevance of irrelevance. In *Proc. International Joint Conference on Artifical Intelligence (IJCAI)*, pages 416–422, 1987.

[128] J. Tenenberg and J. Webber. A statistical solution to the qualification problem. Technical report, Department of Computer Science, University of Rochester, 1989.

[129] D. S. Touretzky. *The Mathematics of Inheritance Systems*. Research Notes in Artificial Intelligence. Morgan Kaufmann, San Mateo, California, 1986.

[130] B. van Fraassen. Probabilistic semantics objectified. *Journal of Philosophic Logic*, 10:371–394, 1981.

[131] J. Weber. *Principles and Algorithms for Causal Reasoning with Uncertainty*. PhD thesis, The University of Rochester, May 1989. Available as University of Rochester Technical Report 287, Department of Computer Science, Rochester, New York, U.S.A.

[132] M. P. Wellman. Probabilistic semantics for qualitative influences. In *Proc. AAAI National Conference*, pages 660–664, 1987.

Index

Page numbers marked with a * indicate that a citation of the author's work appears on that page, but the author's name might not. Page numbers marked with a • indicate that the indexed entry appears in a footnote.

Artificial Intelligence

Patrick Henry Winston and J. Michael Brady, founding editors
J. Michael Brady, Daniel G. Bobrow, and Randall Davis, current editors

AI in the 1980s and Beyond: An MIT Survey, edited by W. Eric L. Grimson and Ramesh S. Patil, 1987

Visual Reconstruction, Andrew Blake and Andrew Zisserman, 1987

Reasoning about Change: Time and Causation from the Standpoint of Artificial Intelligence, Yoav Shoham, 1988

Model-Based Control of a Robot Manipulator, Chae H. An, Christopher G. Atkeson, and John M. Hollerbach, 1988

A Robot Ping-Pong Player: Experiment in Real-Time Intelligent Control, Russell L. Andersson, 1988

Robotics Research: The Fourth International Symposium, edited by Robert C. Bolles and Bernard Roth, 1988

The Paralation Model: Architecture-Independent Parallel Programming, Gary Sabot, 1988

Concurrent System for Knowledge Processing: An Actor Perspective, edited by Carl Hewitt and Gul Agha, 1989

Automated Deduction in Nonclassical Logics: Efficient Matrix Proof Methods for Modal and Intuitionistic Logics, Lincoln Wallen, 1989

3D Model Recognition from Stereoscopic Cues, edited by John E.W. Mayhew and John P. Frisby, 1989

Shape from Shading, edited by Berthold K.P. Horn and Michael J. Brooks, 1989

Ontic: A Knowledge Representation System for Mathematics, David A. McAllester, 1989

Solid Shape, Jan J. Koenderink, 1990

Expert Systems: Human Issues, edited by Dianne Berry and Anna Hart, 1990

Artificial Intelligence: Concepts and Applications, edited by A. R. Mirzai, 1990

Robotics Research: The Fifth International Symposium, edited by Hirofumi Miura and Suguru Arimoto, 1990

Theories of Comparative Analysis, Daniel S. Weld, 1990

Artificial Intelligence at MIT: Expanding Frontiers, edited by Patrick Henry Winston and Sarah Alexandra Shellard, 1990

Experiments in the Machine Interpretation of Visual Motion, David W. Murray and Bernard F. Buxton, 1991

The MIT Press, with Peter Denning as general consulting editor, publishes computer science books in the following series:

ACM Doctoral Dissertation and Distinguished Dissertation Awards

Artificial Intelligence
Patrick Winston, founding editor
Michael Brady, Daniel Bobrow, and Randall Davis, editors

Charles Babbage Institute Reprint Series for the History of Computing
Martin Campbell-Kelly, editor

Computer Systems
Herb Schwetman, editor

The MIT Electrical Engineering and Computer Science Series

Exploring with Logo
E. Paul Goldenberg, editor

Foundations of Computing
Michael Garey and Albert Meyer, editors

History of Computing
I. Bernard Cohen and William Aspray, editors

Information Systems
Michael Lesk, editor

Logic Programming
Ehud Shapiro, editor; Koichi Furukawa, Jean-Louis Lassez, Fernando Pereira, and David H. D. Warren, associate editors

Research Monographs in Parallel and Distributed Processing
Christopher Jesshope and David Klappholz, editors

Scientific and Engineering Computation
Janusz Kowalik, editor

Technical Communications
Ed Barrett, editor